DATE DUE			

D1600112

WILLIAM ELLERY CHANNING

William Ellery Channing

AN INTELLECTUAL PORTRAIT

by
David P. Edgell

GREENWOOD PRESS, PUBLISHERS
WESTPORT, CONNECTICUT

Library of Congress Cataloging in Publication Data

Edgell, David P.
  William Ellery Channing, an intellectual portrait.

    Reprint. Originally published: Boston : Beacon
Press, c1955.
    Bibliography: p.
    Includes index.
    1. Channing, William Ellery, 1780-1842.
2. Unitarians--United States--Biography.   I. Title.
BX9869.C4E3 1983   288'.092'4 [B]   83-18491
ISBN 0-313-24253-4 (lib. bdg.)

Reprinted in 1983 by Greenwood Press
A division of Congressional Information Service, Inc.
88 Post Road West, Westport, Connecticut 06881

Printed in the United States of America

10 9 8 7 6 5 4 3 2 1

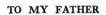

TO MY FATHER

Contents

The frontispiece is from a portrait by Gambardella. Courtesy of the Fine Arts Department of Boston Public Library.

Preface

When William Ellery Channing died in 1842, he was one of the best-known Americans of his day. Testimony to the extent of his reputation is the fact that his collected works in six volumes went through twenty-two editions by 1872 and that the memoir of his life published by his nephew William Henry Channing achieved ten editions by 1874. In addition to constant reprints of his works in a one-volume edition, at least five books of correspondence and reminiscence were published in the last quarter of the century. Interest in Channing's works also continued in foreign countries, for there were two full-scale treatments of his life and works in French and one in Italian during the same period. His work was discussed in Hungary and Sweden as well.

After the publication in 1903 of John W. Chadwick's *William Ellery Channing: Minister of Religion*, interest seems to have dwindled almost to the vanishing point. Channing's memory was, of course, kept green by the Unitarians, who continued to invoke him as one of the founders of their movement; but their interest was of an appreciative rather than analytical nature, displaying itself in sectarian pamphlets, books of religious thought, and articles for religious journals. One suspects that Chadwick's book was the last utterance of those who had known Channing or been directly involved in the religious and social questions that

had absorbed his mind. With the disappearance of Chadwick's generation, the last bonds with the past had been
broken, new and equally pressing problems had appeared,
and a nation that had been coasting on the momentum of
anti-slavery reform for nearly forty years began to interest
itself in the emergent questions of the twentieth century
rather than in the apparently solved difficulties of the nineteenth.

Not only did the twentieth century concern itself with
new questions, but also it demanded new techniques for
their solution. Instead of approaching reform through religion, it increasingly turned to psychological and economic
analyses. Instead of a philosophy of idealism, it chose in-
strumentalism — if not officially, then in practice. Instead
of individualism, it turned to social action. No wonder
that Channing ceased to seem relevant to this new world.
His battles had all been fought and won in a dim and far-off
age, and the methods he had used appeared as obsolete as
the military tactics of the Mexican War. Under these
circumstances, it is surprising that Channing maintained
even a precarious place in men's memory.

But maintain it he did, and not only among Unitarians.
Through the years his name has been mentioned (albeit
cursorily) in most of the major literary and intellectual his-
tories of American life. Some of the more conscientious
anthologies of American literature have included a brief
item or two of his work — usually the Baltimore Sermon or
a selection from the "Remarks on National Literature."
A sprinkling of articles has also appeared in the scholarly
magazines. But it is safe to say that outside of this relatively
limited area his name has been forgotten until recently,

while even within it an apparently unavoidable confusion invariably crops up in card catalogues and bibliographies between Dr. William Ellery Channing (1780–1842) and his namesake and nephew (1818–1901). Even so august an authority as the *Literary History of the United States* contrives to make several mistakes in its two-page bibliography of Dr. Channing.

Whether one relegates the name of Channing to oblivion or regards it as unjustly neglected, one may turn with interest to a re-examination of his place in our national record. Precisely what was his importance to nineteenth-century American life? Has he anything to say to twentieth-century Americans? Whatever our answers to these questions, the fact that scholars and laymen are engaged in redefining the historical components of the American mind assures an interest in the examination of Channing's thought.

Yet, a recovery of the figure of Channing is easier to propose than to accomplish. In the first place, his works are not generally available; in the second place, little of major importance has been published about him since 1903. When we turn to his biographers, beginning with his nephew in 1848 and ending with Chadwick in 1903, we are confronted with the hard fact that they were all so charmed with the elusive figure of his personality that they made no consistent attempt to analyze his thought or to assess his intellectual position. Furthermore, W. H. Channing's *Memoir* of 1848, by far the fullest compendium of Channing's life and thought, is, because of its massive disorganization and lack of index, almost completely useless except as a mine for raw material in the form of journals and letters that would otherwise be unavailable. None of the biographies, except Chadwick's, makes any attempt to go beyond the *Memoir*, and even Chadwick's suffers from excessive reliance on its chief source. Its advantage is that it is both well organized and readable, while the *Memoir* is neither. Chadwick's volume, however, has been out of print for many years and is virtually unobtainable; in addition, the half-century which has passed since its publication has changed our perspective on many facts and interpretations. For one thing, the clerical view of the universe, enlightened as Chadwick's was, no longer seems entirely adequate to the modern reader.

A fortiori, the same criticisms apply to Charles T. Brooks's *William Ellery Channing: A Centennial Memory*, published in 1880, as well as (in addition to the strictures previously mentioned) to W. H. Channing's *Memoir*. Not only have our tastes changed during the period since these books were written, but much new material has come to light. Nor do we any longer have the same Victorian disregard for accuracy which led W. H. Channing to suppress passages from letters and to omit names and dates as unnecessarily personal — suppressions and omissions that have been carefully preserved by all subsequent biographers.

To recover the figure of Channing, then, we must make use of new material as well as what is already available in the standard biographies. And we must also go to sources that were for one reason or another scanted by his contemporaries. Even an examination of the very material used by W. H. Channing in the preparation of his book (at least the part of the material that survived a disastrous railroad fire about 1900, when hundreds of letters and manuscripts were destroyed) enables us to form a more just opinion of Channing. At its lowest level, this examination permits us to assign names and dates to a number of documents hitherto known only by means of the excerpts printed without identification in the *Memoir*.

There are, in addition, many other manuscript sources for a study of Channing that have been ignored, or used only in part, by students of his life. The most important of these sources are the collections of the Houghton Library of Harvard University; of Henry M. Channing of Sherborn, Massachusetts; and of the American Unitarian Association in Boston. Other important documents are in the possession of the Rhode Island Historical Society in Providence and the Massachusetts Historical Society in Boston; the Meadville Theological School in Chicago has on loan a large collection of sermon manuscripts. The Pierpont Morgan Library in New York City has the manuscript of "Slavery," as well as less important material. The Henry E. Huntington Library and Art Gallery of San Marino, California, holds an important letter from Dr. Channing to Hermanus Bleecker (most of which is printed in the *Memoir*).

A second fruitful source of information concerning Channing and his times is, of course, to be found in the veritable flood of memoirs dealing with his contemporaries: Gannett, Dewey, Ware, Mann, Follen, and dozens of others. Such sources as these, ignored by or unavailable to earlier writers on Channing, have been supplemented by new studies of many of his contemporaries, both major and minor figures. Rusk's biography of Emerson, Commager's life of Parker, and Shepard's study of Bronson Alcott will serve as examples of present-day investigations into our nineteenth-century past.

Lastly, with the publication of such journals as those of Emerson and Alcott, we can more accurately assess the importance of Channing to his times than was possible a half-century ago.

The purpose of the present study is twofold: first, to reintroduce Channing as a man of his times, not as the spectral figure the hagiographers have made of him; and, second, to determine as far as possible the nature of his thought and its relevance to the problems of his age and ours. His ultimate importance in American intellectual life will depend, I think, far more on his position as a synthesizer of intellectual and ethical theories than on the secret of his personality.

In the preparation of this study of Dr. Channing I owe much to many people: a full list would be impossible, and a selective list runs the danger of misinterpretation by those who have inadvertently been omitted. It is perhaps needless to say that any inadequacies in the study are to be laid entirely at my door. But among those to whom I owe a special debt of gratitude are Professor Randall Stewart of Brown University; Dr. George H. Williams of Harvard University, whose suggestions have been most valuable; Miss Marion Kesselring of the John Hay Library at Brown University, who has helped both in procuring hard-to-find books and in criticizing the manuscript; Miss Caroline Jakeman of the Houghton Library of Harvard University, who has been unfailingly helpful; Miss Margaret Hackett of the Boston Athenaeum, who has helped to solve many knotty problems of identification; Dr. Frederick May Eliot of the American Unitarian Association, who has kindly put its manuscript collection at my disposal; the Rev. Dana M. Greeley of the Arlington Street Church in Boston, who has permitted me to examine the Proprietors' records of the church and other related materials; the late Rev. Earl C. Davis of Petersham, Massachusetts, for valuable suggestions concerning possible sources of Channing material; and Miss Elizabeth Norton for her kind permission to quote from the Norton Papers at Harvard University.

To Mr. Henry M. Channing of Sherborn, Massachusetts, I am especially grateful for his kind encouragement, his profound knowledge of his distinguished family, his insight into many of the problems faced in this study, and his un-grudging co-operation in making it possible for me to ex-amine the wealth of manuscript in his possession.

D. P. E.

DAVID P. EDGELL, formerly Associate Professor of English at Simmons College, Boston, has also taught at the Windsor Mountain School in Manchester, Vermont. Following a year of independent research at the Bibliothèque Nationale at Paris, Dr. Edgell became a Fulbright Professor of English and Ameri-can literature at Cairo and Heliopolis Universities, Cairo, Egypt. Among his non-academic posts was a two-year stint as editorial assistant at the General Electric Company in Schenec-tady, New York, where he wrote and produced adult-education and public-service programs.

WILLIAM ELLERY CHANNING

CHAPTER ONE

Channing's Life

The Newport, Rhode Island, into which William Ellery Channing was born on the seventh of April in 1780 was not the Newport of twenty years earlier. Then it had been a flourishing town of over nine thousand people, who had somehow crowded themselves into just under a thousand dwelling houses. It had been a town of great wealth, much of it — this was to plague Channing many years later — made in the notorious rum and slave trade. And, as a consequence of its wealth and maritime importance, Newport had been a cosmopolitan town, whose reputation for colonial elegance had extended even to Europe. By 1780 all this had changed: the population had been cut in half by the vicissitudes of the Revolution; those whose houses had survived the guns of the French fleet and the American batteries, as well as the scarcely less formidable occupation by the British and Hessian troops, thought about repairs, while those who had lost their homes wondered where they were going to live. Those whose orchards had been cut down and whose cattle had been driven off dreamed of recouping their losses, while the men of affairs lamented their lost fleets and their ruined docks.

The Second Congregational Church on Clarke Street, where young William Ellery Channing was baptized toward the end of May, was typical of the battered state of New-

port after the occupation. Its pastor since 1755, Dr. Ezra
Stiles, who had left four years earlier at the outbreak of hostilities, had now returned for a two weeks' visit to the congregation, which had never severed its ties with him. He
was shocked at the condition of his church:

> The enemy had run up a Chimney in the middle of the
> Meetinghouse, & demolished all the Pews & Seats below & in
> the Galleries; but they left the Pulpit standg, tho' they de-
> stroyed the pulpit in the other Presb. Meetingh. & in two Bap-
> tist Meetings. My little zealous Flock took down the Chimney,
> & then procuring some Benches & Tables made for the Kings
> Troops Entertainments & left behind. So that we attended di-
> vine Service very conveniently.[1]

The First Congregational Church on Mill Street, Dr.
Samuel Hopkins' meetinghouse, had fared but little better.
Like Stiles, Hopkins had been forced to leave Newport
during the British occupation, and when he returned in
1780, he was met by a greatly reduced congregation whose
life seemed to have gone out of them. Hopkins, however,
determined to stay, even though

> . . . it was a particular discouragement that the meeting house
> was so damaged, by being made a barrack for soldiers, that we
> could not meet in it. The bell was taken away by the British,
> when they left the town; and the pulpit and most of the inside
> work was demolished or taken away. And the few who were
> here had not courage or ability to repair it.[2]

Many years later, Channing was to recall this dismal building, where his father and mother worshiped during the first
six years of his life. Its look of desolation and " in winter
the rattling of the windows," he wrote, " made an impression which time has not worn out." [3]

But more important than the memories of Hopkins'

church was the influence of the Doctor himself on the thinking of young Channing. We shall have occasion to consider the philosophic impact of Hopkins' thought in a later chapter; it is necessary at the moment only to recall that one could readily look from the Channing windows into the Doctor's study, for the two houses were separated only by a garden, and that the small boy often saw the Doctor's candles burning late into the night and even in the early morning just before sunrise. The youngster seems also to have noticed the Doctor's waking hours, since he has left us a vivid picture of the old preacher " as he rode on horseback in a plaid gown fastened by a girdle round his waist, and with a study cap on his head instead of his wig." [4] Not more inviting was Hopkins as a preacher, for Channing went on to say, " His delivery in the pulpit was the worst I ever met with. Such tones never came from any human voice within my hearing. He was the very ideal of bad delivery. Then I must say, the matter was often as uninviting as the manner." [5]

Perhaps the roots of Channing's ultimate repudiation of calvinistic theology spring from these early impressions of the lugubrious tones of a rusty voice croaking messages of doom in an icy, rattling, half-ruined church. Later he was to find much to admire in the Hopkinsian system, but as a youngster he must have reacted to it in the same way that he reacted to that nameless preacher whose fire-and-brimstone sermon convinced the boy that the Last Judgment was at hand. As he left the church after the service, he looked at his father for some assurance of hope. But his father was just then observing to a companion, " Sound doctrine, Sir." There was no hope; it was all true. Half expecting some explanation, the boy climbed silently into the chaise, and the pair drove off toward home, William not daring to open his mouth. They had not been riding long when his father began to whistle. Something strange here – to whistle with hell's mouth gaping! And when they arrived home, there was no family prayer to make ready for the dread summons but rather a calm request for the newspaper, a sigh of relief when the traveling boots were taken off, and a preliminary shake of the paper as his father sat down before the fire to read the latest news.[6]

This discrepancy between the dreadful urgency of the preacher's words and the calm way in which the terrible doctrine was received, Channing remembered later, bred in him the first doubts of the old theology. And these doubts must have been strengthened a thousand times as the youngster came from the decrepit meetinghouse into the cheerful sunshine, from the dark horror of the sermon to the warm radiance of a summer day.

The Hopkinsian eloquence must have grated sadly even on the nerves of his father and mother, for in 1786, when William Patten was ordained pastor of the Second Congregational Church (after Stiles, who had become president of Yale College, had formally dissolved his connection with the society), the family shifted to Dr. Patten's congregation. One suspects that Patten's delivery may have been an improvement on Hopkins'. Whatever his opinion of the newcomer's theological views, Hopkins must have approved of *Christianity the True Religion*, Patten's reply to Tom Paine, published in 1795. But even though Channing spent most of his youth in the Second Congregational Church, Patten's influence apparently remained small. In later life, Channing's thoughts turned to Stiles and Hopkins when he thought of his youth, even though his contact with the former had been relatively slight.

Among the other influences in Channing's early life was his schooling, although this apparently had little effect on his later development, for the few references that remain to us are casual and not particularly revealing. Aside from the fact that his mother's ill health caused him to begin school somewhat earlier than was customary, his course was placid and undistinguished. The first schoolmistress he really remembered, according to her pupil's reminiscence, was remarkable chiefly for a nose that wore two pairs of spectacles, for a figure of immense proportions, and for a reliance on the rod that would have gratified Solomon. Later he attended, presumably in the smock that his brother George bitterly lamented,[7] a second dame school, run by a Mrs. Sayre and her daughter Betsy. His preparation for college was begun at Mr. Rogers' school, an institution of some reputation, since many southern boys who had made the long journey north in order to profit from Yankee learning were enrolled. Young Channing's scholarship does not seem to have been unusual. Indeed, both his brother and his nephew relate a story that he made progress in Latin only after extra-curricular tutoring from a clerk in his father's office. Yet, if not a quick student, he was a thorough one who apparently held a respected place among the boys.

By his twelfth year, however, William seems to have exhausted Newport's educational opportunities, for he was sent to New London, Connecticut, to prepare for Harvard with his uncle Henry Channing, long a preacher in that town. Mr. Channing was, as his nephew's biographer tells us, " of the more liberal body " [8] of preachers. He had been a tutor at Yale but had withdrawn from the college because of doctrinal differences. At the time when young Channing was his pupil, he was strongly moved by one of the manifold revivals that swept over New England during these years. His enthusiasm for religion communicated itself to the boy; it was from this year spent in New London that the mature Channing was to date the beginning of his religious life.[9] Too much weight, however, can be given to this assertion, for, as we shall see, he passed through other periods of religious fervor before his final dedication to a religious career.

Perhaps even more significant in determining the future cast of the boy's life was the unexpected death of his father on the twenty-first of September, 1793. By this misfortune the family was reduced in circumstances to genteel poverty. Though their material standard of living was lowered, the New England tradition of high thinking was maintained; and, after completing his studies with his uncle, Channing was admitted to Harvard College in 1794.

The boy of fourteen who prepared to make the long trip from Newport to Cambridge seems to have been in no way extraordinary. The stories, possibly apocryphal, of his early preoccupation with sermons, his innate gentleness, his boyish sense of justice, of his refusal to go swimming with other boys because his mother told him not to, are balanced by recollections of his good health and lively spirits, by accounts of his climbing the rigging of the ships at Newport, flying his kite, making plans to sleep in an old haunted house, and other such indications of a normal boyhood.

Nor are there any unmistakable signs of intellectual precocity.

The whole family background was influential in the later development of Channing's thinking. The household was typical of many New England families of its class in its paradoxical devotion to political liberty — a devotion coupled with a deep suspicion of all leveling tendencies — and in its religious liberalism. In short, the Channings were Federalists. Grandfather William Ellery, a lawyer, had been a signer of the Declaration of Independence, a member of Congress, and, later, collector of customs at Newport. Grandfather John Channing had been a merchant. His son William, a lawyer, achieved success in his career: he became attorney general of Rhode Island in 1777 and was later appointed to federal office as district attorney for the state.

In such a home, the young Channing must have grown up with political and social discussion constantly in his ears. Later in life he wrote of having been present when the Rhode Island State Convention ratified the Constitution. He remembered Washington's visit to Newport: had not the President stayed at the Channings' house? He met John Jay, too, as well as many other political figures of the day. And yet, with all this talk of liberty and this experience of great men, there were certain unexplained contradictions — slavery, for instance. Dr. Hopkins himself had been bitterly censured for attacking the institution. And there had been slaves in Channing's own family. They were treated well, to be sure, even liberated after the Revolution; but their manumission had been a personal matter, not a question of principle. Then there was the rum trade, by which many of the Newport fortunes had been made.

And the very qualified approval of the French Revolution. William Channing had thought it good as long as it promised to be a Continental version of the American revolt, but when Louis XVI was killed he began to change his opinion.

The boy, of course, was unconscious of these qualifications of the liberal attitude of his home. But his intimacy with those who coupled humanitarianism with a toleration of slavery, belief in the goodness of man with a suspicion of the lower classes, a fine personal morality with an acceptance of the rum and slave trade — this intimate experience was all his life to temper his judgment and to qualify his condemnation of the moral evils which he was to perceive later in life. Hence he was never to achieve the eloquence of a William Lloyd Garrison. Since he could not identify the evil with the evildoer — as more effective, though perhaps lesser, men could — he was destined never to become the patron saint of a movement. And the reason, I think, lies in this early life in cosmopolitan Newport.

The 173 students attending Harvard when Channing arrived in 1794 were plowing through a curriculum very different from that of the present. Joseph Story, who was to join Channing's class in 1795, has left us an account of the formal course of studies:

In Greek, we studied Xenophon's Anabasis, and a few books of the Iliad; in Latin, Sallust and a few books of Livy; in Mathematics, Saunderson's Algebra, and a work on Arithmetic; in Natural Philosophy, Enfield's Natural Philosophy and Ferguson's Astronomy; in Rhetoric, an abridgment of Blair's lectures, and the article on Rhetoric in the ' Preceptor '; in Metaphysics, Watts's Logic, and Locke on the Human Understanding; in History, Millot's Elements; in Theology, Doddridge's Lectures; in grammatical Studies, Lowth's Grammar.[10]

Though it was omitted from Judge Story's list, the Corporation thought one book sufficiently important to be in every student's hands: the *Apology for the Bible*, which was Bishop Watson's reply to Tom Paine's *The Age of Reason*. The Corporation evidently imagined that it had found an antidote for the infidelity of the students and a corrective for what it considered the erroneous ideas being imported from France.

In 1794 both the Corporation and the students took the French menace very seriously. Channing, in later life, recalled his entering days at Harvard: " The French Revolution had diseased the imagination and unsettled the understanding of men everywhere. The old foundations of social order, loyalty, tradition, habit, reverence for antiquity, were everywhere shaken, if not subverted. The authority of the past was gone." [11]

These reflections are what we might expect from one of Channing's background; it is perhaps safe to assume that they were typical of the average undergraduate reaction. All the petty disobediences of the students, every rebellion against the *status quo*, all the natural exuberances of youth were laid at the door of French infidelism and political irresponsibility. Placed in perspective, this attribution seems to be the Federalist cry of alarm against everything it disliked. Harvard, of course, was Federalist; its student body was largely drawn from Federalist homes. Consequently, to the Federalist mind, any deviation from respectability must have been due to a non-Federalist source — and fortunately a scapegoat was at hand in the French.

If Harvard really had been a sink of infidelity and if Channing was (as we know him to have been) conservative both in politics and in religion, we might expect him to have been somewhat aloof from the student affairs of the college. But although he did not board at the school — living instead with his uncle, Chief Justice Dana — he was elected to all the student societies: Phi Beta Kappa, the Speaking Club (later called the Institute of 1770), the Porcellian, the Adelphi (which consisted of the seniors who intended to become ministers),[12] and the Hasty Pudding Club.

Channing's reading at college was also what might have been expected from an intelligent but intellectually unawakened student. We see a mind interested, in college as in later life, in ethical thought; we do not perceive any startling originality in the choice of reading. As his first biographer tells us, he read " Locke, Berkeley, Reid, Hume, Priestley, and especially Price." [13] Equally important to his intellectual development was his careful study of Francis Hutcheson and Adam Ferguson. This bare enumeration of names (some of which we shall have occasion to take up in more detail later) gives us an indication of the direction his mind was taking. Conspicuously absent from this list, however, are the names of the great champion of American theological speculation, Jonathan Edwards, and of his disciple Samuel Hopkins. But Channing could hardly have been unfamiliar with their works.

Perhaps more decisive in the formation of his character was what seems to have been the first of his really profound religious experiences. Channing was accustomed to study near a clump of willows near his uncle's house. One day, while reading Hutcheson, he apparently felt a half-mystical experience, a conviction of " the glory of the Divine disinterestedness . . . the sublimity of devotedness to the will of Infinite Love." Speaking later of this experience, he said, " I longed to die, and felt as if heaven alone could give room for the exercise of such emotions." [14] In such circumstances as these we find interwoven the two threads that made up the texture of Channing's life. The first was his devotion to a life of reason — a devotion exemplified in his reading of Hutcheson. The second was his sense of unity with God — a unity that transcended his rational faculty. All his life, with varying success, he strove to unite these two concepts. To the end of his life he never clearly realized that the two might belong to different orders of experience.

Next to his own problems, however, politics most exercised the young student. In his senior year he was the instigator of a college meeting to pledge the support of the undergraduates to President Adams' administration. The outcome of the meeting was a memorial to the President, written in large part by Channing, assuring Adams of the undying loyalty of Harvard, bitterly resenting the low motives and actions of the French, and approving without reservation the noble and disinterested policy of the United States. When the author and his friends contemplated the French, we are told, " our youthful blood has boiled within us." On the other hand, in defense of America " we now solemnly offer the unwasted ardor and unimpaired energies of our youth to the service of our country." [15]

At commencement time, Channing, whose blood apparently was still boiling within him, was made closing orator, the highest position in the graduating class. In unconscious anticipation of a later discourse with the same title, he spoke on " The Present Age," in spite of a faculty prohibition on any political discussion, and succeeded in making his position clear by referring to the French Revolution. Any local application of his remarks seems to have been left to the ready imagination of his audience, except for the closing words which alluded to the faculty ban: " But that I am forbid, I could a tale unfold, which would harrow up your souls." [16]   And with this declaration, to the applause of his listeners, he concluded his college career.

After graduation Channing went home to Newport for the summer. There he made the acquaintance of David Meade Randolph, of Richmond, the United States marshal for Virginia, who invited the young graduate to live with his family as a tutor to the Randolphs' children and the children of their friends. Channing was delighted to accept the offer, for it seemed to guarantee him both leisure for study and financial independence from his family, who were still in straitened circumstances. Thus, after a summer marked chiefly by nostalgia for the companions of his college days and by a desultory study of divinity, he left Newport for Richmond in October of 1798.

The year and a half that he spent in the South was, in many ways, the most significant period in his personal adjustment. There he met respectable people who were actually Democrats; there he first came into contact with slavery as a system. The hospitality of the Virginians, their urbane manners, and the warmth and color of their civilization were most grateful to him. This contact with the South had much the same effect as a similar experience was to have on Henry Adams some years later — though he was never to conclude, as Adams did, that southern charm was temperamental in its origin rather than intellec-

tual. It was enough for Channing that southern society
sharply contrasted with the staid, somewhat puritanical
(for all its cosmopolitan quality) citizenry of Newport.

Unfortunately, he was unable to blossom as he must
have wanted to in the pleasing warmth of this environment.
His New England conscience forbade him to spend any of
his family's money to buy new clothes, let alone to indulge
himself in any less necessary expenditure. So his clothes
soon grew too shabby for him to present himself in company; his natural shyness did the rest. The not unexpected
result was that he found himself even more alone than he
had been at Newport. The companionship he did not
permit himself to enjoy with people he began to seek in
revery; his intellectual stimulation he looked for in books,
and he threw himself into the study of history. In a letter
to his college friend William Shaw, he speaks of having
read Voltaire's *Louis the Fourteenth* and all of Hume " except the last volume," and says he intends to read " Russell,
Belsham, Mitford, and Ferguson." [17] How much of this
arduous program he finished is not known.

We do know, however, that his tendency to revery got
out of hand. In part, no doubt, a result of his loneliness, it
was abetted by his determination not to lead a sensual life,
as he feared the Virginians were doing. He purposely
mortified the flesh, forced himself to sleep on the floor,
rigidly restricted his diet, and applied himself to his books
so closely that he had no time for exercise. And this regi-
men in turn so stimulated his dreams that he found himself
thinking impure thoughts; consequently, he mortified the
flesh still further. By a tremendous effort of will, he finally
freed himself from this circle, but his health was broken

so badly in the process that his body never completely re-covered from the unwonted strain he put upon it during these months.

In spite of his addiction to revery, Channing made much good use of his time. In addition to the reading in history which he had set himself, he was sufficiently stimulated by the society around him to re-examine his thinking on social and moral subjects. A reading of Godwin's *Caleb Williams* impressed him deeply, as did the writings of Mary Woll-stonecraft and Rousseau's *Eloise*. Channing refuted in his own mind the concept of enlightened self-interest and cried out for a reform of society — even calling, in a letter to Shaw, for a primitive communism. His friends and rela-tives back home naturally viewed with alarm this new de-velopment and accused him of Jacobinism, of being a mem-ber of the Illuminati, and of studying German in order to be unintelligible. In reply to a letter that dealt with God-win, Grandfather Ellery laid down the law: "I am not acquainted with his [Godwin's] moral character. . . . I despise French philosophists. Their system goes to the destruction of all government and all morality." [18] Arthur Walter, a classmate at Harvard, wrote, " Indeed, Channing, your sentiments are too extravagant," [19] and on at least two other occasions criticized him for letting his reach exceed his grasp.

Francis Channing also gave advice, pointing out to his younger brother that Plato and Socrates were only school-masters and that Pythagoras himself confined his sphere to a part of Italy. However, he wrote: " My brother advances with noble ardor to a vaster enterprise. The world is to be his Academy, and all mankind his pupils. . . . I adore it, thou moral Archimedes! but where wilt thou stand to move the mental world? Whither has enthusiasm hurried you? " [20] Apparently not satisfied that William was using his time to the best advantage, Francis also took him to task for his introspection: " You talk of your apathy and stoicism, when you are the baby of your emotions, and dandled by them without any chance of being weaned." [21]

A questioning of the metaphysical and moral basis of society was not William's only sin. He even began, though most equivocally, to question some of the actions of the Adams regime. In a letter to Shaw he wrote, " I blush when I think of the Alien and Sedition Laws. They have only served to show the weakness of government. They were worse than useless." [22] But in another connection he went on to explain that his blushes resulted from the inexpediency of the laws rather than from an objection to them on principle.

The hatred of war, which was to become a theme in Channing's mental development, was already present in his thinking. Shaw might call him " Jacobin, if you please, but I am *not* for enlarging our *standing army*. I wish there was nothing of the kind." [23] His hatred for the French continued, however, and he repudiated the French influence in America as violently as he had repudiated it in his address to President Adams: " I am happy to hear that the same odium is everywhere attached to the name of Jacobin. . . . A *Jacobin* is synonymous with a dishonest, immoral, factious, and disorganizing man." [24] Thus, in spite of the fact that he was no longer willing to rush to arms to defend America and his blood no longer boiled within him, he still repudiated the incursion of foreign thought — when

he was thinking about it. But Rousseau he liked, and Godwin — liked them in spite of Grandfather Ellery's por-
tentous warning.

This tension between his philosophic ideas and his defense of the *status quo,* coupled with his psychological disturbance, was to result in the second of his religious experiences, for in religion he seemed to have found the avenue
of escape that his spirit demanded. Near the end of his
stay at Richmond, Channing wrote to his uncle at New
London, revealing that he had experienced conversion. His
language is most significant. He spoke of " a change of
heart," of " the depravity and rottenness of my heart," and
specifically rejected the doctrine of works in favor of that
of faith. " What liberty," the extract concludes, " so valuable as liberty of heart, — freedom from sin? " [25] Here, it
seems to me, is an orthodox account of an orthodox conversion. It illuminates a state of mind which was not con-
sciously to change for more than ten years — for as late as
1809 we find Channing preaching in these terms, and we
will see abundant evidence that the public thought of him
as an orthodox Hopkinsian, if not an orthodox Calvinist.

With this resolution of his problems, there was no longer
any occasion to delay his theological study. He had probably been able to save most of his salary while at Richmond,
and consequently there would be no insuperable financial
reason why his studies should not be resumed. Furthermore, a young man burning with the desire to enter his
Christian calling could find nothing but spiritual and moral
death in his Virginia friends. Most of them were Democrats — that might perhaps be overlooked. But many of
them were open deists; they neglected the Bible; and even

" those who do not reject Christianity can hardly be said to believe, as they never examine the foundation on which it rests." [26]

The young man who had left Newport eighteen months earlier brought back much more from Virginia than he had taken. His reading had necessarily broadened him, though almost in spite of himself. His Christian experience was to remain with him, though transmuted, through all his days; and his acquaintance with Southern slaveholders, like his acquaintance with the respectable people of Newport, was to affect his view of slavery throughout his life.

Counterbalancing these advantages was his sadly weakened body, which was further strained by the long trip north in a leaky coal sloop. He fell ill early in the voyage and arrived home an invalid. All his life he was to feel the effects of the long self-denial of his Virginia days, aggravated as they were by this unfortunate voyage. He never again knew full health. The precise measure of the effect this physical depression had upon his mental habits can never be fully determined, but that it was most important there can be no doubt.

Channing, like Emerson, who had also taught school, always thought himself a failure in that profession. Yet Mr. Randolph cannot have shared his protégé's view, for he sent his son to Newport to prepare for college under William's tutorship. This responsibility was doubled, for George Channing, William's youngest brother, was also preparing at the same time. One suspects, however, that William took his duties in his stride and spent most of his effort on his own studies.

He had the unrestricted run of the Redwood Library,

which, though still sadly dilapidated as a result of the British occupation, contained a collection of books especially pertinent to his needs. A second source of intellectual stimulation to him was his renewed acquaintance with Dr. Hopkins, the Mill Street pastor. Channing was old enough now to look beneath the surface and to find in the Doctor an intellectual honesty and a rare power of intellect. So close, as a matter of fact, was their intimacy that Channing emerged from the association, at least in the minds of some of his contemporaries, a Hopkinsian. But his acceptance of the Doctor's theories was far from complete; surely what most attracted him was the older man's doctrine of disinterested benevolence, which united for Channing the ethical doctrine he had received so gladly from the English rationalists with the Christian view of the world he had accepted at Richmond. The Doctor's willingness to be damned for the glory of God, as well as his insistence on absolute predestination, Channing — with the eclectic's capacity for picking and choosing — rejected.

Thirty-five years later, Channing was to recall still a third influence of this formative period; at the dedication of the Unitarian Congregational Church in Newport on July 27, 1836, he spoke to his audience of the months he had spent there in his youth. He mentioned the Redwood Library and then went on to speak of the beach and of the power it exercised over him: " No spot on earth has helped to form me so much as that beach. . . . There, in reverential sympathy with the mighty power around me, I became conscious of power within. . . . There began a happiness surpassing all worldly pleasures, all gifts of fortune, the happiness of communing with the works of God." [27]

When, in December, 1801, Channing was elected Regent in Harvard University (an imposing title whose duties were those of a proctorship), he returned to Cambridge as a theological student. He became a member of the church presided over by Dr. Abiel Holmes, the father of Oliver Wendell Holmes, and a man who bore the reputation of a moderate Calvinist. The precise course of studies that Channing followed we do not know. President Willard and Professor Tappan, both "moderate" men, instructed him; but apparently his study was very largely self-directed. His reading seems to have continued in the direction it had taken as an undergraduate, though he now discontinued the course in secular literature that he had set up for himself in Richmond. During this period he wrote a monitory note to himself: "As I find myself full of prejudices on the subject of government and politics, I will lay them aside for a year; and let me not even talk on them except with intimate friends. History I will lay aside for the same time. Let me learn to be silent on subjects where I am ignorant." [28]

In 1802 he received his approbation to preach from the Cambridge Association of Ministers on presentation of a sample sermon and a viva voce examination. Apparently there was no question of his orthodoxy, though there probably was a suspicion that he had a Hopkinsian turn: one may guess as much from the only question he was asked, "Whether he believed that God was the author of sin?" [29] This question was a favorite trap for the unwary, though only the most naïve could have answered an orthodox group in anything but the negative. The existence of whole shelves of controversy testify to the sharpness with which the question was argued. Presumably Channing, with his native caution, was not to be entrapped, and answered the question satisfactorily.

His first sermon was preached at Medford on October 24, 1802. Its text was " Silver and gold have I none, but such as I have give I thee." Contemporary testimony agreed that this maiden effort was entirely satisfactory and that a new light had appeared in the Boston firmament. So complete was Channing's success that he was immediately asked to be a candidate by both the Brattle Street Society and the Federal Street Society. He chose the latter as the smaller church and the lesser responsibility. In his answer to the Brattle Street Church, after thanking them for the honor of the invitation, he pled his ill health as an excuse for declining — the first of a never-ending list of refusals for the same reason.

His acceptance of the Federal Street Church in February, 1803, was followed four months later by his ordination. The participation in that ceremony of Dr. Holmes, Dr. Tappan, and Henry Channing indicates that the young preacher associated himself with the moderate group of ministers, as opposed to the old-line Calvinists. This moderation took various forms, from Arianism to an eclectic acceptance of some of the Hopkinsian doctrines without embracing their doctrinal implications. The moderates as a group were inclined to emphasize the fact that Christianity was a religion of love and that good conduct was the warrant of a Christian life. Naturally they were greatly disliked by the old school, which firmly believed that " In Adam's fall/We sinned all," and that all newfangled ideas were sad fallings-off from the faith of their fathers.

Old Dr. Buckminster, for example — the father of Joseph

Stevens Buckminster, Channing's fellow luminary among
Boston preachers until his premature death in 1812 —
wrote, as early as 1799, to Jedidiah Morse, complaining of
the tendency of ministers to temper the wind of doctrine to
the shorn congregational lamb:

Many persons apprehend that such preaching orthodox Calvinism would affright people from the Gospel, and empty our
churches and religious assemblies at once. Duty is ours, events
are God's. We must preach the preaching that God bids us,
and appeal to the law and to the testimony. The truth sancti-
fies; error may please, but it cannot profit.[30]

And, as all students of Boston history know, Park Street
Church was built a few years later in 1809 to provide a
citadel of orthodoxy where the faithful might gather *in
partibus infidelium.*

Nevertheless, the "Boston religion" — designating somewhat uncritically the beliefs of the moderate and rational
Calvinists, together with those of the quasi-deistical preachers like Jonathan Mayhew — grew less dogmatic and less
emotional (in the narrow sense of the word) as time went
on, until in 1805 its local supremacy was assured by the
appointment of Henry Ware as Hollis Professor of Theology at Harvard. Its triumph, however, was accompanied
by rumblings from the orthodox. Andover Theological
Seminary was founded in 1808 to counteract the abandon-
ment of Harvard to the infidels. Moses Stuart, fresh from
New Haven in 1810, contrasted Boston religion with that
of the faithful in Connecticut:

Before I came here, I had no idea, that these regions were so
near the North Pole! Cold, distant, benumbing as death, The

Dons here, with their cocked hats, & old wigs, & formidable cloaks, & *angular* manners, & frigid precision, & distant civility, & high ideas of Massachusetts superiority, and Bunker Hill spirit, absolutely put one upon trial. Let any man be warmly engaged for religion here, & he is at once a Hopkensian [*sic*], or an enthusiast. O what a wonderful difference between this, and my dear people at N. Haven! [31]

The *Panoplist,* right-wing organ of the orthodox party, also emitted discontented noises, though it was not to erupt openly until 1812, when it demanded the prompt formation of ecclesiastical tribunals to put down the upstarts.

For the first ten years of his pastorate, Channing took little open notice of the ecclesiastical storm brewing under his nose. He was, of course, temperamentally allied with the moderates, if not with the extreme liberals. His view of Christ had always been Arian; in Boston this occasioned no great comment, though in what Oliver Wendell Holmes was later to call "the huckleberry districts" it might have been fatal to his ministerial prospects. He was also, in many respects, a Hopkinsian, and was recognized as such by much of the public. Furthermore he did not, for some years, indicate that his disagreement with the orthodox was a matter of great significance. And, as a matter of fact, the impetus to the separation of the Unitarians from the Trinitarians was to come from the latter. Just how far Channing disagreed with the orthodox position, aside from his Arianism, is not entirely clear. In what C. T. Brooks called his first Thanksgiving Sermon (presumably delivered in 1803), Channing spoke of "the *ruins of human nature,*" and went on to say: "There is nothing in us to recommend us to God. Sinners as we are, we are vile in his sight. Our sins cry to God for unmingled vengeance." [32]   And five years

later, in a sermon preached at the ordination of John Codman, Channing said, speaking of the minister's duties toward his parishioners: "He sees immortal beings, com-
mitted to his care, advancing with rapid steps to the brink
of an abyss, from which they are never to arise. And can
he be unconcerned? Can he read of that fire which is
never quenched, of that worm which never dies, and yet
see without emotion fellow beings . . . hastening forward
to this indescribable ruin?" [33]

Admittedly, these notes are not dominant in Channing's
thinking, even at this time. But that they exist at all is
ample testimony to the fact that he had not yet, even in his
own mind, thought of his own position as incompatible
with that of the conservative ministers of the town.

Yet Channing's moderation and his desire to see the best
in every point of view did not protect him or his colleagues
from the attack of the orthodox. This attack was not personal (at least in public), but its tenor was unmistakable.
The call of the *Panoplist* for what amounted to heresy trials
seems to have awakened Channing and his friends to action,
for they began to sound out their colleagues concerning a
new magazine, one which was to be (as Channing described
it a few months after its founding) "a publication . . . for
the purpose of promoting a spirit of charity and serious-
ness, and of increasing attention to the Scriptures. . . .
The friends of this publication wish to do something towards changing what they think the prevalent bad spirit of
the age, a spirit of narrowness, intolerance, and denuncia-
tion, more dangerous to Christianity than any other
cause." [34] Such were the motives for the founding of the
Christian Disciple, a magazine that was to continue under

that name until 1824, when it became the *Christian Examiner* until its death in 1869. The *Christian Disciple* was edited by Noah Worcester. Channing became one of its leading contributors.

The necessity of writing for publication and of taking a specific position naturally clarified Channing's ideas, while the controversy between the two parties forced him to choose between them. His interest in ethical behavior, a constant note in his intellectual development dating from his college days, made his decision a foregone conclusion. Except, however, for a certain amount of sparring between the two points of view, matters went on in much the same way for nearly two years.

The armed truce came to an abrupt end in 1815, when Jedidiah Morse [35] took it upon himself to open hostilities in dead earnest. He had printed a pamphlet excerpting a chapter on American Unitarianism from Thomas Belsham's biography of Theophilus Lindsey, the English Unitarian. Morse evidently thought the chapter summed up in a compact manner all the more odious doctrines of Unitarianism. He added ten pages of his own to the thirty-eight of the original selection and endowed it with a resounding title page:

American Unitarianism, or a Brief History of " The Progress and Present State of the Unitarian Churches in America." Compiled, from Documents and Information Communicated by the Rev. James Freeman, D.D., and William Wells, Jun. Esq., of Boston, and from other Unitarian Gentlemen in this Country, By Rev. Thomas Belsham, Essex Street, London. Extracted from his " Memoirs of the Life of the Reverend Theophilus Lindsey," published in London, 1812, and now published for the benefit of the Christian Churches in this country, without note or alteration.

The pamphlet itself apparently caused little stir. Not so the review produced by Jeremiah Evarts, the editor of the *Panoplist*. It attempted to show that English and American Unitarians shared the same beliefs — a proposition that was manifestly untrue, since the British variety, both material- istic and necessitarian, absolutely denied any divine quali- ties to Jesus, while the American version was Arian. Evarts also insinuated that the Americans were afraid to admit the true extent of their infidelity for fear of losing their posi- tions. He concluded with a call to all true Christians to separate from the infidels and deny communion to them.

Channing rose to the defense of the " liberal Christians," as Evarts had called them, in a pamphlet entitled *A Letter to the Rev. Samuel C. Thacher, on the Aspersions Contained in a Late Number of the Panoplist, on the Ministers of Bos- ton and the Vicinity*. In it he categorically denied all of Evarts' charges, pointing out his own complete disagree- ment with the metaphysical and theological basis of Belsham and Priestley. In answer to the second charge, that of hypocrisy, Channing — perhaps protesting too much — wrote, " We have only followed a general system, which we are persuaded to be best for our people and for the cause of Christianity; the system of excluding controversy as much as possible from our pulpits." [36] And in refuting the third point, Channing called for unity among all Chris- tian churches: the areas of agreement were so wide, while the points of disagreement were so few.

It was a pamphleteering age. Samuel Worcester, an orthodox minister from Fitchburg who had lost his pulpit to liberals, took up the cudgels in a series of three pamphlets, two of which were answered by Channing. The struggle between the two forces had begun, though the liberal wing remained on the defensive for the next three years. Not until 1819 did it take the offensive. On May 5 of that year, Channing journeyed to Baltimore to deliver the ordination sermon for Jared Sparks. Its text was: " Prove all things; hold fast that which is good." The sermon itself will be dealt with later; at the moment, we can best estimate its importance by the reactions it provoked.

Baltimore, in the second decade of the nineteenth century, was apparently a citadel of orthodoxy. Unitarians were looked upon with loathing by the respectable Protestant ministers of the place. We have ample testimony of this fact in a letter that John Ware, a Duxbury dentist and friend of Andrews Norton, sent to Norton early in 1817. Dr. Freeman, the Unitarian minister of King's Chapel, had recently visited Baltimore, and Ware quoted from a friend's description of the ministerial reaction:

Duncan, one of the Ministers in the city, calls Unitarianism a star in the North of ill-omen. He addressed his congregation particularly on Dr. Freeman. Among other things I heard him say — 'That he — Dr. F. — told a tale at which Solon would have frowned, Lycurgus blushed and Socrates have wept.' — Dr. Inglis in an introductory lecture declaring the objects of a monthly prayer meeting lately established in this city mentioned as one to protect us from bestial error and heresy. There are many bigotted [sic] Scotch here. I heard an old lady say — the boys ought to break his windows and stone him through the streets. One minister publicly threatened to excommunicate any one of his society who should have the presumption to hear Dr. Freeman.[37]

Ware added that his correspondent told him that " the Unitarians there will probably build a place of worship." They

did, and two years later Channing's manifesto was pronounced within its walls. Samuel A. Eliot, another friend
of Norton, wrote a full account of Spark's ordination ceremony. It deserves to be quoted at length because of its
appealing mixture of clerical gossip, personal reaction, and
description of the reception the Baltimore clergy (mentioned in the Ware letter) gave to the affair:

Wednesday at about ½ past 10 the services commenced, and
everybody was very much interested and pleased. I have seen
no one who was not gratified. The sermon was an hour and a
half long, and was an effort of uncommon boldness and decision
for Mr. Channing. He defended some of the most important
points of Unitarianism and spoke in just terms of the opposite
doctrines. He was certainly very able and in his manner more
than usually animated. The discourse will without doubt be
printed. Mr. Palfrey's right hand of fellowship was worthy of
him and of the occasion, and more need not, I think, be said
to convey the idea that it was appropriate, judicious, affectionate; in short that it was excellent. . . . Dr. Ware's ordain-
ing prayer was, I thought, exceedingly good. . . . Dr. Porter
delivered the same charge which he gave to Mr. Pierpont, with
some few trifling alterations. I am in hopes that it will be
printed that we may not hear it again. Dr. Thayer made an
address to the society which was of about the same stamp; however it *took* very well. The other performances were very
good, though there was nothing particularly striking in
them. . . . It was well worth coming 400 miles for, at least
that and what was connected with it. It is very encouraging to
see the progress of truth, and its advances are very perceptible
here, notwithstanding the violent efforts of the clergy to ob-
struct it. None of them have had the decency to call upon any
of the gentlemen from New England, though Mr. Channing,
Mr. Edes, and Mr. Palfrey went to hear Dr. Inglis preach last
Sunday and thought the Dr. promised to visit both Mr. P. and
Mr. C. They often declaim against the Unitarians from the
pulpit, and still more in private circles; Duncan even went so
far as to say that his people ought not to shake hands with an

Unitarian. . . . On Saturday we shall go together to Philadelphia, where Palfrey is to preach, vice Mr. Channing, too lazy. I have just heard that Dr. Glendy, (who with Dr. Inglis attended the ordination) is exceedingly outraged by Mr. Channing's sermon, says that he was invited to be insulted, etc. etc. though he thinks all the other performances very excellent. As for being insulted, I am sure it would have been impossible for any one to have spoken with more moderation of the opposite doctrines than Mr. Channing did; but it must be confessed to be an unhappy thing when the bare mentioning what a man believes cannot but be regarded as an intentional insult.[38]

In the North, Channing's sermon was received with equal horror by the conservatives but with much rejoicing by the " liberal Christians." To the former it was another battle in the eternal struggle between the forces of evil and those of good, and pens scratched away in many a ministerial study in an attempt to refute this latest eruption of godlessness. As was the custom in theological controversies, one pamphlet begot another until whole volumes had been filled. Moses Stuart, wise now in the ways of the Boston world and, as the title page of his pamphlet tells us, " Associate Prof. of Sac. Literature in the Theol. Sem., Andover," wrote 180 pages both in sorrow and anger, rising in his peroration to the climactic question: " When shall we bring a united offering to our common Lord, if men like you, who stand in eminent and responsible stations, treat those whom they profess to own as *Christian brethren*, in such a manner, and strive to degrade and render them contemptible! " [39]

Stuart's pamphlet defended the doctrine of the Trinity on scholarly and textual grounds which Channing, no Biblical scholar, was not competent to answer; therefore the burden passed into the able hands of Andrews Norton,

whose article in the *Christian Disciple* was baldly entitled
" Statement of Reasons for Not Believing the Doctrine of
the Trinitarians." With the battle joined, the orthodox
wheeled up their biggest gun — Dr. Leonard Woods, Ab-
bot Professor of Christian Theology in the Theological
Seminary at Andover. Woods endeavored in his pamphlet
*Letters to Unitarians Occasioned by the Sermon of the
Reverend William E. Channing at the Ordination of the
Rev. J. Sparks* to defend four of the five points of Calvinism: total depravity, reprobation, vicarious atonement, and
election. Professor Ware of Harvard took up the cudgels
for the liberals in his *Letters Addressed to Trinitarians and
Calvinists, Occasioned by Dr. Woods' Letters to Unitar-
ians.*[40]

It is idle to pursue the details of these wordy battles, except to note that they were still going strong in the early
1830's, and that — what is perhaps more important — an
economic and legal difficulty had arisen which much increased the heat of the controversy. In 1820, in the famous
Dedham case, arose the question: In the event of disagreement between church and parish, when the majority of the
parish wanted to become Unitarian but the majority of the
church wanted to remain Trinitarian, which party was to
get the ecclesiastical property? The Supreme Court of
Massachusetts decided the matter in favor of the parish,
much to the chagrin of the faithful and the delight of the
liberals.

Channing himself, though the target of much abuse from
the orthodox, remained in general aloof from the arena.
Nevertheless, he contributed to the excitement with several
papers, which, though they studiously avoided personal

reference, were body blows against the orthodox. Conspicuous among them were the " Moral Argument Against Calvinism," which appeared in the *Christian Disciple* in 1820; the sermon preached at the dedication of the Second Unitarian Church of New York on December 7, 1826, " Unitarian Christianity Most Favorable to Piety "; and the Election Sermon of 1830. Significant in all these controversial papers was Channing's appeal to the moral nature of the universe. The grounds for his rejection of Calvinism were only incidentally theological or Biblical in nature; they rested on a philosophical theory that was not specifically Christian, though it wore the clothes of Christianity. Its ultimate basis was rational ethics, not theology.

The sixteen years between 1803, when Channing assumed his pastorate, and 1819, when he became the acknowledged leader in the Unitarian movement, had been comparatively uneventful ones. More than with most men, Channing's life was led in the mind. The external happenings of these years were completely unremarkable. He had taken the parsonage on Berry Street provided by the church and invited his mother and her family to live with him there, sharing his salary of twelve hundred dollars. His presence in the Federal Street pulpit had proved magnetic; as a result, in 1809 a new church had to be built to hold the enlarged congregation. The next year he was saddened by the premature death of his older brother Francis; and two years later his friendly rival, Joseph Stevens Buckminster, died. Channing and his friend S. C. Thacher immediately busied themselves in editing Buckminster's sermons for publication. Channing's own reputation was steadily growing through these years; the outward sign of the inward grace was an increase in salary which enabled him to be financially independent. His personal affairs were so well in hand by 1814 that he summoned courage enough to ask a childhood friend and cousin, Ruth Gibbs, to marry him.

Her acceptance was destined to free him from all financial worry, for she shared in the possession of a large fortune as well as an estate near Portsmouth, Rhode Island, called " Oakland," [41] where they were henceforth to spend long summer vacations. His marriage also enabled him to move to larger quarters, for his mother-in-law asked him to make his home with her family, presumably on Beacon Street.[42] Channing did not seem to change his personal style of living, though we do see him relying less and less upon his salary from the Federal Street Church — for as early as 1817, we find him asking the Proprietors for an assistant, who was granted him.[43]

For the purpose of this study Channing's domestic life may be passed over lightly. It was marked by the happiness of marriage and birth and the sorrow of death. The death of his sister Ann, who was married to the painter Washington Allston, occurred in 1815, five years after that of Francis. In 1816 the Channings had a daughter, who died in infancy; in 1818 a second daughter was born. In 1819 a son was born, only to die in infancy. In 1820 was born a second son, William Francis Channing, who was to attain a measure of fame in his own right as an inventor.

Outward honors, during these years, came to Channing

as the result of his pre-eminence as a preacher. In 1812 he was chosen to be the lecturer on the Dexter Foundation at Harvard; but he relinquished the appointment the next year because his health did not permit him to fulfill the duties he set himself. Harvard, unwilling to lose him altogether, made him a member of the Corporation, a post he held for thirteen years. In recognition of his standing in the community and his services to education, Harvard also granted him a D.D. degree in 1820. In the same year he was invited to become minister of the First Congregational Society of New York, but he declined.

More important to the development of his thought in this period was his first introduction to German Transcendentalism. Like that of most Americans, his acquaintance was not direct but through Mme. de Staël's *De l'Allemagne* (published in 1813) and through Coleridge's *Biographia Literaria* (published in 1817). Wordsworth's poetry was also Channing's constant companion; indeed, he seems to have been one of the first in Boston to recognize the poet's value. This reading reinforced a judgment Channing had made even in his college days. Speaking, many years later, to Elizabeth Peabody about Transcendentalism, Channing said of the English Unitarian Richard Price:

Price saved me from Locke's philosophy. He gave me the Platonic doctrine of ideas, and like him, I always write the words Right, Love, Idea, etc., with a capital letter. His book, probably, moulded my philosophy into the form it has always retained, and opened my mind into the *transcendental depth.* And I have always found in the accounts I have read of German philosophy in Madame de Staël, and in these later times, that it was cognate to my own. I cannot say that I have ever received a new idea from it; and the cause is obvious, if Price was alike the father of *it* and of *mine.*[44]

He was perhaps interpreting his intellectual development too simply when he saw it as a straight line from his college days to his maturity; Andrews Norton had noted in a letter to George Bancroft in Göttingen that Channing had made great strides between 1815 and 1820. Norton wrote: " Mr. Channing whose views were but imperfectly formed when he wrote in controversy with Worcester has since improved infinitely, as you may judge from his late writings." [45] Norton probably had Channing's theological opinions in mind when he wrote this letter, but his judgment was true of Channing's whole mental development.

The strain of controversy, of his regular parochial duties, and of his new life as a public figure had begun to tell upon Channing's never robust health. He had had an assistant in the church since 1817, but even this lessening of his responsibilities had failed to give him strength. Therefore, in the summer of 1821 he tried the nineteenth century's remedy for any and all ailments — a trip. He journeyed through New Hampshire and Vermont into New York; but, though he was impressed by the scenery, his health did not improve. In 1822 he found himself obliged to ask for a year's leave of absence; it was willingly granted. The Proprietors appointed Orville Dewey, then on the threshold of his career as a minister, to the vacant place; and they voted a thousand dollars extra to Channing to help him with the expenses of his journey.

He and Mrs. Channing sailed at the very end of May in 1822 for Liverpool, using the leisure of the voyage to study chemistry in what was then a new history of the subject by Playfair and Brande. Upon landing at Liverpool, they were introduced to the local society; but, finding the exertion too much for the Doctor's health, they set out almost immediately for the Lake District, where they hoped to meet Wordsworth. The meeting did take place, much to the satisfaction of both parties, as Channing's letter home described the interview:

After an interview of great pleasure and interest, I set out to return, and, unwilling to lose Mr. Wordsworth's society, I accepted his proposition that we should walk together until I was fatigued. At the end of half a mile my strength began to fail, and finding my companion still earnest in conversation, I invited him to take a seat with me [in the cart in which Channing had come], which he did; and in this state we reentered the charming valley. . . .

Mr. Wordsworth's conversation was free, various, animated. We talked so eagerly as often to interrupt one another. And as I descended into Grassmere near sunset, with the placid lake before me, and Wordsworth talking and reciting poetry with a poet's spirit by my side, I felt that the combination of circumstances was such as my highest hopes could never have anticipated.[46]

The Channings returned to London in August and then went to Paris, where they seem to have stayed for a few weeks before going on to Switzerland. They were much impressed by the Alps, but they were to hear such sad news from home that Catherine Norton feared that it would " counteract the good effects of Swiss air and exercise." [47] Mrs. Norton's premonition was all too true: the unexpected death of their oldest son and of their sister-in-law Barbara, the wife of Walter Channing, upset them so much that we look in vain in the letters home for any mention of the impression that persons and places made upon the travelers. They spent the winter months at Florence, Rome, and Naples, but before sailing home went back to London.

There Channing met Coleridge, to whom he had brought a letter of introduction from Washington Allston. Again the meeting was successful, though Coleridge, as was his wont, did all of the talking. A newspaper correspondent some years later was to say that Channing's ideas for his essay on Napoleon came from this conversation; but Channing denied the allegation.[48]

After their return to America in the summer of 1823, Channing retired to Oakland until the fall. When he returned to Boston, leaving Mrs. Channing still in Rhode Island with her mother and sister, he asked the church to provide him with a full-time colleague, since he did not feel equal to the demands of his growing pastorate. Contemporary testimony, however, spoke of the renewal of his health. Catherine Norton reported that she heard " he said last Tuesday that he felt better than he had since he came home," and he seemed to her " stronger and more animated " [49] than she had ever seen him before. And a young man who was just then beginning to study for the ministry wrote to his Aunt Mary (whose staunch Calvinist mind can hardly have been gratified by the news) that " Dr. Channing is preaching sublime sermons every Sunday morning in Federal Street one of which I heard last Sunday, and which infinitely surpassed Everett's eloquence." [50]

Young Ralph Waldo Emerson was, within a few months, to begin his theological study with Dr. Channing. Their association seems to have been relatively informal, even though Emerson got a reading list from the Doctor, for he refers to himself as taking a " hebdomadal walk " to Dr. Channing, " for the sake of saying I am studying divinity." [51]

His private pupil can hardly have taken much of Channing's time, and when Ezra Stiles Gannett accepted an invitation from the Federal Street Church to become Channing's assistant, the older man, for the first time in his mature life, was able to work for his own interests. His success as a preacher had been remarkable; but he had a kind of fear of being labeled " a preacher " and hence of having his arguments anticipated as soon as his sect became known. In 1812 he took himself to task for this, saying that the great objection he had to writing letters was that it was impossible to keep from preaching: " I have composed sermons till I can with difficulty write anything else." [52] Now, with a certain amount of leisure, he began to make forays into secular fields.

The *Christian Examiner* — recently metamorphosed from the *Christian Disciple* in order to give the magazine a more popular tone and a wider circulation — was the chief vehicle for Channing's thought. In its pages appeared many of the essays that were to give him an international reputation as a leader of American culture. The " Remarks on the Character and Writings of John Milton " appeared in 1826. In 1827 and 1828 were published the two parts of the " Remarks on the Life and Character of Napoleon Bonaparte," the essay that drew the fire of Hazlitt in the *Edinburgh Review*. The " Remarks on the Character and Writings of Fénelon " appeared in 1829, and the paper on " The Union " in the same year. " Remarks on National Literature " was published in 1830 — a foreshadowing of Emerson's " The American Scholar."

In the same year, Channing, with due clerical modesty (which seems akin to the Elizabethan passion for publishing only at the request of friends), consented that some of his more striking efforts be gathered together and printed under the title *Discourses, Reviews, and Miscellanies*. In this volume were printed the Milton, Fénelon, and Bonaparte articles, as well as a selection of sermons, including the Baltimore Sermon of 1819, and an appendix of extracts from other sermons and notices. In 1832 appeared a second volume of sermons. These publications were destined, several years later, to draw down the lightning of the *Edinburgh Review* a second time, with Lord Brougham in 1839 assuming the role of *Jupiter Tonans*. Brougham's attack, of course, was not so much directed against the actual publications as against Channing's English reputation, which had grown enormously.

To this period we also owe two of Channing's greatest sermons, sermons showing a growing awareness of the problems of the age and a social consciousness which, though not entirely lacking in Channing's earlier work, nevertheless now demonstrated the distance from the prevailing religious and social orthodoxy his thought was taking him. The first, "Likeness to God," preached at the ordination of Frederick A. Farley in Providence, Rhode Island, on September 10, 1828, was the strongest statement Channing ever made of the Transcendental position — "the creation is a birth and shining forth of the Divine Mind." "Thus," Channing added, "God's infinity has its image in the soul; and through the soul, much more than through the universe, we arrive at this conception of the Deity." [53] The second sermon, "Spiritual Freedom," showed the distance Channing had traveled from the Federalism of his youth — even from the modified Federalism of his article on "The Union," published in May of 1829. "I am shocked," Channing now said, "at the imprisonment of the honest debtor; and the legislation, which allows a creditor to play the tyrant over an innocent man, would disgrace, I think, a barbarous age. . . . the thief is sent to prison, and the dishonest bankrupt lives perhaps in state. . . . I cannot but remember how much of the guilt of the convict results from the general corruption of society." [54] Such sentiments were not calculated to endear him to the men of position in the community.

Paul Revere Frothingham, minister of the Arlington Street Church from 1900 until 1926, repeated an anecdote which probably sums up the attitude of conventional Boston toward Channing's new tack. A layman of the period is quoted as saying, " when Dr. Channing used to preach about God and the soul, about holiness and sin, we liked him; that was Christianity. But now, he is always insisting on some reform, talking about temperance or war. We wish he would preach the Gospel." [55]

Though Channing's opinions about society might be changing — and with them his relationship with his parishioners — his physical condition remained much the same. The five years between 1825 and 1830 had been strenuous ones, climaxed by the publication of his *Discourses* in 1830. Mrs. Channing's health had also begun to fail, and another journey was prescribed, this time to St. Croix in the West Indies. Emerson received the news incredulously, relaying it with expressive exclamation points and an inaccuracy to his brother William: " Dr. Channing, I learn goes to Cuba this winter for his *wife's* health!! " [56]

Before Channing and his wife sailed, some time in November, 1830, he had asked the Proprietors to cut his salary to eight hundred dollars a year. They agreed, with the proviso that henceforward he would not have to pay a pew tax. Thus, with his absence atoned for by the sacrifice of half his salary (already pared down by a four-hundred-dollar cut a few years earlier), he began a voyage which was to inaugurate a new activity for him — an activity that would render even more tenuous his connection with his church. His stay in St. Croix was to be Channing's reintroduction to the horrors of slavery; he had seen them more than thirty years ago, but his realization of them had lain dormant.

The St. Croix visit, however, was not altogether taken up with reflections on slavery. The climate was mild and refreshing, and Channing could not resist comparing his condition with that of Andrews Norton in Massachusetts: "Sitting as I now am in an open room, in my summer dress, and inhaling a soft delicious air, I cannot easily think of you all as hovering over your fires, and looking out on a leafless, desolate country." [57] And there was a contingent from Boston: a Mr. and Mrs. Derby were expected, while Edward Emerson was already there, "a very pleasing companion, who is rapidly regaining health." [58] But even in this idyllic atmosphere the fact of slavery corrupted Channing's enjoyment. Had, he asked himself, Christianity failed? And though he was forced to admit that the condition of the northern operatives was often no better than that of the slave, he did not use that argument, as the defenders of slavery did, to extenuate it.

The echoes of the 1830 revolution in France reverberated in the West Indies, and Channing heard them with a new

wisdom, far removed from the condemnation of all innovation in society with which he had indulged himself in previous years. After speaking of the European revolutions
and sensing that they were a great, fundamental upheaval
in the way men thought, he went on, in another letter to
Andrews Norton, to give his views of the meaning of these
events for America:

I have no great solicitude however about our country, for
whilst the people have hardly the conception that liberty and
the publick weal are moral goods, and whilst I see little but
immorality in our politicians and government, I still recognise
in the instinctive feelings and unconscious habits of the community, in their respect for private rights, in their indignant
sympathy with the injured, oppressed man of whatever condition, in their stern demands for the equal, impartial operations
of law, I recognise in these things, germs or elements, which
time I trust is to develop, of a true understanding and of an
enlightened invinc[ible] love of freedom — [59]

So deep was this concern in Channing's mind for social
questions — with slavery the greatest of them — that after
his return he preached his first sermon on his experiences in
St. Croix. He spoke of slavery, condemning it unequivocally — though with a preoccupation with mental and moral
degradation that sounds strange to our ears and must have
sounded strange to W. L. Garrison, whose *Liberator* was
then only six months old. But temperate as the words were,
they incensed the solid businessmen of State Street who
composed so large a part of Channing's congregation.
Their preacher had already begun to show that he was
politically unreliable; now he had begun to meddle with
an institution whose fate affected New England's own tex-
tile industry.

The conflict is an old one, perhaps insoluble: How far can a preacher, who is in effect a pensioner of the wealthy men of the church, go in questioning the basis of their wealth? P. R. Frothingham, many years later, was to tell his congregation:

It is well known of Dr. Channing that during the latter years of his life he lived in partial retirement on his farm in Rhode Island, preaching but seldom. The reason for that retirement is not well known. It has generally been attributed to ill health and declining strength. But the real reason was that the people of this church did not like his utterances on slavery. The atmosphere of the Federal St. Church was hostile to him, and he found it convenient to stay away.[60]

Certain it is that when Channing's dearest friend, Charles Follen, was drowned in the wreck of the *Lexington*, the Federal Street Church denied their minister's request to permit the Massachusetts Antislavery Society to hold a commemoration service in the church. It is perhaps significant that immediately after the refusal of this permission Channing severed his last financial connection with the society, though he remained its nominal minister.[61]

The Federal Street Church might look upon its senior minister as a dangerous radical, but the Abolitionists thought of him as a tool of the moneyed interests. Maria Weston Chapman, one of the Abolitionist faithful, wrote as late as 1878 that Channing " had been selected by a set of money-making men as their representative for piety, as Edward Everett was their representative gentleman and scholar, Judge Story their representative jurist and companion in social life, and Daniel Webster their representative statesman and advocate looking after their interests in Congress." [62]

Others echoed Mrs. Chapman's appraisal. Elizabeth Peabody, who was most inaccurate, reported to Channing that Garrison had accused the Doctor of living on blood money derived from his father-in-law's ownership of a distillery engaged in the famous triangular trade. Channing admitted the distillery, and somewhat weakly sought to justify Mr. Gibbs's position. In a postscript he asked, " Have you any authority but rumor for saying that Garrison made the gross charge against me? To rumor I give no weight. I do not believe he said this." [63] But the anecdote that perhaps does most justice to both Channing and the Abolitionists comes from the pen of one of the chief actors in the Abolition movement, Samuel J. May. May had been at Channing's house and had spent the evening listening to the Doctor complain that the Abolitionists were too precipitate, that they lacked tact, that they were, in short, too violent. May, unable to control his impatience any longer, broke out:

Dr. Channing, I am tired of these complaints. . . . It is not *our fault* that those who might have conducted this great reform more prudently have left us to manage as we may. It is not *our fault* that those who might have pleaded for the enslaved so much more wisely and eloquently, both with the pen and with the living voice than we can, have been silent. We are not to blame, sir, that you, who, more perhaps than any other man, might have so raised the voice of remonstrance that it should have been heard throughout the length and breadth of the land, — we are not to blame, sir, that you have not spoken. And now that inferior men have begun to speak and act against what you acknowledge to be an awful system of iniquity, it is not becoming in you to complain of us because we do it in an inferior style. Why, sir, have you not taken this matter in hand yourself? [64]

Channing, unable to answer the rebuke, accepted the challenge, saying, " I have been silent too long." This event took place in the fall of 1834. The next year Channing published his pamphlet " Slavery "; and from that time on, though never an out-and-out Abolitionist, he was to be found unequivocally on the side of the anti-slavery movement.

The publication of " Slavery " was doubly significant because it followed the pro-slavery riots in Boston by only a few weeks. In the face of hysterical public opinion, the book demonstrated once and for all that the anti-slavery agitation was not the work of a few crackpot incendiaries. Garrison could be dismissed as a fanatic, Maria Chapman as a flighty woman, S. J. May as a backwoods parson — but the Rev. Dr. William Ellery Channing, minister of the Federal Street Church and acknowledged leader of the American Unitarian movement, was unassailable. An attempt, of course, was made to denigrate him; we have seen the response his own church made. Parishioners cut him in the streets, and it was rumored that the Doctor had been bitten by the political bug. Whittier, many years later, summed up the extent of Channing's action in a letter to W. F. Channing: " As to the matter of courage and self-sacrifice very few of us have evinced so much of both as thy father. He threw upon the altar the proudest reputation, in letters and theology, of his day." [65]

From this year on, the topic of slavery bulked large in Channing's thought. In 1836 he published " The Abolitionists," an open letter to James G. Birney, in which he defended with some qualification the Abolitionist position. The following year saw two notable actions by Channing.

The first was the open letter to Henry Clay on the " An-
nexation of Texas," for which Harriet Martineau claimed
to be the inspiration — a pamphlet of such force that she
thought its moral effect great enough so that " the annexa-
tion of Texas was unquestionably deferred for two
years." [66] The second step, requiring a measure of physical
courage that one might not expect in so cautious a figure,
was Channing's part in the Faneuil Hall meeting held on
December 8, 1837, to protest the murder of Elijah Lovejoy
by a pro-slavery mob in Alton, Illinois. Channing took a
leading part in forcing the city government to throw open
the hall to the meeting — a course they were unwilling to
adopt because of the fear of violence. He also spoke at the
meeting and wrote the resolutions which were the cause of
an outbreak of heckling. The attorney general of Massachusetts, James T. Austin, rose to condemn the purpose
for which the meeting was held, maintaining that Lovejoy
had died as the fool dieth, and closing with the astonishing
statement that the Alton mob was acting in the same spirit
as the fathers of the American Revolution.

Austin's speech, inflammatory in the extreme to the respectable citizens of Boston who had tasted their own mob
violence only two years earlier, called forth a great uproar.
Jonathan Phillips, Channing's good friend and chairman of
the meeting, asked the Doctor, " Can you stand thunder? "
Channing answered, " Such thunder as this, in any measure." [67] Then Wendell Phillips rose to his feet, and poured
out such a flood of eloquence that the hecklers were shamed
into silence, and the meeting proceeded quietly to its close.

Channing, of course, immediately was publicly identified
with the Abolitionists. He wished to reject the identifica-

tion, since he was not entirely in agreement with the extreme Abolitionist position; consequently, he wrote a letter to the *Liberator* explaining his views and questioning some of the principles of Garrison and his friends, *as he understood them.* S. J. May had gone to some lengths to explain that Channing's distrust of the Abolitionists was based chiefly on misconceptions about their use of violence and invective. When these were shown to him to have been false, he withdrew the charges.[68]

Garrison dismissed Channing's argument categorically with the statement that it " was defective in principle, false in its charity, and inconsistent in its reasoning." [69] And so it must have seemed at the time, and so it may perhaps seem at the present. Channing's endless qualification, his insistence on seeing every possible facet of a problem, seemed to some of his contemporaries a form of moral cowardice. And in our day Arthur M. Schlesinger, Jr., has written: " The work of Channing in sabotaging the liberal impulses of his day by his theory of ' internal ' reform, with its indifference to external social change, has never been properly appreciated." [70]

If these opinions are accurate, we must obviously dismiss Channing (as Maria Chapman did) as a tool, conscious or unconscious, of the dominant business interests of his day. If the critic is positivistic, he must dismiss all idealists as corrupt because they are idealists. In this view Channing was corrupt — but so were Emerson, Alcott, and Thoreau. To such a judgment there can be no effective answer because there can be no agreement on premises.

But even the sympathetic critic cannot fail to be disturbed by the lack of fire and the superabundant caution which are all too evident in Channing's social views. His blood apparently boiled only once, and then in an ungenerous cause, though it could not have seemed ungenerous to him at the time. His offer to shed his blood and that of the rest of the Harvard students for John Adams and Federalist principles was never repeated in quite such impressive terms. We have seen how his whole environment, his whole disposition, militated against violence, either in thought or in expression. That this tendency, in a sense, played into the hands of those opposed to any reform must be evident. But there is another aspect to be considered. When a man so essentially conservative in action as Channing moved, his shift was consequential and therefore of great weight.

His fear of being misunderstood, his reluctance to adopt a position until he was absolutely sure of his moral ground, may in the long run have been wise — for he thus escaped the usual fate of reformers by escaping the trap of cant phrases and narrowed perceptions. Channing was not a man, like Dr. Johnson, to estimate the value of his controversial efforts by the number of attacks his work inspired; he looked at human affairs *sub specie aeternitatis*, was confident that the truth would prevail, and did not wish to exacerbate prejudices any more than human prudence could help. If this was a fault, it was the fault of the liberal and rational tradition to which he belonged rather than of an individual.

With all his caution, however, Channing was in advance of his times in most of his opinions. In an age of military conquest, he preached against war as the worst of evils; in an age of faith, he headed a petition for the release of Abner Kneeland, who had been imprisoned by the authorities for

atheism. He was concerned with intemperance, and realized that poverty was one of its main causes — that it was
not entirely a moral issue. He found time to lecture on
" Self-Culture " for the Franklin Institute in Boston, and
to amplify his thoughts in two lectures in 1840 " On the
Elevation of the Laboring Classes."

The most mature statement of Channing's views of the
relation of classes and of the need for reform is to be found
in his speech given before the Mercantile Library Company
of Philadelphia on May 11, 1841. In this address we can
measure the distance that Channing had moved from the
Federalism of his youth. He dealt, not with abstract considerations of progress, but with a defense of revolution and
a condemnation of a business society. " It is not only on
the field of battle that men fight," said Channing, " they
fight on the exchange. Business is war, a conflict of skill,
management, and too often fraud; to snatch the prey from
our neighbour is the end of all this stir." [71] A moment
earlier he had spoken of the way in which the word " revolution " was used to frighten the promoters of any social
reform. Where, he had asked, did the French Revolution
originate? He answered:

. . . it came from the intolerable weight of misgovernment and
tyranny, from the utter want of culture among the mass of the
people, and from a corruption of the great too deep to be
purged away except by destruction. . . . In offering this plea
for the multitude I have no desire to transfer to the multitude
uncontrolled political power. I look at power in all hands
with jealousy. I wish neither rich nor poor to be my masters. What I wish is, the improvement, the elevation of all
classes. . . . The mass must not be confined and kept down
through a vague dread of revolutions. A social order requiring
such a sacrifice would be too dearly bought.[72]

But the greater part of Channing's effort during these last years of his life — years that saw him grow more and more flexible in his thinking — was devoted to the most pressing social problem of the age: the problem of slavery. In 1840 he had continued the work of the previous five years by writing a pamphlet defending emancipation in the West Indies. Two years later he wrote two papers on the *Creole* case, the legal and moral explosion touched off by the mutiny on the slaver *Creole* and her flight to British territory. The question arose whether the slaves were property or whether, as men, they gained their freedom by touching soil where slavery was not recognized. And his last effort — the address given in Lenox, Massachusetts, on the first of August, 1842 — was a celebration of the emancipation of slaves in the West Indies four years earlier. In this final speech, Channing went to the heart of the southern objection to emancipation. It was not, he pointed out, fear of a servile insurrection that determined the southern reaction but a callous determination to hang on to property, whatever the moral cost:

It is not because they are so fierce, but so profitable, that they are kept in chains. Were they meek angels from God's throne, imprisoned for a while in human frames, and were they at the same time worth twelve hundred millions of dollars [Henry Clay's estimate of the value of the slaves] in the market, comparatively few, I fear, would be suffered to return to their native skies, as long as the chain could fetter them to the plantation.[73]

It was useless, Channing thought, to attempt to combat slavery on a political basis. His solution was remarkably like that of Thoreau, and one may assume that his reaction to the Fugitive Slave Law, had he lived until 1850, would have been similar to Emerson's. His program in 1842 was twofold: " First, we must free ourselves . . . from all constitutional or legal obligations to uphold slavery." And, " should a slave-hunter ever profane these mountainous retreats by seeking here a flying bondman, regard him as a legalized robber." [74] In the second place, " The North has but one weapon, moral force. . . . I do not say that this alone is to subvert slavery. . . . All social changes come from mixed motives, from varied impulses, and slavery is to fall through various causes." [75]

The effort of making the speech took its customary toll of Channing's strength, but he soon recovered and early in September began the journey back to Boston. He chose to travel, as he had done more than twenty years before, through Vermont. This time, however, he was fated to go only as far as Bennington, where he was attacked by typhoid fever. He lingered for nearly a month, but the disease finally conquered him on October 2, 1842. After initial services in the Bennington church (from which Channing's friend Joseph Stevens Buckminster had been buried thirty years earlier), his body was taken to Cambridge for burial in Mount Auburn Cemetery.

The *odium theologicum* of some members of the orthodox party pursued him even after his death, for the usual rumor was inspired that on his deathbed he had seen the errors of his heterodoxy and had repented, dying in the bosom of a strictly Calvinist faith. There was no evidence for this change of heart, and W. H. Channing effectively scotched the rumor in 1848 in a brief but emphatic appendix to the biography of his uncle.

Needless to say, the impact of the news of Channing's death, both in this country and abroad, was enormous. Lowell and Whittier responded with poems which unfortunately testify rather to their respect for the deceased than to their divine afflatus. At least fourteen published sermons in this country and thirteen in England bore testimony to the respect in which Channing was held by his colleagues. The *Dial* printed a brief notice of the Doctor's death as a stopgap until an article could be prepared, either by Margaret Fuller or by Emerson. They both finally agreed that Margaret should make the effort, but after some procrastination the project fell through, and the *Dial* never fully recorded the memory of the man whom Emerson, speaking for " the Newness," had called " our Bishop."

For some years after his death, Channing's influence increased rapidly. His collected works in six volumes (the first five published in 1842 and the sixth in 1843) went through twenty-two editions, both English and American, by 1872. As early as 1854 the Unitarian Association reported that 100,000 copies of Channing's *Works* had been sold. In 1875, the Association published a one-volume edition of his writings, which was superseded in 1886 by a " complete " edition containing *The Perfect Life*, a series of twelve sermons edited for publication by W. H. Channing in 1872. The *Memoir* itself went through ten editions by 1874.

Channing's foreign reputation was hardly inferior to his American. George Bancroft had introduced his writings into Germany as early as 1836; but ten years before that, Beethoven became so interested in a newspaper report of one of the Doctor's addresses that he hoped to see the whole pamphlet.[76]   And Baron von Bunsen in his *God in History*, published in 1857–58, spoke in the highest terms of Channing.

England, of course, had known of Channing almost as soon as he became a public figure in America.   His articles on Napoleon and Milton had introduced his name to a wide British public, and thereafter many of his writings were published in Great Britain as soon as they appeared.   We have already mentioned the attention the *Edinburgh Review* granted to Channing during his lifetime.   Immediately following the publication of the Channing *Memoir*, James Martineau reviewed the work in the *Westminster Review*.   Besides these formal notices, Channing was known to many English literary figures.   He was in extensive correspondence with the Roscoes of Liverpool, Joanna Baillie, Felicia Hemans, Lucy Aikin, Joseph Blanco White, and many others.   Queen Victoria herself indicated her pleasure in his writings.

It was the same in France.   Channing was in correspondence with Baron de Gérando in 1830, with Chateaubriand in 1837.   His "Remarks on National Literature" were translated into French in 1838.   An anonymous author (probably a Mrs. Holland) had published in 1857 a panegyric entitled *Channing, sa vie et ses oeuvres* with a preface by Charles de Rémusat.   In 1862 Renan answered this interpretation with a somewhat more temperate approach published in his *Etudes d'histoire religieuse;* but French enthusiasm grew apace following Lavollèe's biography and exegesis, *Channing, sa vie et sa doctrine*, in 1876.   And six years later M. Laboulaye translated some of Channing's works under the title *Oeuvres sociales*.

Channing's book on slavery was published in Spain in 1864. In Italy, Carlo Cossu had, the year before, published his *Channing, le sue opere e le sue dottrine unitarie*. In Switzerland, Sismondi knew Channing well and was in correspondence with him for a number of years. And in Hungary — as one might perhaps expect because of its native Unitarian tradition — Channing's name and works were also known.

In America, the many books published about Channing testify to the continuing interest his countrymen felt in his life. In 1874, Roberts Brothers of Boston published the *Correspondence of William Ellery Channing, D.D., and Lucy Aikin*. Six years later, probably to take advantage of the publicity offered by the centenary celebration of his birth, the same firm brought out Elizabeth Peabody's *Reminiscences of Rev. Wm. Ellery Channing, D.D.* In that year, Roberts Brothers also published Charles T. Brooks's *William Ellery Channing: A Centennial Memory*; and three years later came *Channing's Note-Book: Passages from the Unpublished Manuscripts of William Ellery Channing*. Needless to say, the memoirs and biographies of the nineteenth century are full of recollections of Dr. Channing. But from 1887 until 1903 there was a lull in books devoted exclusively to him. In that year appeared the last full-scale biography, John White Chadwick's *William Ellery Channing*, a book that deserves reprinting. Until recently, the last half-century has seen only a sprinkling of scholarly articles and pious references in works of literary history to a man who once stood high in the esteem of the American people.

There have been signs, however, of a reawakening of interest. We are exploring our cultural past with a new vigor these days; as we explore, the figure of Channing looms larger and larger as a man who unites in his own person the two eras of American history that Henry Adams saw wrenched asunder. In Channing we see clearly a man of the Enlightenment face to face with practical problems of poverty, slavery, and the new industrialism. We meet a man whose whole life demonstrated his faith in the natural goodness of man and in the power of reason and good will to solve human difficulties. In these last decades, when there have been so many vain attempts to escape responsibility for our lives by flying into the arms of obscurantism and authoritarianism, we have cogent reasons for examining anew the intellectual life of a great and good man who was, as a colleague remembered him, " always a learner."

CHAPTER TWO

The Rational Christian

The eighteenth century, like the Renaissance, has been all things to all men. Such a wealth of scholarship and interpretation has been lavished on the period that it has become almost impossible to make any generalization that will illuminate the age. And yet, when one reads the words "eighteenth century" or "Enlightenment," one willynilly makes an intellectual response — perhaps, a critic will say, to an inaccurate symbol, but perhaps also to a group of ideas more typical of this epoch than of any other. These ideas, when closely examined, often appear self-contradictory, ill-reasoned, superficial, contrary to experience, and murkily phrased. Who, for example, can read the opening paragraph of the Declaration of Independence without being painfully aware of all these qualities?

Today the ideas of the Enlightenment are under attack. They are assailed from one direction as weak and offensive platitudes which mock the real inequality of man and hinder the strong from achieving their goal; they are attacked from another direction as pernicious jargon employed by the cynical to mask their own selfishness; they are scorned by religious groups, both Catholic and Protestant, as arrogantly humanistic and failing in reverence before the Lord. Yet these ideas endure. Deep in American life — perhaps essential to it — we discover certain fundamental concepts: a conviction that human life is intelligible, that mankind has infinite capacity for good, that human progress is possible, that justice is possible, and that all men *are* created equal and endowed with inalienable rights, among which are life, liberty, and the pursuit of happiness.

These terms, to be sure, are not strictly definable; they resist close intellectual examination; they cannot be included in a catechism. And because of this evasive quality, the words have been misused, often by the forces most inimical to the concepts for which they stand. As John Dewey has said:

> It would be difficult to estimate the harm that has resulted because the liberal and progressive movement of the eighteenth and earlier nineteenth centuries had no method of intellectual articulation commensurate with its practical aspirations. Its heart was in the right place. It was humane and social in intention. But it had no theoretical instrumentalities of constructive power. . . . This deficiency played into the hands of the reactionary and the obscurantist.[1]

Channing's importance in American intellectual history lies in his attempt to establish these deeply felt concepts on a valid basis. He succeeded only in maintaining a precarious equilibrium among three more or less irreconcilable forces — Christianity, the "rationalism" of the English Enlightenment, and the self-reliance of the Transcendentalists.[2] He could not permanently unite such disparate elements; he could only teeter back and forth as now one and now the other of them threatened his intellectual balance. At one moment he refused the logical consequences of his Christianity, at the next he shrank from the implications of romantic self-reliance. Nor did he ever completely account himself a rationalist. The result of this unconscious wavering was failure. But though it was failure, it casts a good deal of light on the evolution of what Gunnar Myrdal has called the " American Dream."

No one, I think, can effectively deny the desirability of Channing's goals. He preached and wrote with all his strength against slavery, he defended freedom of thought with all his power, he emphasized that we are all members of one another, and he held that love and tolerance are better tools for reform than hatred and bigotry. His heart, as Dewey said, was in the right place. Perhaps he had not a " method of intellectual articulation commensurate with . . . [his] practical aspirations " but this is the paradox of all great figures. From the vantage point of a few years we think we can mark the crudities and inconsistencies of their basic philosophies. On such a foundation, we wonder, how could they live meaningful lives and perform significant actions? How can their lives and thoughts have any importance for us, who see so clearly the error of both their assumptions and their logic?

The other side of the paradox is the fact that only under the influence of these same assumptions and logic could the man have developed as he did. Without the ethical insights of Christianity, without a firm conviction of the value of reason, and without the independence of mind that came from his Transcendental leanings, Channing could not have become the significant figure he was. His life and his works have been, there can be no doubt, empirically justified — yet they rest on a very dubious intellectual foundation.

It seems to me, however, that this judgment does not detract from Channing's importance, for the lives of all of us stem from the same mixture of truth and error. We are

what we are both because of and in spite of the influence of
the past upon us. To understand that past, then, becomes
both an obligation and a necessity — a necessity because the
past acts upon us whether we will or no; an obligation
because, unless we feel that life is utterly without meaning,
we must believe in the power of human intelligence to
comprehend at least some of its significance. And human
intelligence ought, on these premises, to concern itself with
understanding the conditions of our being.

This was Channing's belief; it modified his Christianity
to such an extent that by some sects he ceased to be regarded
as a Christian. The Doctor preferred to think of himself
as a " rational Christian " and was capable of saying when
hard-pressed, " I am surer that my rational nature is from
God, than that any book is an expression of his will." [3]
The natural result of such a belief, of course, was to render
him somewhat more rational than Christian, at least by
orthodox definition. Yet there is no doubt that Channing
regarded himself first and foremost as a Christian minister.
He had ample excuse for thinking of himself in that light,
for he had, after all, been graduated from a theological
school and had been approbated to preach by the Cambridge
Association of Ministers, none of whom had questioned his
beliefs. And his intellectual masters had been, almost without exception, men of the cloth. Francis Hutcheson,
though he seems to have refused to become a member of the
Church of England, was licensed to preach, and had studied
theology at the University of Glasgow. Joseph Butler
was sufficiently orthodox to become Bishop of Durham.
Richard Price was a dissenting minister who had received a

D.D. degree from the University of Glasgow. And in this country it would be a brave man indeed who would have dared to suggest that the Rev. Samuel Hopkins, D.D., was not a Christian.

Yet the most conspicuous element of the writings of all these men was not their testimony to the sovereignty of God and a blind subjugation to his will. They were all occupied in justifying (in the modern sense of the word) the ways of God to man — in proving that God acted, not capriciously, but in accord with a rational system. Implicit in all their argument was the assumption that God *must* act in accord with the " nature of things " and that this " nature of things " was intelligible. At once, of course, the religious center of gravity shifted from the will of God to a concept of natural law.

John Calvin's opinion of such weakening of the sovereignty of God's arbitrary will had been scathing:

. . . how exceedingly presumptuous it is only to inquire into the causes of the Divine will; which is in fact, and is justly entitled to be, the cause of everything that exists. For if it has any cause, then there must be something antecedent, on which it depends; which it is impious to suppose. For the will of God is the highest rule of justice; so that what he wills must be considered just, for this very reason, because he wills it. When it is inquired, therefore, why the Lord did so, the answer must be, Because he would. But if you go further, and ask why he so determined, you are in search of something greater and higher than the will of God, which can never be found.[4]

One may compare such an unqualified statement of God's magnificent irresponsibility with Shaftesbury's equally unqualified assertion of the idea that even God is responsible:

For whoever thinks there is a God, and pretends formally to believe that he is *just* and *good*, must suppose, that there is independently such a thing as *justice* and *injustice*, *truth* and *falsehood*, *right* and *wrong*, according to which he pronounces that *God is just, righteous*, and *true*. If the mere *will, decree* or *law* of God be said absolutely to constitute *right* and *wrong*, then are these latter words of no significancy at all.[5]

Hopkins himself bore unwilling witness to this point of view in *The System of Doctrines* when he wrote:

The infinite excellence, beauty and glory of God, consist wholly in his moral perfections and character. Infinite greatness, understanding and power, without any rectitude, wisdom and goodness of heart . . . would not be desirable and amiable; but worse than nothing, and infinitely dreadful.[6]

Needless to say, Channing's position was analogous. He was a Christian because he regarded Christianity as the religion best fitted to develop the potentialities of the human race, not because he took revelation as a datum. And his chief objections to the Calvinist theology against which he rebelled were precisely those points on which true-blue Calvinists most prided themselves — belief in the Trinity, total depravity, and predestination. Whereas Calvin had said that these concepts, though repugnant to human reason, were manifestations of the illimitable sovereignty of God and hence not to be questioned, Channing held exactly opposite views. If doctrines were repugnant to human reason, they could not be true, not even if they bore the name of revelation.

Like his master Richard Price, Channing believed that morality is " eternal and immutable," that it " depends upon no will or power," and that " omnipotence does not consist in a power to alter the nature of things." [7] He claimed, of course, that these conclusions were Christian; one can imagine what Calvin's reaction to the claim would have been.

In such a concept can be discerned the fusion of two elements: a belief that the universe is constructed according to rational principles and a belief that the fundamental nature of the world is moral. We are to deal only with the developed version of this theory; hence it is not necessary to trace its genesis in detail. Suffice it to say, once responsibility has been transferred from an incomprehensible deity whose will is law to a rationally ordered, moral universe it becomes necessary to establish some modus vivendi with this abstract " nature of things." Piety is no longer enough, nor is simple obedience sufficient, for the complexity of the world has become too great to present a unified and consistent whole to the inquirer. And for exactly the same reasons, the idea of " self-evidence " fails to satisfy. The old deistic criterion of universal acceptance as a guide to moral behavior was bound to fall of its own weight once mankind became thoroughly aware of the irreconcilable differences in belief and practice among the several peoples of the world.

Shaftesbury, with the publication of *An Inquiry Concerning Virtue, or Merit* in 1711,[8] is generally credited with the introduction of the concept of a specific moral sense into English ethical theory. This moral sense, which was supposed to provide an infallible touchstone for distinguishing between true and false perceptions of the nature of things, was developed by Francis Hutcheson into the cornerstone of his *A System of Moral Philosophy*. Hutcheson held that the moral sense was analogous to the other senses and that one perceived morality just as one perceived a physical object. And extending this somewhat tenuous analogy, he came to the conclusion that, " if we can any way reason concerning the *original Nature* from what we feel in our own, or from any of our notions of excellency or perfection, we must conceive in a Deity some *perceptive power* analogous to our *moral sense*, by which he may have self-approbation in certain affections and actions rather than the contrary.[9]

Hutcheson's conception of a moral sense was obviously difficult to maintain in an unqualified form. Shaftesbury had not emphasized his version; consequently it escaped the adverse notice of Richard Price's *Questions in Morals*, undoubtedly the most influential book in the whole course of Channing's intellectual development. Price, however, did seize upon Hutcheson and made him bear the brunt of the attack on the moral sense.

Price opened with a refutation of Hutcheson by pointing out that the concept of a moral sense relieved agents of any moral worth — for the morality, or lack of it, became a matter of the successful or unsuccessful functioning of a sense; it did not involve choice on the part of the agent. Price's solution, anticipating Kant's, was to distinguish between the perception of the senses and the understanding. The understanding intuited the concepts of substance, duration, space, causation, infinity, and (very conveniently) the ideas of morality. Nor was the understanding to be confused with reason, for this latter " consists in investigating certain relations between objects, ideas of which must have been previously in the mind: that is, it supposes us already to have the ideas we want to trace; and therefore cannot give rise to new ideas." [10]   This distinction, of course, is to be met with among the Transcendentalists — though among them, unhappily for clarity, the nomenclature is reversed.

The nature of the right and wrong to be intuited by the understanding was, as we have seen, " eternal and immutable."   Furthermore, " Virtue and vice . . . from the *natures of things*, are the immediate and principal, and the most constant and intimate causes of private happiness and misery." [11]   The recognition of this fact was the source of virtue in mankind; people were not virtuous because of " publick utility or inutility," while those who depended on their conception of the will of God, independently of a prior morality, as the source of moral obligation were actually utilitarians in disguise, for they were really motivated by the hope of future reward or the fear of future pain.[12]

Channing, it will be remembered, told Miss Peabody that Price had saved him from Locke's philosophy.   The debt is perhaps overstated, though there can be no doubt that Price's distinction between the reason and the understanding provided a way out of the skepticism in which Hume had left the sensationalist school.   But fertile though Price's suggestions proved, the understanding was to turn out, in the light of later philosophic thought, to be as fallible a guide as the will of God or sensory perception had been to other generations.   In Channing's day, however, it seemed like a key to the secret of the universe, and he adopted it gladly.

He also subscribed to another tenet of Price's thinking: that one could train the moral understanding to a more perfect comprehension of the nature of things.   Price's reason-

ing was appealing, if not logical: " Our *speculative understanding* is evidently capable of infinite improvement; and
therefore our *moral understanding* must be so likewise; for
these being only different views of the same faculty . . .
cannot be conceived not to influence each other." [13] Channing most completely developed his doctrine of the conscience (or moral understanding) in an argument with
Theodore Parker, which was reported by the latter. The
discussion centered around the educability of the conscience — a theory that Parker, with true Transcendental
fervor, repudiated. One suspects that logic was also on
Parker's side, for it is difficult to conceive why an intuitive
faculty in direct contact with the nature of things needs to
be educated. According to Parker, however, Channing
said:

. . . it must be educated, like the understanding. But upon
being asked if more was needed than this, that the understanding should be rendered capable of presenting the case distinctly
to conscience, he seemed to favour the hypothesis. I asked him
if conscience were not an infallible guide. He seems to doubt
it. . . .   He said conscience was like the *eye*, which might be
dim, or might see wrong. . . . But conscience, when the facts
are fairly before it, acts *directly* and not *mediately*, and therefore it is not liable to the same mistakes with the eye.
He seemed inclined to admit this, yet denied that we needed
an infallible guide. . . .
He thought a man late in his life (in a case I put), who had
not hitherto consulted his conscience, would, coming to that
adviser, make great mistakes, and therefore be punished for his
past sin of neglect. Upon the whole, he believed if a man
should begin early to ask for the right, with sincere wish to
find it, he never would get far out of the way. . . .
Conscience is the last appeal. Never go beyond that; even if
it says wrong, the man is degraded who disobeys it. But if a
man's conscience tells him something different from other

men's, he is not to forego it, but to recast its plans, examine the subject anew, but at last adhere to conscience.[14]

The Transcendentalists made one improvement on this doctrine: they claimed that the conscience, reason — or whatever name they chose to denote the intuitive faculty — *was* infallible. And sometimes they went even further. Emerson, for instance, in his Divinity School Address announced, " If a man is at heart just, then in so far is he God; the safety of God, the immortality of God, the majesty of God do enter into that man with justice." [15] Channing, of course, recoiled from such a view, just as he recoiled from Parker's view of the conscience; but unless he was prepared (as he most definitely was not) to adopt an empirical view of reason, the assumptions he shared with Price inevitably led to the Transcendental extreme.

Yet Channing thought he had discovered a halfway house in which he could preserve the virtues of historical Christianity and at the same time give shelter to the new and more sophisticated rationalism of the age. He identified himself with " the community of free minds, of lovers of truth, of followers of Christ." And, he went on, " I desire to escape the narrow walls of a particular church, and to live in the open sky, in the broad light, looking far and wide, seeing with my own eyes, hearing with my own ears, and following truth meekly, but resolutely." [16] So had he spoken in 1828; so was he to speak again more than a dozen years later in his discourse on " The Church," the address which best sums up his view of institutional religion.

Unlike Emerson and the more extreme Transcendentalists, Channing could agree only partially with Tom

Paine's war cry, " My own mind is my own church." But nearly three decades of religious controversy had taught Channing that religious truth did not lie in sectarian claims; nor was he unaware of the role played by economic and class forces in the life of the church. A letter to his English friend Lucy Aikin written within a few weeks of the delivery of the discourse on " The Church " clearly shows his consciousness of the importance of these factors. Speaking of the fear of a lower-class uprising, Channing was not slow to put his finger on the perversion of the church into an instrument of class warfare:

How we ought to rejoice to lift up our depressed brethren! But no; we hate and fear them the more because they have caught the idea of some better, higher lot. We strengthen State authorities, Church authorities, to keep them down. We make religion hateful to them by using it for their own subjugation.[17]

As we have seen, Channing's conviction that religious groups were often used to further secular purposes was not entirely a matter of theory.[18] Hence, it is no surprise to see him concerned with this very problem in " The Church." Admitting freely that " few religious societies . . . would knowingly make the minister a slave," he added in warning:

Still, the members of a congregation, conscious of holding the support of their teacher in their hands, are apt to expect a cautious tenderness towards their known prejudices or judgments, which, though not regarded as servility, is very hostile to that firm, bold utterance of truth on which the success of his ministry chiefly depends.[19]

For Channing, then, the church was neither the vehicle of a particular class nor the formalized expression of a set of dogmas. It was a society of men like-minded in their search for truth. Large enough in its view of truth to include all men of good will, such a church could admit to fellowship all who tried to follow the precepts of Christ. Metaphysical and theological differences faded away in the face of a common goal, making it possible for Channing to say:

> Do not tell me that I surrender myself to a fiction of imagination, when I say, that distant Christians, that all Christians and myself, form one body, one church, just as far as a common love and piety possess our hearts. . . . There *is* one grand, all-comprehending church; and if I am a Christian, I belong to it, and no man can shut me out of it.[20]

This is the real catholic church; the individual religious society has no particular efficacy, for the " adaptation of the church to the promotion of holiness among men is its grand excellence; and where it accomplishes this end its work is done, and no greater can be conceived on earth or in heaven." [21]

So conceiving the excellence of the church, Channing felt that the success of any particular sect lies in two sources — the character of the minister and the spirituality of the congregation. The minister is teacher and guide. He acts on his flock by inspiring them with his example and by bringing their minds into contact with the minds of great spiritual leaders. The congregation in its turn must exercise a " quickening power " on its own members,[22] a power which, in the last analysis, exists to awaken the voice of reason, of conscience, the " voice within them, which they cannot silence." [23]   Thus, Channing's ecumenical church, the institutional embodiment of his thought, is indeed a halfway house, logically as well as practically. Able to conceive of a universal Christian church, he could not completely transcend — as Emerson had done a few years earlier — the Christian framework of his thinking. Yet he so expanded this framework that in this same discourse he could write: " Goodness, purity, virtue, this is the only distinction in God's sight. . . . It owes nothing to time, to circumstance, to outward connexions. It shines by its own light. It is the sun of the spiritual universe. It is God himself dwelling in the human soul." [24]

By thus broadening his concept of the church, Channing was able to remain Christian and still preserve his independence of mind. But he did not seem to see how close he had come to rendering supererogatory the institutional church as well as theological Christianity.

He could, for instance, brush off the argument for Christianity from revelation by saying that the argument from nature and reason was so convincing that he would use it instead of the traditional evidences of Christianity.[25] Yet, a few years earlier, he had given the Dudleian lectures at Harvard on " The Evidences of Christianity." That was in 1821; now, in 1828, he was asking:

Whence do we derive our knowledge of the attributes and perfections which constitute the Supreme Being? I answer, we derive them from our own souls. The divine attributes are first developed in ourselves, and thence transferred to our Creator. The idea of God, sublime and awful as it is, is the idea of our own spiritual nature, purified and enlarged to infinity. In ourselves are the elements of the Divinity.[26]

This was obviously Transcendental doctrine; it was also a reflection of Hutcheson's thought.[27] As a theological view, it belonged to the *via affirmativa* which maintained the possibility of predication about the nature of God. More than that, it created God in man's image and could not avoid the trap of creating a God who was the reflection of the mind of his creator. Thus Channing's God became a sweetly reasonable being, loath to judge, ready to love, and universally benevolent. Emerson's God, on the other hand, was very like Emerson writ large.

This view of God as the lengthened shadow of a man was naturally repugnant to the orthodox. Princeton was especially alarmed and did its best to put down the infidels. Identifying the doctrine as tending to atheism, if not worse, Princeton exposed it to public horror:

> While it retains the name of God, and does not, therefore, at once startle and shock the feelings like open atheism, it teaches its disciples to deify themselves and nature, and to look upon all phenomena alike, whether of the material universe or of the mind of man, as manifestations of the Deity. Every emotion of the heart is an acting forth of God, and every indulgence of a passion, however depraved, becomes an act of worship.[28]

Princeton had Carlyle and Emerson in mind when it issued this blast, but the argument was obviously applicable to this facet of Channing's thought.

Admittedly Channing was at his most extreme in the 1828 sermon from which the above quotation was taken; but one could cite dozens of instances in which the chief idea was adumbrated. The concept of a God in the likeness of man is characteristic of Channing's view.[29] Bearing this fact in mind, it is easy to understand Channing's rejection of Calvinist theology. The sum of his objection was that Calvin's God is an inhuman monster. As Channing rejected Calvin, he also drew away from his old master Samuel Hopkins.

Hopkins was just as conscious as Channing that the Calvinist view of the Deity was repugnant to our human concept of morality — indeed, of simple decency. Still, the Bible was the inspired word of God, and clearly, on strict Biblical terms, the Lord was something of an enigma, filled sometimes with hatred for mankind, sometimes with pity and love, and sometimes with an inexorable desire for vengeance. Hopkins made it his task to reconcile these varying attributes of God, as well as some of the corollaries that energetic divines had deduced from the Bible's sacred and infallible word, with contemporary ethical doctrine. The result of his labors was *The System of Doctrines, Contained in Divine Revelation. Explained and Defended. Shewing Their Consistence and Connexion with Each Other. To Which Is Added, a Treatise on the Millennium.* Hopkins endeavored in this book to relieve God of the arbitrariness with which Calvin had endowed him. He achieved his goal, not by denying the authenticity either of revelation or of Pauline Christianity, but by marrying them to the Enlightenment's theory of disinterested benevolence.

The possibility of the marriage depended, of course, on a rejection of Calvin's God as the *ne plus ultra* of philosophical inquiry. Hopkins, like Channing and some of the English ethical writers, had perforce to substitute a hypothetical "nature of things" for God's arbitrary will in order to render the Deity more acceptable to the human mind. For otherwise, in spite of all denial, God became the author of evil — a position most unacceptable for the-

ology to take in unqualified form. Hopkins, then, cut the
Gordian knot by admitting that the problem of the author-
ship of evil could not be answered " to the satisfaction of
a rational, inquisitive mind, or the difficulty in any measure
solved, unless it be supposed and granted, *That all the evil
which does take place, is necessary for the greatest possible
general good; and therefore on the whole, all things considered, wisest and best that it should exist just as it does.*" [30]
In other words, God is bound by the nature of things to
act in the way he does. But if God was thus exonerated,
the nature of things was not, and the dilemma remained —
especially if Calvinism's five points proved to be as firmly
based on the new ground as they were on the old. It did
the sinner no good to be told that, although he was utterly
corrupt and his own efforts could do nothing to redeem
him, his fate was determined by the " divine decrees, which
is of all other possible plans the wisest and best." [31]   Dr.
Hopkins, like Dr. Pangloss, had no answer to Candide's
question, " Si c'est ici le meilleur des mondes possibles, que
sont donc les autres? "

Channing, as we have seen, had been much influenced
by Hopkins — more, perhaps, by the old man's personal
character than by his explanation of the universe. In practice, Hopkins' philosophical and theological asperity was
tempered by the disinterested benevolence of his actions.
Disentangled from its Calvinist trappings, his theory of
benevolence was remarkably similar to that of Francis
Hutcheson, who had written: " That disposition . . .
which is most excellent, and naturally gains the highest
moral approbation, is the calm, stable, universal, good-will
to all, or the most extensive benevolence. And this seems

the most distinct notion we can form of the moral excellency of the Deity." [32] Translated into theological terms, the sentiment was obviously that of Hopkins and Channing. And even closer to Hopkins' conviction that disinterested benevolence to being in general required the sacrifice of many of its parts, was Hutcheson's example of a judge who acquitted criminals because he was tender of heart; we might applaud such pity, but a moment's reflection would convince us that its misuse caused "violence and outrages" to abound. Furthermore:

A more extensive view of a publick interest shews some sort of pity to occasion more extensive misery, than arises from a strict execution of justice. Pity of itself never appears deformed; but a more extensive affection, a love to society, a zeal to promote general happiness, is a more lovely principle, and the want of this renders a character deformed.[33]

This disregard for the sufferings of the individual in the interest of a somewhat abstract "being in general" was more than equaled in Hopkins' thought. In perhaps the only passage of his works that is remembered today he wrote:

And if he [the man who is disinterestedly benevolent] could know that God designed, for his own glory and the general good, to cast him into endless destruction; this would not make him cease to approve of his character; he would continue to be a friend of God, and to be pleased with his moral perfection.[34]

No wonder that Dr. Holmes could call Hopkins a "poor, dear, good old Christian heathen!" and add, "Meant well, —meant well. Juggernaut." Holmes, an inveterate foe of religious orthodoxy, whether Old or New Light, continued by saying:

Parson Channing put a little oil on one linchpin, and slipped it out so softly, the first thing they knew about it was the wheel of that side was down. T'other fellow's at work now, but he makes more noise about it. When the linchpin comes out on his side, there'll be a jerk, I tell you! [35]

In spite of the levity of the image, Holmes accurately assessed Channing's role in the breakdown of orthodoxy. Channing's common sense seized on the elements of Hopkins' and Hutcheson's work which provided a reasonable theodicy; but it stopped short at the psychological absurdity with which the former, at least, carried his theory of disinterested benevolence to its logical conclusion that we ought to be glad to be damned. The catch, obviously, is that those worthy of damnation on Hopkinsian principles would never have agreed to their fate, while the elect who were capable of accepting damnation *ad majorem Dei gloriam* were probably in no danger of eternal fire.

The image of the linchpin was perhaps a little dubious. It took more than oil to slip it loose, and Channing, in his day, made as much theological noise as Parker in his. But Holmes — who prided himself on the belief that like stimuli ought to provide like responses — had written four years earlier, in 1855, " The Deacon's Masterpiece or, The Wonderful ' One-Hoss Shay ' A Logical Story! " in which the wagon motif was also used as a device to record the collapse of Calvinism. The " shay " of the poem disappeared a great deal more suddenly than its theological prototype, which is with us still, though its rejection by religious liberals was not due to its logical faults, any more than the collapse of the " shay " resulted from the failure of its structure. But still,

You see, of course, if you're not a dunce,
How it went to pieces all at once, —
All at once, and nothing first, —
Just as bubbles do when they burst.

End of the wonderful one-hoss shay.
Logic is logic. That's all I say.

Channing, of course, played his part in perfect innocence.
He thought it possible to repudiate both the Old Light Calvinists and the New Light followers of Hopkins without af-
fecting Christian unity, and it was with an air of pained
surprise that he realized he was considered an apostate by
both parties. He had never accepted Calvin's doctrine of an
arbitrary God; he had, for a time, found in Hutcheson and
Hopkins a satisfactory explanation of the fact of evil, and
parts of their teaching he retained until his dying day. It is
impossible to discover any consistent chronological development in Channing's religious thought. He assimilated from
others the elements in their thinking that were congenial to
his nature; the uncongenial corollaries and implications he
ignored. He was surprised when others of a more logical
turn insisted that if he said A, then B must inevitably follow.
Not concerned with logic or consistency himself, he looked
upon the assaults of the Calvinists and Hopkinsians with
amazement, and never ceased to wonder at their reaction to
his eclecticism.

The impression in early nineteenth-century Boston that
Channing was a Hopkinsian was probably chiefly derived
from his constant use of the words " disinterested benevolence," a phrase that was almost the hallmark of the group.
But, as we have seen, the idea of benevolence was a com-

monplace in English ethical thought. There is no need to review the controversy between the devotees of self-love as the mainspring of all human actions and those who regarded disinterestedness as essential to truly ethical behavior; Shaftesbury and Hutcheson are perhaps the best-known examples of the latter school, while Hobbes and Mandeville are representative of the former.

Hopkins eagerly adopted the distinction between self-love and disinterested benevolence, adding to it a theological qualification — all mankind was *naturally* motivated by self-love. The gift of grace, however, enabled a man to become disinterestedly benevolent and hence in tune with God's purpose. It followed that whatever men did of their own accord, without grace, was purely selfish and consequently deserving of no moral credit. Good actions, then, were good only when their motivation was disinterested. Thus Hopkins avoided the imputation of Arminianism which was hurled at Channing.

It is not clear whether Channing ever translated the ethical distinction between self-love and benevolence into theological terms. Nevertheless, his audience almost surely did, and their identification was probably sufficient in itself to relegate him to the Hopkinsian camp. The resemblance between Channing's thought and that of Hopkins was further strengthened by the younger man's evident piety — a characteristic of the New Lights viewed with alarm both by the old-line Calvinists and by the rationalists. Remember Moses Stuart's comment, " Let any man be warmly engaged for religion here [in Boston], and he is at once a Hopkinsian or an enthusiast." [36] Furthermore, there was just enough of the traditional phraseology in Channing's writing to give color to the belief that he was a follower of Hopkins. Such a belief, of course, became untenable once the Unitarian movement had asserted itself, though even in his later sermons Channing was capable of writing:

We dedicate it [this church] to the King and Father Eternal, the King of kings and Lord of lords. We dedicate it to his Unity, to his unrivalled and undivided Majesty. We dedicate it to the praise of his free, unbought, unmerited grace. We dedicate it to Jesus Christ, to the memory of his love, to the celebration of his divine virtue, to the preaching of that truth which he sealed with his blood.[37]

Nothing in those lines could terrify the orthodox, while many of the expressions would gratify the most devout Calvinist as well as the most rigorous Hopkinsian. Yet they are drawn from the peroration of the sermon " Unitarian Christianity Most Favorable to Piety," delivered in 1826.

Nine years earlier, in 1817, Channing had written a letter to a Portland clergyman, a Mr. Nichols, proposing a series of ministerial meetings, and adding, " Men do not need so much to be taught what to do, as to be quickened and revived to do it — The fault is in the heart and will and not in the understanding." [38] This was pure orthodox as well as pure Hopkinsian doctrine, for Calvin had said: " The blinding of the wicked and all those enormities which attend it, are called the works of Satan, the cause of which must nevertheless be sought only in the human will, from which proceeds the root of evil." [39] And Hopkins, writing of the creation of man, held that we were created in God's *moral* image, without which our intellectual qualities would be as nothing.[40] He reinforced this separation of pure intelligence from right disposition of the heart in his discussion of the wisdom of God: " It is certain that this wisdom is a moral excellence, and belongs to the heart, and therefore does not consist in mere speculation, or that knowledge or understanding which may be without any rectitude or goodness of disposition or heart." [41]

It is possible, however, that Channing was not using the conventional words in their traditional meaning, even though his audience probably apprehended them in their usual sense. Perhaps when he wrote such phrases as " they [preachers] have addressed men as mere creatures of intellect," [42] using the words in a pejorative sense, he was thinking of the intellect in a Pricean manner, holding with his mentor that:

Reason alone, (imperfect as it is in us) is by no means sufficient to defend us against the danger to which . . . we are exposed. Our Maker has, therefore, wisely provided remedies for its imperfections; and established a due balance in our frame by annexing to our intellectual perceptions sensations and instincts, which give them greater weight and force.[43]

There is no sure way of deciding the question; more important is the fact that much of Channing's preaching could be interpreted in Hopkinsian terms without wrenching the words out of context. And the public tendency to affix labels must have been strengthened by the knowledge that Channing was a good friend of Hopkins, that the older man lent his pulpit to the younger on more than one occasion, and that he was a kindly critic of Channing's sermons and theological opinions.

Throughout his life Channing warmly remembered Hopkins, and referred to him in friendly terms on more than one occasion. His own view of Hopkins' theology was surprisingly generous; he paid public tribute both to the man and his theology in the sermon " Christian Worship," delivered at the dedication of the First Unitarian Church in Newport, in 1836. Not only did Channing's statement avow his own indebtedness to Hopkins, but also it provided an excellent summary of the meaning of Hopkins' teaching in Channing's own thought; the statement therefore deserves quotation *in extenso:*

His [Dr. Hopkins'] name is indeed associated with a stern and appalling theology, and it is true, that he wanted toleration towards those who rejected his views. Still in forming his religious opinions, he was superior to human authority; he broke away from human creeds; he revered reason, the oracle of God within him. His system, however fearful, was yet built on a generous foundation. He maintained that all holiness, all moral excellence, consists in benevolence, or disinterested devotion to the greatest good; that this is the character of God; that love is the only principle of the divine administration. He taught that sin was introduced into the creation, and is to be everlastingly punished, because evil is necessary to the highest good. To this government, in which the individual is surrendered to the well-being of the whole, he required entire and cheerful submission. Other Calvinists were willing that their neighbours should be predestined to everlasting misery for the glory of God. This noble-minded man demanded a more generous and impartial virtue, and maintained that we should consent to our own perdition, should be willing ourselves to be condemned, if the greatest good of the universe, and the manifestation of the divine perfections should so require. True virtue, as he taught, was an entire surrender of personal interest to the benevolent purposes of God. Self-love he spared in none of its movements. He called us to seek our own happiness as well as that of others, in a spirit of impartial benevolence; to do good to ourselves, not from self-preference, not from the impulse of personal desires, but in obedience to that sublime law, which requires us to promote the welfare of each and all within our influence. I need not be ashamed to confess the deep impression which this system made on my youthful mind. I am grateful to this stern teacher for turning my thoughts and heart to the claims and majesty of impartial, universal benevolence. From such a man, a tame acquiescence in the established theology was not to be expected. He indeed accepted the doctrine of predestination in its severest form; but in so doing, he imagined himself a disciple of reason as well as of revelation. He believed this doctrine to be sustained by profound metaphysical argumentation, and to rest on the only sound philosophy of the human mind, so that in receiving it, he did not abandon the ground of reason. In accordance with his free spirit of inquiry, we find him making not a few important modifications of Calvinism. The doctrine that we are liable to punishment for the sin of our first parent, he wholly rejected; and not satisfied with denying the imputation of Adam's guilt to his posterity, he subverted what the old theology had set forth as the only foundation of divine acceptance, namely the imputation of Christ's righteousness or merits to the believer. The doctrine that Christ died for the elect only, found no mercy at his hands. He taught that Christ suffered equally for all mankind. The system of Dr. Hopkins was indeed an effort of reason to reconcile Calvinism with its essential truths. Accordingly his disciples were sometimes called, and willingly called, Rational Calvinists.[44]

We can discover in this interpretation of *The System of Doctrines* many features of Channing's own thought. The self-reliance of a man who dared to make his own interpretation of the Bible, his insistence that revelation ought to make rational sense, his belief in benevolence as the foundation of the universe, his rejection of Adam's responsibility for the sinful actions of his descendents, his denial that Christ was the redeemer of a chosen few — all the items in this list (if taken out of context) might come from Channing's own writings. In context, however, Hopkins' theology was not less appalling than Calvin's. A few words have been rearranged: God's purposes have become benevolent instead of mysterious; we are not damned for Adam's guilt, though his lapse involves us all in sin and hence we deserve damnation; Christ may have died for all, but only a few are saved. In short, though the terms have changed a little, " The world, it is the old world still."

Channing displayed in this interpretation his customary approach to the writings of other men. He found in them only what he chose to find; always his own face looked back at him, no matter which way he turned. A believer in disinterested benevolence, he could welcome its appearance even though the words concealed a narrow and vindictive view of life which could not be tortured into rationality by Hopkins' most determined efforts. Yet, in spite of Channing's failure to unite a supernatural world view with a reasonable one and thus produce the anomaly of a " rational Calvinist," he did perceive the fundamental significance of his old friend's *The System of Doctrines.* Abortive though the attempt was, the mere fact that Hopkins had caused a revolution in American theology by his insistence that the ways of God must be held accountable at the bar of reason prepared the way for Channing's further liberation of religious thinking, and ultimately for the religious (though perhaps not Christian) beliefs of Transcendentalism.[45]

Channing's own revolution was a continuance of the Hopkinsian revolt. The new movement not only consolidated the gains of its predecessor, but also moved on to new positions — the denial of the Trinity, the virtual denial of hell, a belief in the perfectibility of man and the spiritual efficacy of good works, a faith in progress, and finally a new conception of the value of man as the source of whatever is truly divine.

Like Hopkins, however, Channing was interested not so much in revolution as in morality. The changes that each made in the prevailing doctrine of the day were not primarily philosophical necessities; they were adaptations of the theological structure to changing social and political views. Channing, much more than Hopkins, was alert to the new currents of his day. A broader, more sensitive figure — though much less the scholar — Channing sought a faith that would embody not only the rationalism of the Enlightenment but also the humanitarianism of the nineteenth century. In addition, he had to deal with the new political ideology exemplified in the government of the United States as well as to adjust his thought to the problems of an emergent capitalism.

All of these influences tended toward secularization, and Channing's concept of Christianity showed the strain. He tried to accommodate the formal structure of his religion to the new stresses, persuading himself that in his accommodations he was sacrificing nothing essential. But neither his contemporaries, nor, I suspect, the majority of professing Christians today, could accept the greater part of his emendations of the traditional dogma. We have seen his often-repeated assertion that revelation must be acceptable to the rational faculty before it can command belief. This is a far cry from Calvin and, indeed, from a tradition at least as old as Tertullian's *Credo quia impossibile est*. Channing, however, succeeded in convincing himself that revelation, properly interpreted, was consonant with reason, and was thus enabled, as he thought, to preserve Christianity intact.

His confidence extended neither to his followers nor to his opponents. The former, in the person of Theodore Parker, abandoned revelation almost entirely. The latter, in the doughty Andover champions, Leonard Woods and Moses Stuart, smote Channing hip and thigh for apostasy from Bible Christianity. Channing's Baltimore Sermon of 1819 dealt with his method (if it can be dignified with so logical a term) of interpreting Scripture. He began, bravely enough, by saying:

We regard the Scriptures as the records of God's successive revelations to mankind, and particularly of the last and most perfect revelation of his will by Jesus Christ. Whatever doctrines seem to us to be clearly taught in the Scriptures, we receive without reserve or exception. We do not, however, attach equal importance to all the books in this collection. Our religion, we believe, lies chiefly in the New Testament.[46]

Channing added that whatever Jesus taught was held by Unitarians to be of divine authority. And then he proceeded to take up the charge that Unitarians were said " to prefer our own wisdom to God's." [47] In language strongly reminiscent of Tom Paine, Channing then defended the use of reason in the interpretation of the Bible: " We believe that God, when he speaks to the human race, conforms . . . to the established rules of speaking and writing." [48] It follows, therefore, that God's words, phrases, and sentences ought to be subject to the usual criteria. Furthermore, Bible passages must be considered in context. Some of the language is poetical rather than scientific; much of it is marked by the habits of the age in which it was written. Therefore, thought Channing, it was necessary " to look beyond the letter to the spirit." [49] If this course was taken, the Bible would be found to be perfectly self-consistent.

But since apparent contradictions existed, we must make use of reason. Channing described the technique:

> From a variety of possible interpretations, we select that which accords, with the nature of the subject and the state of the writer, with the connexion of the passage, with the general strain of Scripture, with the known character and will of God, and with the obvious and acknowledged laws of nature.[50]

The Doctor felt that to maintain the divine authority of Scripture without these rational qualifications would prove impossible.

The orthodox fell with infinite zeal on these contentions. Moses Stuart immediately put his finger on the weak point of Channing's argument by contending that though reason was essential to the interpretation of Scripture, its role ended there:

> In short, the Scriptures once being admitted to be the word of God, or of divine authority; the sole office of reason in respect to them is to act as the *interpreter* of Revelation, and not in any case as a *legislator*. . . . Philosophy has no right to interfere here.[51]

Stuart's real thunder was reserved for some of the deductions Channing drew from his rational interpretations of the Bible — particularly his view of the unity of God. This unity, according to Channing, was that of a simple being; it was not a complex conception of three in one, or a threefold being, or three aspects of the same being. Such a conception was fundamentally irrational; therefore it could not supply a true idea of God. Furthermore, the idea of a trinity distracted the mind; it was a form of polytheism and gave rise to a species of idolatry.

If these deductions were granted, Jesus necessarily became a being — unique, to be sure — but clearly inferior to God. Stuart might have been willing to admit, as a matter of form, that reason was necessary in the interpretation of Scripture — but when sacrilege resulted, it was time to call a halt. He rebutted Channing by pointing out what the Unitarian minister already knew: that the Calvinists also insisted on the unity of God. Channing would have agreed, though he felt the Calvinists who flattered themselves that they could at one and the same time have both unity and trinity were either using language in an indefensible manner or indulging in the crudest of sophistries. Stuart confessed the difficulty, saying:

> The *fact* that a distinction exists [among the persons of the Godhead], is what I aver; the definition of that distinction is what I shall by no means attempt. . . . I confess myself unable to advance a single step here, in explaining what the distinction is. *I receive the* FACT *that it exists, simply because I believe that the Scriptures reveal the* FACT. And if the Scriptures do reveal the fact that there are three persons in the Godhead . . . then it is, like every other fact revealed, to be received simply on the credit of divine revelation.[52]

But because a proposition is undefinable, said Stuart, there is no reason for assuming it to be unintelligible. And historically there has been such a proposition, both in Scripture and in the earliest sacred writings. Hence, in the doctrine of the Trinity we had one of those mysterious truths which it has pleased a divine Providence to reveal to us.

Such a revelation could not be judged by reason, once it

was admitted that the Bible did contain such a statement. Stuart hammered his point home with relentless logic. To Channing's contention that the double nature of Christ was "repugnant to common sense,"[53] his adversary countered:

Do you mean, that common sense may determine first, independently of Revelation, that the doctrine cannot be true; and then maintain the impossibility that Revelation should exhibit it? If so, then we are able to decide, *a priori*, what can be revealed, and what cannot: consequently what we may believe, and what we must disbelieve. It follows, then, that a Revelation is unnecessary.[54]

The remaining sections of Stuart's pamphlet were devoted to the question of the precise revelation concerning the Deity in the Bible. Needless to say, he found his own position entirely justified — and no doubt he rested from his labors confident that he had utterly driven Channing from the field.

Stuart, however, had concerned himself only with the nature of the Trinity. The gravamen of Channing's charge lay in his description of Calvinism as an immoral theology. The concept of the Trinity was in itself not of primary importance to Channing. He challenged it as a symbol of the inhumanity of orthodox doctrine and as detracting from the true knowledge of God. Orthodoxy, as he described it, " take[s] from us our Father in heaven, and substitute[s] for him a being, whom we cannot love if we would."[55] And, in spite of Channing's affinity with Hopkins, the New Lights received their share of his censure. Mentioning total depravity, election, limited atonement, effectual calling — omitting only predestination — Channing stated that a belief in such doctrines was pernicious. And such a faith must have an " unhappy influence ":

It tends to discourage the timid, to give excuses to the bad, to feed the vanity of the fanatical, and to offer shelter to the bad feelings of the malignant. By shocking, as it does, the fundamental principles of morality, and by exhibiting a severe and partial Deity, it tends strongly to pervert the moral faculty, to form a gloomy, forbidding, and servile religion, and to lead men to substitute censoriousness, bitterness, and persecution, for a tender and impartial charity.[56]

Unitarianism, on the other hand, was open to none of these objections:

. . . we regard it as more friendly to practical piety and pure morals than the opposite doctrines, . . . it gives clearer and nobler views of duty, and stronger motives to its performance, it recommends religion at once to the understanding and the heart, . . . it asserts the lovely and venerable attributes of God, . . . it tends to restore the benevolent spirit of Jesus to his divided and afflicted church, and . . . it cuts off every hope of God's favor, except that which springs from practical conformity to the life and precepts of Christ.[57]

To the defense of orthodoxy and, incidentally, of the Hopkinsians (the two groups having dropped their internecine war to unite against this common enemy), Leonard Woods of Andover devoted his *Letters to Unitarians Occasioned by the Sermon of the Reverend William E. Channing at the Ordination of the Rev. J. Sparks.* Woods employed 160 pages to demolish Channing's criticisms of Calvinism. He began — as was the ministerial custom in the first stages of a pamphlet war — with a disclaimer of any sectarian spirit; it was against his will to be drawn into a controversy, but he could not sit idly by while the character of his faith was traduced by Unitarians. He then proceeded to justify the Calvinist and Hopkinsian views by claiming that his God was not immoral but benevolent. And God's benevolence was proved by the death of Christ on the cross, for " To forgive sin in any other way, than through *the shedding of blood*, would not consist with a due regard to ' the interests of virtue.' " [58]

It was precisely this attitude, which could find benevolence conclusively established by the shedding of blood, that Channing was objecting to. He wanted no part of a theodicy, a logic, or a religion based on so fantastic an inversion of ordinary morality. Moreover, Woods asked:

What human father, possessing even a common degree of paternal kindness and compassion, would ever treat his children, as God treated his rational offspring, when he destroyed the world by a deluge, or Sodom by fire, or when he caused the earth to open and swallow up the company of Korah? Would a compassionate father drown his children, or consume them by fire, or bury them alive in the earth? [59]

Channing could answer only that if no human father could act in so revolting a manner, then a fortiori no God worthy of the name could do so. But Woods had used his questions only as a rhetorical device to prove that Channing's analogy between a divine and human father was faulty.

Having established that " God is love," and having considered " what stress the Orthodox lay upon the moral perfection of God," [60] Woods proceeded to his next point — the irrefragability of the doctrine of total depravity. After admitting the difficulty of understanding why a good God should treat his creatures so harshly, he concluded:

But our being unable, by the mere exercise of reason, to discover the consistency between these facts and the infinite goodness of God, is no proof that the facts do not exist, and

no proof that they are in reality inconsistent with divine goodness.[61]

Woods, following this contention with a description of the
evils flesh is heir to, asserted triumphantly that evils were
facts which no a priori argument about the nature of God
could change. Twenty-two pages of scriptural authority
in favor of the total depravity of the human race concluded
the argument on this score.

Channing had said that Calvinism "teaches, that God
selects from this corrupt mass a number to be saved, and
plucks them, by a special influence, from the common ruin;
that the rest of mankind, though left without that special
grace which their conversion requires, are commanded to
repent." [62] Woods, needless to say, found these doctrines
acceptable enough; turning to Bible texts for aid, he inquired why the Unitarians could not see that Scripture
bore ample testimony to the orthodox position. But the
modern reader detects a note of uneasiness — even of petulance — in Woods's defense of the doctrine of election. He
permitted himself a little clerical impatience at the end of
the seventh letter by complaining:

Indeed, a man in some instances, can hardly find himself at
liberty simply to repeat the texts of Scripture, which support
the doctrine, without being attacked. . . . I trust my readers
will be sensible, that the state of mind, which is exhibited in
such cases, is altogether at variance with Christian candor, and
in a high degree unpropitious to the cause of truth.[63]

And at the end of the eighth letter, speaking of the Unitarian repugnance to the idea of election, he slyly remarked:
"Were it not for this repugnance, which plainly shows the
moral disorder of the human mind, no man, we think, could

be found, who would not regard the doctrine with the most cordial acquiescence." [64]

Channing's objection to the orthodox view of the atonement was the next item on Woods's agenda. Here, too, he showed a certain weakness, for he was quick to admit that, although God's punishment of sin did *sound* somewhat like the actions of an angry and revengeful man, in reality they were not — because God's motives were different from those of men. Furthermore, Channing and the other Unitarians would do well to remember that much of the Biblical language on this topic was metaphorical; some of this Eastern riot of imagination might conceivably have crept into the orthodox description of the doctrine. In short, Woods seemed to be a trifle uneasy in his defense of the doctrine of atonement. A similar uneasiness revealed itself in his letter on irresistible grace. Channing had rejected " the doctrine of irresistible divine influence on the human mind, moulding it into goodness, as marble is hewn into a statue. Such goodness . . . would not be the object of moral approbation, any more than the instinctive affections of inferior animals or the constitutional amiableness of human beings." [65] Woods again took refuge in a semantic defense: " irresistible," he said, meant convincing. And furthermore, even it if did mean irresistible, man's moral freedom would be intact, for in the phrase " irresistible grace " there is no hint of coercion: " When we represent the influence of the Holy Spirit in sanctifying the hearts of men, as *irresistible,* or *overpowering,* we speak solely with reference to that, which is supposed to make resistance, or is to be overcome." [66] Since no one supposed that the moral sense itself provided any resistance to grace, it followed that the freedom of moral agency was not in any way impugned.

Woods concluded his pamphlet with two more letters in answer to Channing's general conclusions. Both Unitarians and orthodox, he maintained, agreed on the role of Jesus in promoting a moral life. They agreed also that enthusiasm was often damaging to the cause of true religious affection and that love for Christ was essential for a truly Christian spirit. Channing's contention that Calvinism was not conducive to piety Woods refuted with a point-by-point comparison with Unitarianism, in which he easily proved to his own satisfaction that the orthodox were absolutely correct and that their system was infinitely superior to Channing's. Significantly, Woods rested a great part of the burden of his defense on the ground that orthodoxy had been misrepresented:

Should I, in these Letters, impute to you as a Society of Unitarians, all the extravagancies of opinion, which some German, English, or American Unitarians, have held, and all the rashness and violence of language, which they have employed; you would doubtless think me guilty of acting contrary to fairness and equity.[67]

The Unitarians, thought Woods, had done just exactly that in their strictures on orthodoxy.

Since this charge of misrepresentation was to bulk large in orthodox rebuttals of Unitarian attacks as well as in Unitarian rejoinders to orthodox forays, a word or two from the perspective of the next century may not be amiss. Both sides cried misrepresentation as a matter of course. And since both parties were actually engaged in a warfare whose larger issues they understood imperfectly, much of their argument was on the level of name-calling. This was particularly true of the Unitarians. They could — as Channing did in 1819 — pick out some of the more unattractive features of orthodox belief, list them, call them immoral, and think they had won the argument. And, taken in the Unitarian sense and based on premises that the Unitarians themselves were seldom fully conscious of, such orthodox doctrines were, if not immoral, at least highly unattractive. But not only did the Unitarians ignore the libraries of qualifications and justifications with which the orthodox surrounded their creeds, but also they were arguing on premises which they themselves would have rejected if they had been conscious of them — which, in fact, most of them did reject when Theodore Parker brought them into public view more than twenty years later.

Bare, unqualified orthodoxy, confronted with rational humanitarianism, must seem offensive to the rational humanitarian. The conflict between the two points of view, however, is not an intellectual one; it is a conflict of attitudes in which neither one can possibly understand the other unless he realizes the grounds of the opposition. Woods did comprehend the issue and put his finger squarely on it when he wrote:

The Bible, we believe, contains a harmonious system of truth, eternal truth, unmixed with error. If our reason seems to see inconsistencies, we charge not the appearance of those inconsistencies to any fault in the Scriptures, but to the weakness and obscurity of reason, and we have no doubt it will entirely vanish, when our reason acquires a higher degree of improvement. I must refer it to the christian public to determine, whether Unitarianism teaches its disciples to treat the word of God with this kind of reverence and submission.[68]

The plain fact is that Unitarianism did not so teach its disciples; it was sitting on a logical fence. If it made up its mind to climb down on the side of the Bible, the orthodox bull was waiting to gore it with scriptural authority and logical argument; if it tried to climb down on the other side, it was met with cries of infidelity and secularism — taunts that it was unwilling, as a body, to face.

In Channing's Baltimore Sermon and in the Andover replies to it lay the gist of the Unitarian controversy with the orthodox. When Channing four years earlier had replied to Evarts' review in the *Panoplist* and in his skirmish with Dr. Worcester, his tactics had been defensive. The "liberal Christians" had resented being consigned to the outer darkness by the orthodox; their energies were spent in denying imputations of heresy. But the 1819 Baltimore Sermon was a declaration of war to which the blasts and counterblasts that followed added nothing of doctrinal importance. Ware endeavored to rout Woods with Bible texts, and Norton unfurled his immense erudition in defense of the unity of God. Channing himself, though he repeated many of his points in the "Moral Argument Against Calvinism," added nothing new to the controversy, which simmered along until 1826.

"Unitarian Christianity Most Favorable to Piety" was the title of Channing's sermon at the dedication of the Second Congregational Church in New York. The title was innocuous; the contents did not differ markedly from those of the Baltimore Sermon or those of the "Moral Argument Against Calvinism." And yet, Channing wrote to Lucy Aikin, "that production has drawn upon me more angry criticism than anything I have published." [69] The reason for the *furor theologicus* lay in a graphic image of the orthodox view of the universe:

> Suppose, then, that a teacher should come among you, and should tell you that the Creator, in order to pardon his own children, had erected a gallows in the centre of the universe, and had publicly executed upon it, in room of the offenders, an Infinite Being, the partaker of his own Supreme Divinity; suppose him to declare, that this execution was appointed, as a most conspicuous and terrible manifestation of God's justice, and of the infinite woe denounced by his law; and suppose him to add, that all beings in heaven and earth are required to fix their eyes on this fearful sight, as the most powerful enforcement of obedience and virtue. Would you not tell him, that he calumniated his Maker? Would you not say to him, that this central gallows threw gloom over the universe; that the spirit of a government, whose very acts of pardon were written in such blood, was terror, not paternal love; and that the obedience which needed to be upheld by this horrid spectacle, was nothing worth? [70]

Though hedged with disclaimers of offense, this picture irritated the orthodox — irritated them the more, perhaps, because there was no effective rejoinder. A disquisition on the infinite benevolence of the Deity did not have half the emotive power of Channing's analogy, and to murmur of this interpretation of their ingeniously elaborate logic, " That is not what I meant at all, / That is not it, at all," would scarcely have been effective.

Channing's analogy was irritating enough. But four years later, climaxing more than a decade of controversy, appeared his volume entitled *Discourses, Reviews, and Miscellanies*, containing a section from the controversy with Dr. Worcester; the Baltimore Sermon; the *Christian Dis-*

ciple article on the " Moral Argument Against Calvinism ";
the " Objections to Unitarian Christianity "; " Unitarian
Christianity Most Favorable to Piety "; and the " Discourse
at the Installation of the Rev. F. A. Farley " (which we
shall presently have occasion to consider in some detail).
Worse than the inclusion of all this heretical material in one
volume was Channing's preface, in which he said that circumstances rather than a love for disputation forced him
to write so much controversial material. With the spirit of
religious persecution rampant, he had no choice but to
write:

Opinions, which I thought true and purifying were not only
assailed as errors, but branded as crimes. Then began, what
seems to me one of the gross immoralities of our times, the
practice of aspersing the characters of exemplary men, on the
ground of differences of opinion as to the most mysterious articles of faith. Then began those assaults on freedom of thought
and speech, which, had they succeeded, would have left us only
the name of religious liberty. Then it grew perilous to search
the scriptures for ourselves, and to speak freely according to the
convictions of our own minds. I saw that penalties . . . were,
if possible, to be attached to the profession of liberal views of
Christianity . . . and that a degrading uniformity of opinion
was to be imposed by the severest persecution, which the spirit
of the age would allow. At such a period, I dared not to be
silent.[71]

Moses Stuart once again rose to the attack, and published
*A Letter to William E. Channing D.D. on the subject of
Religious Liberty.* Stuart maintained that the orthodox had
no intention of suppressing dissent: they merely wished
the dissenters to remember that the orthodox possessed the
right of self-defense. He wished, too, that the dissenters

would modify their language, referring to Channing's gallows image as that "awful paragraph." [72] And he indignantly denied the truth of Channing's allegation:

I know that what I have said is incapable of being contradicted, on any grounds of evidence. *I do know that the accusations which you stand pledged to support are* NOT TRUE. I aver that THEY ARE NOT, before heaven and earth.[73]

Bernard Whitman replied for the Unitarians, while the Rev. Dr. Samuel Cheever broke a lance for the orthodox. Occasional sniping, of course, continued from both sides, but this was the last pamphlet war in which Channing was engaged. The next major outbreak was the work of Theodore Parker.

Two of Channing's controversial religious works are occasionally read today — or at least sometimes included in the more conscientious anthologies of American literature. These are the Baltimore Sermon and the "Moral Argument Against Calvinism." The orthodox pamphlets are completely forgotten, which is as it should be, for the great majority of Americans are no longer intimately concerned with theological niceties. Channing did not overbear the orthodox with argument; he merely substituted new premises for old, though he was not completely aware of the substitution. The significance of the whole controversy lies for us, not in the fact that the old logic was once again chopped over or that it made any practical difference whether God was one or triune, but in the formal recognition of a new humanitarian morality so strong that the nature of the Deity itself had to be redefined.

Thomas Malthus neatly put his finger on the crux of the whole matter. On borrowing Lucy Aikin's copy of Channing's New York dedication sermon, he slipped it into his pocket, saying, " It is a system which every good mind must wish to be true, but I think there are considerable difficulties from some of the texts." [74] And so there were. Channing could ignore the difficulties; his opponents could not. Yet the humanistic leaven was working even in the orthodox mind. At the beginning of the controversy Channing had noted: " It is well known that the old fashioned Calvinists in general regard the ' new divinity ' of the Hopkinsians with great horrour [sic]; but it is also true that ' a peculiar brotherhood is established ' between these two classes of Christians in New-England. They both by mutual consent take shelter under the name of ' orthodox.' " [75] Channing suspected that the union of Hopkinsians and Calvinists smacked of hypocrisy and an unchristian desire to crush the Unitarians. Actually, however, the alliance measured the distance theology had moved since Calvin's time.

All three parties, whatever their theological differences, were united on the premise that reason was essential to the interpretation of Scripture. All three agreed substantially on the evidences of Christianity, and all were convinced of the benevolence and justice of God. But they differed on the conclusions that the use of reason enabled them to draw from an inspired Bible, and they were at sword's points over the meaning of such words as " benevolence " and " justice." Each sect, sure that it had worked out its own salvation, failed to perceive that no unanimous agreement was possible once secular terms like " reason " and " benevolence " had been introduced into the equation. And each failed to see that it was equally guilty with the rest of substituting human ideas for the word of God. The fact that the American Calvinists of the early nineteenth century could unite with their Hopkinsian brothers against the Unitarian heresy is ample proof that the old rigor had departed.

The descent into secularism had proved easy. Calvin had taken a long step in this direction by breaking away from papal authority and by denying transubstantiation — to mention only two points which involved " considerable difficulties from some of the texts." Hopkins had gone much farther, even limiting the transcendent sovereignty of God by the " nature of things." When Calvinism and Hopkinsianism found it possible to live together, American religious thought had — unconsciously, to be sure — prepared the way for Unitarianism. Needless to say, none of these groups was in any way conscious of abandoning the traditional concepts of Christianity. Each at first was shocked by the latitudinarianism of the other, though we can now see that the development, for better or for worse, was almost inevitable. None of the movements involved a break with the past; all were evolutions from it, though the shocked horror with which each in turn was received might cause the casual observer to think otherwise.

The distance between Channing's Christianity and that of Hopkins out of which it grew is the difference between the eighteenth century and the nineteenth. The eighteenth century in its ethics, in its psychology, in its theology, and in its science was chiefly interested in establishing general principles, in discovering codes of behavior. It thought in abstractions more than in concrete instances; it was not by accident that its literature indulged in abstract personifications and descriptions that had little individuality. The eighteenth century was suspicious of enthusiasm; it believed in a reason which was really a magnified common sense. By exalting a priori principles and the concept of a mechanical universe ruled by a compulsive natural law, it tended to lose sight of men as individuals. A. N. Whitehead's comment on its science is applicable to its whole mode of thought: " It is the defect of the eighteenth century scientific scheme that it provides none of the elements which compose the immediate psychological experiences of mankind." [76] Hopkins, an eighteenth-century figure, had, as he thought, established the benevolence of God; but it was a benevolence so remote from the " immediate psychological experiences of mankind " that Channing could not accept the explanation.

Channing was trying to restore religion to man the individual — not to man representative of a species. His theological contribution was analogous to the poetical revolution begun by Wordsworth and Coleridge. It was the reaffirmation of the whole individual as the center of the universe. Channing, of course, did not find it necessary to repudiate the eighteenth century, or even to revolt against it. He did attempt to make the whole impersonal fabric of eighteenth-century thought significant to the individual in terms that were at once private and universal. Enough the child of his age to dislike excessive individualism, he still sought to reconcile the values of the eighteenth century with the nascent Transcendentalism of the nineteenth.

In 1828 Channing preached at the installation of the Rev. M. I. Motte a sermon called " The Great Purpose of Christianity." The great purpose, as Channing saw it, was not the glorification of God; it was not even the redemption of man from the flames of hell; rather, it was the development of the human mind. God's " great purpose in revealing himself is, that he may exalt and perfect human nature." [77] The term " human nature," as Channing employed it, covered a multitude of ideas, of which the chief was that of moral and intellectual virtue. This virtue was a quality of the mind, and the " highest existence in the universe is Mind; for God is mind; and the development of that principle which assimilates us to God, must be our supreme good." [78] A few pages later, Channing wrote, " God as he is manifested by Christ, is another name for intellectual and moral excellence." [79] This was perilously close to Emerson's identification of God with justice in the Divinity School Address. And, in fact, the whole tenor of Channing's discourse was one with Emerson's in its insistence that religious benefits were not external, but part and parcel of the individual himself.

Even heaven and hell, Channing thought, were not external to the mind:

Men are flying from an outward hell, when in truth they carry within them the hell which they should chiefly dread. The salvation which man chiefly needs, and that which brings with it all other deliverances, is salvation from the evil of his own mind. . . . How slowly do men learn, that heaven is the perfection of the mind, and that Christ gives it now just as far as he raises the mind to celestial truth and virtue.[80]

In Channing's thought, these states of mind constituting heaven and hell apparently would continue after death — though even beyond the grave they would apparently still be mental in character. But Channing's emphasis was almost entirely on our mundane life; he dismissed the future life almost cursorily.

A second sermon preached in 1828 also insisted on the spiritual or mental purposes of Christianity. This discourse, "Likeness to God," Channing's most Transcendental utterance, was preached at the ordination of the Rev. F. A. Farley in Providence. The sermon is remarkable in that it seems to cast some doubt on Channing's dualistic view of nature — dualistic, that is, in its psychological expression, which was usually so unequivocal. How are we to take the statement ". . . the creation is a birth and shining forth of the Divine Mind, a work through which his spirit breathes"? [81] Or, even more startling: "He [God] penetrates all things, and delights to irradiate all with his glory. . . . How much of God may be seen in the structure of a single leaf, which . . . is itself a revelation of an omnipotent mind! God delights to diffuse himself everywhere." [82] A second Transcendental assertion, almost pantheistic in its phrasing, can be found in only one other place in Channing's writings, in the second chapter of *The Perfect Life*, edited and published in 1872 by W. H. Channing. The Doctor had written, some time during the last decade of his life: "This lesson of moral and religious truth is that there is in human nature an element, truly divine and worthy of all reverence; that the Infinite which is mirrored in the outward universe is yet more brightly imaged in the inward spiritual world." [83]

This view of the universe as an emanation of God was like that expressed in Emerson's *Nature*: "The world proceeds from the same spirit as the body of man. It is a remoter and inferior incarnation of God, a projection of

God in the unconscious." [84]   But this view was not Channing's usual conception of the relation of the Deity to his work.   Nevertheless, one can hardly wonder that when the Doctor preached such sermons, "not a few within Channing's denomination, and his own congregation even, criticised them as 'transcendental.'" [85]

No less Transcendental was Channing's statement of the relation of man to God and hence to God's universe:

That unbounded spiritual energy which we call God, is conceived by us only through consciousness, through the knowledge of ourselves. . . . God is another name for human intelligence raised above all error and imperfection, and extended to all possible truth. . . . The same is true of God's goodness. . . . The same is true of all the moral perfections of the Deity.[86]

The genesis of these ideas, which represent the most advanced outpost of Channing's mind, is obviously in the eighteenth-century revival.   We have seen Hutcheson's contention that our moral perceptions are in some sense analogous with those of God.[87]   Richard Price, in addition to making the human mind the source of the chief categories of thought, had suggested that "truth, not being itself a *substance*, nor yet *nothing*, it must be *a mode of a substance; or the *essential wisdom and intelligence of the one, necessary Being*." [88]   From this, it was but a step to Bishop Berkeley's idealism in which existence itself depended upon the perception by "*the one, necessary* Being."   Nevertheless, only Price had suggested that man exercised a genuinely creative power in the universe of which he was a part.   It is Channing's distinction that in American thought he bridged the gap between the incipient Transcendentalism of the eighteenth century and the absolute idealism of Emerson and Thoreau.

It is significant that Channing's two most Transcendental utterances should precede by a year the famous introduction which the Rev. James Marsh wrote for the American edition of Coleridge's *Aids to Reflection* in 1829. How much Channing owed to his contemporary and friend Frederic Henry Hedge, who had studied German philosophy in its native land from 1820 to 1822, we cannot guess, any more than we can accurately gauge his debt to Coleridge. The only certainty is that the direction of Channing's thought had for years been toward Transcendentalism and that some combination of circumstances pushed him into an overt statement in 1828. Perhaps his friendship for Charles Follen, the German refugee whom he had met two years earlier and whom he had grown to love, was the catalyst.

The problem of Channing's Transcendentalism is not made any easier by the fact that only in a few sermons did he make such unqualifiedly Transcendental assertions. And, as we shall see in his relations with Parker and with Emerson, Channing was often anxious to tone down similar statements when they were made by others. But from 1815 until his death in 1842 Channing's fundamental bias was Transcendental: he was, with certain inconsistencies, an ideal monist; he conceived of the physical universe as emblematic of the moral world; he thought of man as partaking of the divine essence; evil to him was privative; he believed in the perfectibility of man; and the human mind, in which he included conscience and intuition as well as the intellect, to him was sacred as an end in itself.

To this Transcendental attitude he added a conviction that man was primarily a social being, that he was educable in the usual sense of the word (as opposed to the Transcendental reliance on intuition), that revelation was as important as nature and insight for knowing the truth, and that God (however inconsistently with the Transcendental interpretation) was personal.

If these views appear to cancel each other, the defender of Channing can appeal only to Emerson's dictum on consistency. Fortunately, in one pregnant paragraph in *The Perfect Life*, Channing appealed to all his authorities at once:

Wisdom is omnipresent. The greatest truths meet us at every turn. Jesus came to reveal the Father. But is God, the infinite and universal Father, made known only by a single voice, heard ages ago on the banks of the Jordan, or by the sea of Tiberias? Is it an unknown tongue that the heavens and earth forever utter? Is Nature's page a blank? Does the human soul report nothing of its Creator? Does conscience announce no authority higher than its own? Does reason discern no trace of an Intelligence, that it cannot comprehend, and yet of which it is itself a ray? Does the heart find in the circuits of creation no friend worthy of trust and love? [89]

Since Channing did not live to write the great work in which he proposed to put his ideas into coherent order, it is not perhaps quite fair to attempt to reconstruct a system from sermons, speeches, and articles which were written for specific occasions and therefore present his thought only in fragments. But even if he had lived, it is questionable whether he could have brought such disparate elements into any order.

A quarter-century after Channing's death, Hedge tried

to identify the source of his power — and could not. Channing, he said, was " without learning, without research, not a scholar, not a critic, without imagination or fancy, not a poet, not a word-painter, without humor or wit, without profundity of thought, without grace of elocution." [90]

A formidable indictment — yet Hedge managed to extract some comfort by mentioning two foci of Channing's thought: " the goodness of God and the dignity of man." All else was corollary, and dependent on " that overwhelming personality which pervades all his speech, so that you can nowhere separate between the word and the man." [91] When only an echo of the personality remains, no precise reconstruction of a philosophy dependent upon it is possible; but certain themes, thanks to their constant reiteration, impress themselves on the reader's mind. Hedge isolated two of them: the goodness of God and the dignity of man. A third is a faith in what Channing called " reason."

The first theme, it seems to me, and the third are dependent on the second. In Channing's mature thought, one is immediately struck with the primacy he gives to individual worth. His conception of God as a person was an expression of this primacy which infused his whole philosophy. This exaltation of the human soul explains Channing's Transcendentalism, which was never a philosophy in the German sense, but a poetic attitude, a lyric emphasis on mankind's potentialities. When this emphasis was foremost, Channing could write, " I may become partaker of the very mind from which it [the universe] springs." [92] And he could set down his belief that " God's infinity has its image in the soul." [93] Though I have drawn these examples from a single sermon, the same thought is explicit in much of the

Doctor's writing and implicit in all of it, except the earliest.

Thus, his insistence on the infinity of the private man did not stem from Transcendentalism, except in so far as it was adumbrated in Price. It originated, rather, in Channing's instinctive perception that neither the orthodox theology of his youth nor the rationalism of the eighteenth century was able to provide an adequate basis for the optimism and the faith in progress so characteristic of nineteenth century America. Whatever his secondary objections, Channing's essential revulsion from orthodoxy was the result of its insistence on the depravity of man. Rationalism in its mechanistic form he found almost as repulsive, even when it was coupled with Unitarian theology. In 1831, he wrote to Lucy Aikin explaining his feelings: " Now Priestley's system of materialism, of necessity, and of the derivation of all our moral sentiments from *sensations* variously modified by association, does seem to strike a blow at our most intimate and strongest moral convictions, whilst it robs our nature of all its grandeur." [94] The Hopkinsian attempt to graft rationalism onto an orthodox scion in order to make the Calvinist dispensation more palatable was equally repugnant to Channing, once he had reached intellectual maturity. Reason itself, when considered solely as intellectuality, seemed an insufficient guide, for as Channing wrote in his Charge at the ordination of J. S. Dwight in 1840, " something more than the action of intellect is needed to secure you a living knowledge of Christian truth." [95]

This " something more " was an amalgam of the Christian doctrine of grace (in its Universalist dress) and the identity of the soul with God. A direct relationship with the Deity was no figure of speech with Channing. When he referred to God as the Father, he meant, of course, that the relation was a spiritual one which displayed all the mysterious connections of the physical relationship. It was even closer, for, as he wrote in 1831, " I can enjoy God only insofar as I receive the divine mind into my own . . . I must inhale, if I may so speak, the spirit that breathes through his works and his word. . . . It is only by this diffusion of himself through my spiritual nature . . . that God becomes to me the enduring and the highest good." [96] This spiritual oneness with God, Channing thought, was not the only reason that all men were deserving of respect. In his sermon " Honor Due to All Men," he wondered if mankind was truly conscious of this fundamental brotherhood: " Do we feel ourselves to be derived from one Heavenly Parent, in whose image we are all made, and whose perfection we may constantly approach? Do we feel that there is one divine life in our own and in all souls? This seems to me the only true bond of man to man." [97]

In both these passages, of course, we see a Transcendentalism not fully emerged from the religious chrysalis. But it is not a long step from this view of the relation between the individual and God and the relation between the individual and his fellow men to Emerson's vision in " History ":

There is one mind common to all individual men. Every man is an inlet to the same and to all of the same. He that is once admitted to the right of reason is made a freeman of the whole estate. What Plato has thought, he may think; what a saint has felt, he may feel; what at any time has befallen any man, he can understand. Who hath access to this universal mind is a party to all that is or can be done, for this is the only and sovereign agent.[98]

Channing was not interested in reducing the Deity to " universal mind " except for illustrative purposes. His theism was more complicated than that. Yet, in order to bring his God within human reach, he found it necessary to exalt man to godlike proportions — in fact to make him a participator in the Godhead. The Transcendentalists could not do more.

The vagaries of romantic Transcendentalism verging on solipsism held no attraction for Channing. Nor did the absolute idealism of Schelling and Hegel interest him as it interested Alcott, Margaret Fuller, and — to a lesser extent — Emerson and Thoreau. Not for him were the distinctions between the " me and the not-me " or the mysteries of Hegel's dialectic. In fact, his eighteenth-century training served him well here, for he insisted all his life on the integrity of his own mind, eschewing the complacently passive optimism of Emerson or Thoreau, as well as the passivity they sometimes displayed in their acceptance of the Oversoul or Higher Law. Indeed, Channing specifically repudiated this form of idealism — suspecting, perhaps, that like the orthodoxy and the rationalism he had outgrown, it diminished the position of man. In one of his last essays, the introduction to the collected edition of his works in 1842, he wrote:

There are, indeed, philosophical schools of the present day, which tell us, that we are to start in all our speculations from the Absolute, the Infinite. But we rise to these conceptions from the contemplation of our own nature; and even if it were not so, of what avail would be the notion of an Absolute, Infinite existence, an uncaused Unity, if stripped of all those intellectual and moral attributes, which we learn only from our own souls. . . . The only God, whom our thoughts can rest on, and our hearts can cling to, and our consciences can recognize, is the God whose image dwells in our own souls.[99]

Although the concept of the dignity of man stood at the center of Channing's thinking, his faith in reason was almost equally important. His use of the term was remarkably consistent. In his sermon " Christianity a Rational Religion," he set down his definition of the concept. It was most emphatically not mere common sense, for Channing, taking a leaf from Price and the Transcendentalists, thought reason to be " the highest faculty or energy of the mind." [100] It had, he thought, two principal characteristics. Reason enabled man to understand universal truths; it also applied these truths to the particulars of experience: " Thus reason is perpetually at work on the ideas furnished us by the senses, by consciousness, by memory, associating them with its own great truths, or investing them with its own universality.[101] Its other function was that of reducing thoughts to " Unity or Consistency. . . . It carries within itself an instinctive consciousness, that all things which exist are intimately bound together; and it cannot rest until it has connected whatever we witness with the infinite whole. . . . It corresponds to the unity of God and the Universe, and seeks to make the soul the image and mirror of this sublime unity." [102]

The modern critic of Channing's thinking may perhaps ask why reason is thus divided into two functions, since the unifying power of reason seems to be merely an extension of its ability to combine the data of sensory experience, consciousness, and the memory. But the point is not important because the real significance of Channing's position is his interpretation of the mind as creative. Here again he was following Price, who had written: " The power, I assert, that *understands;* or the faculty within us that discerns *truth,* and that compares all the objects of thought, and *judges* of them, is a spring of new ideas." [103]

The coherence of this view of the role of reason with Channing's reiterated statement of the innate divinity of man is obvious. Man possesses a creative reason of infinite potentiality; he also shares, in a manner of speaking, the infinity of God, but this sharing is accomplished through the reason itself: " God delights to communicate himself; and therefore his greatness, far from inspiring contempt for human reason, gives it a sacredness, and opens before it the most elevating hopes. The error of men is, not that they exaggerate, but that they do not know or suspect, the worth and dignity of their rational nature." [104]

Since Channing was a dualist in his psychology, holding that the mind or soul was the essence of the individual and the body was accident, and since he made the further distinction that the spirit was higher than the body, it is clear that when he spoke of human worth he meant the worth of human reason. Thus his faith in man was his faith in reason, and his faith in reason was his faith in man. Both aspects of this belief were Transcendental, in the widest sense of the word, because neither was derived from experience. The mind created its primary ideas from itself, and the value of the individual lay in his relationship with the Deity.

Like Emerson in *Nature,* Channing started with the proposition that the universe was intelligible. Nor did either of them ever doubt that it was beneficent. We have already encountered Channing's faith in disinterested benevolence as the perfection of God's qualities; it followed, therefore, that such a benevolence was the height of reason, since God was a reasonable being. One may doubt whether Channing himself tried to examine logically the question of God's goodness. To him the proposition must have seemed self-evident. And yet, as we have seen earlier, this doctrine, too, is derived (though perhaps unconsciously) from the Doctor's unconquerable faith in the supreme worth of the individual.

In an attempt to sum up his opinions as a preface to the collected edition of his works, Channing set down his own criteria of judgment on his writings. He spoke of the fact that many of his themes seemed repetitious — adding that repetition and emphasis themselves, however, were clues to the individuality of a writer. He went on:

So, to learn what a man is, it is not enough to dissect his mind, and see separately the thoughts and feelings which successively possess him. The question is, what thoughts and feelings predominate, stand out most distinctly, and give a hue and impulse to the common actions of his mind? What are his great ideas? These form the man, and by their truth and dignity he is very much to be judged.[105]

The supreme worth of the individual, a faith in what the Doctor called reason, an assurance of the goodness of God — these three are Channing's " great ideas." Seen in the matrix of the larger intellectual world of which he was a part, these ideas can be assigned to Transcendentalism, to the rationalism of the eighteenth century as it was expressed in the writings of Richard Price, and to Channing's interpretation of Christianity. Each of these elements, of course, influenced and partially transformed the others. The product of their interaction was not the simple sum of the three parts. It was something unique — something not quite Christian (in the orthodox sense), not quite rational (in the eighteenth-century sense), not quite Transcendental (in the philosophic sense). The ambiguous equilibrium of Channing's philosophy could not endure, for it was maintained, as Hedge pointed out, only by Channing's personality. But it did its part in helping to break down the old orthodoxies, whether of theology, politics, or economics.

CHAPTER THREE

Channing
and the Transcendentalists

We must now turn to Channing's personal relationship with the men of the Transcendental movement, for it was in them that the seed he planted finally came to maturity. Whatever controversy there has been concerning Channing's precise relation to the Transcendental movement,[1] there can be none concerning his association with the men most closely connected with Transcendentalism. In fact, he could hardly have escaped knowing them, for Boston in the third and fourth decades of the nineteenth century was a small place, and Elizabeth Peabody, his amanuensis and friend, was at the center of the movement. And in addition there is much contemporary testimony to Channing's association with the Transcendentalists, the most unequivocal of which seems to be a letter from his old friend Andrews Norton:

Will you do me the favor to accept and read the accompanying pamphlet. I have regretted that your views respecting the transcendentalism that has been making its way among us as they were expressed to me in conversation some time since and have been otherwise indicated should be so different from my own. You have evidently not regarded as I have done, either its characters, relations or tendencies; and the party that has distinguished itself by the vague doctrines and loose declamation which may be summed up under that name, has publicly and privately sought to shelter itself under your high reputation by claiming you as its head. I beg you earnestly to give attention to the existing state of things under a sense of the good or evil which your mode of acting and teaching may occasion; and I have thought you would not be indifferent to the manner in which as appears from the pamphlet I send, that state of things is regarded at a distance by men as able as the authors of the articles contained in it.[2]

If Norton, no friend of Transcendentalism, identified Channing with it, and if Elizabeth Peabody, one of its most ardent adherents, also claimed him, we may reasonably suppose that some connection did exist. Nor was this connection limited to the world of ideas. There was close personal contact between Channing and most of the people popularly identified with the Transcendentalists — Emerson, for example. Channing, as minister of the Federal Street Church, could hardly have failed to be acquainted with William Emerson, minister of the First Church in Boston and, consequently, with his family. The name of Dr. Channing was a familiar one in the record of the Emerson household as we have it in the form of letters and of Emerson's journal. As early as 1817, young Ralph Waldo, writing to his brother Edward, informed him that Mr. Channing's health was "feeble."[3] And six years later, Emerson was taking his "hebdomadal" walks to Channing to study divinity. Emerson's Aunt Mary shared her nephew's interest in the Doctor, but for different reasons: she was sure that free thought and humanitarianism led to no good ends, and she suspected Channing of both. Throughout her life she kept up a running fire of objections to Channing's doctrines, though near the end of his life she relented enough to complain to her nephew that he hadn't sent any Channing pamphlets in her package.[4]

Emerson's association with Channing continued as long as the older man lived, though it was destined never to be close. But then, Channing was intimate with very few people indeed. If intimacy were the requirement for associating him with any group, we should have to label him a solitary. In 1867 F. H. Hedge bore convincing testimony to Channing's aloofness:

> The action of this quality [his uncompromising honesty] in private made conversation with him, to a young man especially, somewhat embarrassing. You missed those smooth insincerities which hide or soften milder disagreements and facilitate colloquial intercourse. You made your statement; if he accepted it, it was well; he was sure to furnish, from the riches of his mental experience, some apt comment, illustration, or application. If he rejected it, it was equally well; there was then opportunity and scope for friendly debate. But the chances were that he would neither accept nor reject, but receive it with dumb gravity, turning upon you that calm, clear eye, and annoying you with an awkward sense of frustration, as when one offers to shake hands, and no hand is given him in return.[5]

This impatience with the normal amenities of conversation was itself typical of the Transcendentalists; they scorned to utter what they did not feel. Obviously, such an attitude did not make for intimacy. They must often have felt among themselves as G. W. Curtis did on one of his visits to Emerson's home when the host, and Hawthorne, Alcott, Thoreau, and himself were eating apples together, all munching silently, mentally inquiring of themselves, " Who will now proceed to say the finest thing that has ever been said? " [6]

Expecting so much of his fellow man, Channing, like those other apostles of good will, Emerson and Thoreau, often found personal relationships unsatisfactory. Like them, too, he did not trouble to conceal his disappointment when a friend had not met his expectations. This was the case in his relationship with another leader of the Transcendentalists, Bronson Alcott. With his customary rhetorical abandon, Alcott had characterized the Boston of 1828 as having a purer morality than any other city in America. " Channing," he went on, " is its moral teacher. His system of instruction is that of Christ." [7] Farfetched as this was, it was only an unconscious echo of Emerson's scarcely less rapturous view a year or so earlier: " I am glad when God touches with fire such minds as Channing." [8] Too, Alcott had been in Boston only a year; when his experience had deepened after five years of residence in Boston, he thought again, and wrote in his journal: " The splendid genius of Channing is inadequate to break through the remaining clouds of prejudice and intolerance which linger in its horizon." [9] By 1836, Alcott had met Emerson and had decided that " He is superior to Channing." [10]

The cooling off of Alcott's admiration for Channing bore a direct relation to the Doctor's opinion of Alcott's school. At first the project had had his approval and support, but after Elizabeth Peabody had published her *Record of a School* in 1835 and showed it to Channing, he began to have reservations about Alcott's method: " I want proof that the minds of the children really act on the subjects of conversation; that their deep consciousness is stirred. Then I want light as to the degree the mind of the child should be turned inward. The free development of the spiritual nature may be impeded by too much analysis of it." [11]

Channing had apparently made the same objections to Alcott, rousing that gentleman's sense of injustice, for in the same letter Channing wrote that he had spent a visit with the philosopher and that " I only regretted that so much of the time was spent in controversy."

The controversy did not diminish with the passing of time, for some years later Alcott demoted Channing entirely from his select list of first-rate men — a list containing only two names: that of Emerson and that of Alcott himself. In the second category appeared Channing, along with Dewey, Follen, Garrison, and Walker. They were all, thought Alcott, good men, but the second were " practical, and therefore less efficient. The first apprehend things in their principles; the second in details." [12]

Nevertheless, these disagreements did not completely alienate the two from each other any more than similar disagreements were to alienate Emerson from Thoreau or from Alcott. Proof of this fact was the historic meeting of the " Symposeum," as Alcott called it, at Ripley's house in Boston on September 19, 1836. Present were a long list of Transcendental notables, including Alcott, Hedge, Emerson, Orestes Brownson — then in his Unitarian and Transcendental phase — and Ripley himself. With these and two or three others as the nucleus, it was decided to invite others whose ideas might be sympathetic to join them. Those others included Channing, who, because of his ill health and solitary disposition, never came. But the fact that he was invited to join what was nicknamed the " Transcendental Club " is itself significant.

And during these years Channing was keeping up with " the Newness " in all its forms. As early as 1835 he had shown interest in Emerson's public lectures, though, since he was hard of hearing, he did not attend them.[13]   Margaret Fuller was a frequent visitor, often reading aloud to her host; in fact, says Elizabeth Peabody, Channing gave Miss Fuller part of the plan for her Conversations.[14]   Elizabeth Peabody herself must have kept the Channings *au courant* with the latest Transcendental gossip, which must have been entertaining even if it was not particularly accurate.

More significant than personal relationships, perhaps, was Channing's intellectual sympathy.   During these years he was reading, or having Elizabeth Peabody read to him, such Transcendental stock pieces as Carlyle's *Sartor Resartus* and *The French Revolution* (Emerson had suggested in 1837 that Channing might subscribe to the latter book), Jean Paul Richter, Coleridge, Jouffroy's *Cours de Droit Naturel*, Wordsworth (a continuing love with Channing), Taylor's *Van Artevelde, Don Quixote*, and Goethe.

Channing's sympathetic response to Carlyle is particularly revealing when one contrasts it to the reaction of such gentlemen as Professor John Brazer of Harvard and the Rev. Charles W. Upham of Salem.   Professor Brazer had, in 1836, been reading the *Christian Examiner*, and was alarmed by what he read.   Such was his consternation at the latest form of infidelity that he sat down to write Andrews Norton a letter, in which, after a few derogatory remarks about " a certain class of mind . . . ostensibly . . . Christians," he buckled down to his real business, an attack on heresy:

I do not know that *Mr. Carlyle* is the hierophant of this new sect, since it is not easy to learn what his opinions are, or whether he has any, amidst the affectation, and straining after effect and attempted *intensive* force of diction which so unfortunately characterize his later productions; — but I do know that his admirers belong to the class of persons above alluded to.[15]

Also from Salem came the letter written to Norton two days earlier by the Rev. Mr. Upham, who enjoyed a contemporary reputation, at least in the eyes of Longfellow and Charles Sumner, as " a fat, red, rowdy chap," and as a " smooth, smiling, oily man of God." [16]   He lives in political history as the man who had Hawthorne removed from the Salem customhouse to make room for his own political cronies, and in literature as the putative original of Judge Pyncheon in *The House of the Seven Gables.*   Upham determined that the new philosophy should be exposed and indicated his conviction in no uncertain terms:

> I am deeply impressed with the conviction that the philosophical speculations, which have been brought into vogue of late, and which are considered as resting upon such authorities as Coleridge, Carlisle [*sic*], and the German writers from whom they were borrowed, are not only vulnerable in point of reasoning, and puerile in the manner in which they are expressed, but absolutely, and not remotely, of infidel tendency and import.[17]

Three years later, Upham was still concerned about the ravages of infidelity, and informed Norton that " Dr. Channing favors the new views, as they are called." [18]

In the midst of all this thunder from the right, some of which surely must have reached him, Channing remained calm, confirming Upham's worst suspicions by confessing to Miss Peabody that he found Carlyle most stimulating and his *Sartor Resartus* a work of positive genius.   Still, he observed, "it gave me no new idea, but it was a perfect quickener of *all* my ideas. . . . I do not wonder at the effect it has produced." [19]   And two years later he was finding much to admire in *The French Revolution*.

So closely were the ideas of Carlyle and Channing associated in the literary chitchat of the day (or such was the thinness of Boston culture) that Emerson commented wryly on the fact to Margaret Fuller, telling her that he " was at Medford the other day at a meeting of Hedge's Club [Alcott's " Symposeum "]. . . . The poverty of topics the very names of Carlyle Cambridge Dr Channing and the Reviews became presently insupportable. The dog that was fed on sugar died." [20]

But Emerson's mood did not last long. Within eighteen months he was considering, along with Margaret Fuller, George Ripley, Theodore Parker, and Frederic Henry Hedge, the establishment of a magazine that would reflect the interest of the Club. As one might expect in a society devoted to the discussion of " Carlyle Cambridge Dr Channing and the Reviews," the name of the Doctor popped up again, this time in a proposal that Margaret should get Ripley " to write a Declaration of Independence. When he has tried, suppose we apply to Dr Channing." [21]   But whether Channing was asked we do not know. It is certain that neither he nor Ripley provided the introductory manifesto for the first issue of the *Dial:* that task fell to Emerson.

Channing never contributed to the *Dial*, and though he was sympathetic with the project, it was the sympathy of an optimist who looked hopefully on all experiment. When the magazine actually appeared, the Doctor was not impressed — but very few were. Emerson himself was not satisfied,[22] and Carlyle's strictures are well known.[23]   Channing's objection was that of any carefully conscientious man who has developed the habit of weighing every word and every thought.   He found the glowing intuitions of the Transcendentalists insufficiently considered.   Specifically, he objected to Alcott's " Orphic Sayings ": " I do not care much for Orpheus in the ' Dial,' — his flights there amuse rather than edify me, — but Orpheus at the plough is after my own heart." [24]   Like Hawthorne, Channing disliked the calm assumption of genius in which a great many of the minor-league Transcendentalists indulged themselves.   He had seen somewhat too much of this particular type of irresponsibility in his own nephew and namesake.   Had the Doctor known the opinion of Ellery that Hawthorne confided to his notebook, he must have agreed (as he doubtless would have agreed with Hawthorne's generalization on Emerson's followers):

There is nothing very peculiar about him [Ellery] — some originality and self-inspiration in his character, but none, or very little, in his intellect. . . . these originals in a small way, after one has seen a few of them, become more dull and commonplace than even those who keep the ordinary pathway of life.   They have a rule and a routine, which they follow with as little variety as other people do *their* rule and routine; and when once we have fathomed this mystery nothing can be more wearisome.[25]

As violently as he was capable of disliking anything, Channing disliked the assumption that whatever was spontaneous and deeply felt was therefore divine in its origin. He saw through — as Emerson often did not — Charles King Newcomb, Anna Parsons, and the other bright young people who flocked to Concord and fluttered around Emerson's light. But he was fully sympathetic with the Transcendental idea when it was presented in a reasonably coherent and responsible form. Therefore he found Emerson's poems " The Problem " and " The Sphinx " entirely satisfactory, in spite of the rejection of a formal church in the first and the suggestion of pantheism in the second. Channing usually made the distinction between man as a partaker of divinity and divinity itself, while the Transcendentalists were prone to confuse their own intuition with the whole of divinity. Channing, in a conversation with Miss Peabody, brought out this point, saying that Emerson made such a distinction in " The Problem " and " The Sphinx." " But," he went on to say, " many of his professed followers *do not*, and fall into a kind of *ego-theism*, of which a true understanding of Jesus Christ is the only cure, as I more and more believe." [26]

In this view of Transcendentalism, Channing was at one with Hedge, who had withdrawn his support of the *Dial* when he found that the public temper did not approve of its philosophy. In a letter to Margaret Fuller, Hedge declared that he did not want to be identified with atheism. Nor did he agree entirely with some of the ideas of Emerson and Alcott.[27] And yet he confessed to being much interested in the journal and its success. Such an attitude was not completely creditable in one who had early been considered for the editorship, but it does sum up the position of a great many of the Christian Transcendentalists who feared that the excesses of some of the satellites like Charles Newcomb and Ellery Channing might bring the whole philosophy into disrepute.[28] It is likely that Channing was not particularly worried about the public reputation of the *Dial;* it is certain that he found himself in disagreement with its extreme individualism, and therefore did not give his unqualified endorsement to it.

Though Channing was unwilling to cast his lot unequivocally with the Transcendentalists, he was usually numbered among their supporters on specific questions. According to Elizabeth Peabody, he approved of Emerson's honesty of purpose and moral integrity in leaving the Second Church because he felt himself unable to administer Communion. Even more marked was Channing's respect for Emerson's position as announced in the Divinity School Address of 1838 — though he did not entirely understand what his former pupil meant by the statement that historical Christianity is " an exaggeration of the personal, the positive, the ritual. It has dwelt, it dwells, with noxious exaggeration about the *person* of Jesus. The soul knows no persons." [29]

For some reason, not quite clear at the distance of more than a hundred years, reaction to Emerson's address seems to have centered upon this paragraph. Whether God was a personality exercised the minds of the critics of 1838; today we find quite another message in the Divinity School Address, and the rebuttal sermon by Henry Ware, Jr., " The Personality of the Deity," appears irrelevant to the chief point of Emerson's speech. But both Channing and Elizabeth Peabody were concerned — she to defend Emerson, he to discover precisely the meaning. Channing's chief objection was the ambiguity of Emerson's phraseology; he was sure that Emerson did not mean to deny personality to God and thought that Ware was "fighting with a shadow." But, he felt, though Emerson should take no direct notice of the adverse criticism, he might well take advantage of his next opportunity "to express clearly whether by 'impersonality' he means 'moral impartiality.'" [30]

Channing also took pains to dissociate himself from the critics who felt that Emerson had taken unfair advantage of the students in the Divinity School by using a Christian platform to promulgate heresies. Channing *had* said that if Emerson did not believe in the veracity of the New Testament, he ought not to have been invited to a platform dedicated to the preaching of that book. "But," he told Miss Peabody, "what I said was hypothetical. I pronounced no judgment on Mr. Emerson." [31]

A comparison between Emerson's address and the one preached by Channing twelve years earlier at the dedication of Divinity Hall shows that the two are remarkably similar in thought. They differ in degree rather than in kind: Emerson was far more willing to pursue his thought to its logical conclusion than Channing had been, while Emerson's talent for epigram gave his discourse a snap and vitality that Channing's more measured diction usually lacked. The older man scorned the affective use of language. He was concerned primarily with lucidity, Emerson with stimulating his audience.

Miss Peabody retailed an anecdote which perfectly illustrates this difference:

I said I was visiting at Mr. Emerson's when he was correcting the proof-sheets of his Address. He came to us one day and read the paragraph which begins, "But by this Eastern monarchy of a Christianity," etc., and said, " How does that strike your Hebrew souls? " I replied, " I like it; but put a large F to designate Jesus as the ' Friend of souls! ' " He reflected a moment, and then said, " No; directly I put that large F they all go to sleep."

On hearing this anecdote, Channing smiled, adding that " Mr. Emerson seems to be gifted to speak to an audience which is not addressed by any of the rest of us." [32]

In a sense, Channing's reaction, in spite of its condescension, was accurate. Emerson spoke for those who found the old molds of religious thinking cramping to the free exercise of the spirit, while Channing felt that Christianity, liberally interpreted, provided room enough for the most rebellious soul. Yet the two Divinity School discourses are much alike. Both, as the circumstances of their delivery might indicate, deal with substantially the same subject — the function of the minister and his place in society. Both writers were aware that the ministry often lags behind the society of which it is a part, and both expressed their feeling in much the same way. As so often when one reads the two men on the same topic, the phraseology might be the work of either. It would be difficult to say whether Emerson or Channing wrote this sentence: " Let those who are to assume the ministry be taught, that they have something more to do than handle old topics in old ways, and to walk in beaten paths."

And both men pointed to the corrosive effect of institutionalized religion on men's minds. Emerson took, for once, the more general position: that preaching is dead and spiritless. " Men," he said, " have come to speak of the revelation as somewhat long ago given and done, as if God were dead. The injury to faith throttles the preacher; and the goodliest of institutions becomes an uncertain and inarticulate voice." [33] Channing, more realistic about the grasp of religion on people's minds, concerned himself with the minister's abuse of power:

> The panic-smitten hearer, instructed that safety is to be found in bowing to an unintelligible creed, and too agitated for deliberate and vigorous thought, resigns himself a passive subject to his spiritual guides, and receives a faith by which he is debased. Nor does the teacher escape unhurt; for all usurpation on men's understandings begets . . . a dread and resistance of the truth which threatens its subversion. Hence ministers have so often fallen behind their age, and have been the chief foes of the master spirits who have improved the world. They have felt their power totter at the tread of an independent thinker. By a kind of instinct, they have fought against the light . . . and have received their punishment in the darkness and degradation of their own minds.[34]

Explicit in Emerson's argument and implicit in Channing's was the conclusion that each mind must receive divine truth for itself. But where Emerson brushed away all mediators, even Jesus himself, as obstacles to this direct intuition, Channing maintained that the preacher, that the Christian revelation, can do much to stimulate the soul to its own activity. The preacher's " great purpose . . . is, to give vitality to the thought of God in the human mind; to make his presence felt; to make him a reality, and the most powerful reality to the soul." [35] The human soul cries for divine knowledge; to " bring the created mind into living union with the Infinite Mind " is the function of both nature and a true ministry.[36]

And, finally, both men agreed on the dangers of imitation and warned against the influence of the teacher, no matter how great he might be. " Thank God for these good men," said Emerson, speaking of the world's saints, " but say, ' I also am a man.' " [37]   Channing's words lack Emerson's cutting edge, but the thought is the same: " Accumulate teachers and books, for these are indispensable. But the best teacher is he who awakens in his pupils the power of thought, and aids them to go alone." [38]   And, a page later, " The first duty of a rational being is to his own intellect." Emerson, perhaps, could have written this with greater effectiveness, but he could not have said more.

Nor is the similarity in thought between Emerson and Channing confined to these addresses. Scattered throughout their writings are passages that might have come from either. As we have seen, these correspondences of thought are not accidental — since they rest on a similar philosophic basis. There is, I think, no evidence of the direct influence of one on the other, particularly in the case of Emerson's " The American Scholar " and Channing's " Self-Culture," since the older man delivered his address more than a year after Emerson had made the Phi Beta Kappa oration at Harvard in 1837. But one part of Emerson's speech recalls an article that Channing had written nearly a decade earlier for the *Christian Examiner*. That part (in reality not the dominant note of the address) was said by Oliver Wendell Holmes to be America's " intellectual Declaration of Independence." [39]   (Holmes, of course, was given to the striking phrase. Did he not say that a half-truth is often better than a whole truth, just as a half-brick carries better than a whole one in an argument?) Actually, Channing's " Remarks on National Literature," as we shall see, deserves Holmes's descriptive phrase rather more than does Emerson's " The American Scholar," which is really a call for self-reliance in the student. Only once did Emerson specifically refer to nationalism in literature — in the well-known passage beginning, " We have listened too long to the courtly muses of Europe."

Channing's " Remarks on National Literature," published in 1830, was a reasoned examination of the precise meaning of the term " national literature," which the Doctor defined as the " expression of a nation's mind in writing . . . the manifestation of a nation's intellect in the only forms by which it can multiply itself at home, and send itself abroad." He did not restrict literature to belles-lettres, but broadened its definition to include any " expression of superior mind in writing." [40]   With this point clearly established, and buttressed by the opinion that in literature was to be discovered the most influential force of the age, Channing went on to ask whether America had as yet a literature of her own. The answer, in 1830, was bound to be that she had not, though the names of Franklin and Edwards were of international significance. But " Whilst clamoring against dependence on European manufactures, we contentedly rely on Europe for the nobler and more important fabrics of the intellect." [41]

The reasons for this dependence on Europe, thought Channing, were not far to seek. The utilitarian temper of the country found literature unnecessary: if some people wanted literature, they could find it in foreign books; America had no time for such foolishness. Channing shied away from so narrow a definition of utility, feeling that the " idea of beauty is an indestructible principle of our nature." [42] The mind itself, he went on, was capable of infinite improvement in many directions; therefore a society that called itself good would cherish institutions devoted to the training of scholars, historians, mathematicians, and other intellectual laborers.   Like Emerson, Channing held no brief for arid scholarship: " We have no desire to rear in our country a race of pedants, of solemn triflers, of laborious commentators on the mysteries of a Greek accent or a rusty coin." [43]

The view that America could not afford universities and provide help for worthy scholars and writers met with Channing's deep scorn.   Admitting that these facilities were lacking, he demanded that they be established, asking, " Where lies our poverty?   In the purse, or in the soul? " [44]

But admitting all this, why should we not continue to import our books?   Because, said Channing, " We are inclined to believe, that, as a people, we occupy a position, from which the great subjects of literature may be viewed more justly than from those which most other nations hold." [45]   Here in America we had no outmoded class structure, no monarchial system, no established religion, nor any of the superstitious inheritance of the past which rendered Europe unfit to interpret the new age that was beginning to dawn.   Echoing a tradition going back to the Puritan colonists, who regarded themselves as a peculiar people set apart by God to accomplish some great end denied to the rest of the world, Channing set down his own version of the American dream:

We should have no heart to encourage native literature, did we not hope that it would become instinct with a new spirit. We cannot admit the thought, that this country is to be only a repetition of the old world.   We delight to believe that God, in the fulness of time, has brought a new continent to light, in order that the human mind should move here with a new freedom, should form new social institutions, should explore new paths, and reap new harvests.[46]

Here, then, rather than in " The American Scholar," is America's " intellectual Declaration of Independence."

More strikingly Emersonian in both style and subject is Channing's " Self-Culture," which bears the subtitle " An Address Introductory to the Franklin Lectures, Delivered at Boston, Sept. 1838." The different circumstances of the address account for some of the differences in approach between this speech and that of Emerson before the Phi Beta Kappa Society. Channing's audience was composed for the most part of laborers and mechanics; he did not need to dwell, as Emerson had, on the dangers of book learning, though he was equally conscious of them. Books were invaluable, he thought, but " When they absorb men, as they sometimes do and turn them from observation of nature and life, they generate a learned folly." Nor are books absolutely necessary: " Homer, Plato, Demosthenes, never heard the name of chemistry, and knew less of the solar system than a boy in our common schools." [47] Channing also shared Emerson's suspicion of great teachers, pointing out that " Even the influence of superior minds may harm us, by bowing us to servile acquiescence and damping our spiritual activity." [48]

Yet Channing was far from writing " Whim " upon his door, though he advised his hearers to think for themselves and to give " reverent heed " to ideas which seem to be important and to spring from a " higher order." Such ideas, " intimations from our own souls of something more perfect than others teach," give us a force not experienced by those " who march, as they are drilled, to the step of their times." But this intimation of immortality is not the sole criterion of value:

Do not trust it blindly, for it may be an illusion; but it may be the Divinity moving within you, a new revelation, not super-natural but still most precious, of truth or duty; and if, after inquiry, it so appear, then let no clamor, or scorn, or desertion turn you from it. Be true to your own highest convictions.[49]

In these sentences lies the chief difference between Emerson and Channing. The former, in an apparently unbridled individualism, was willing to be the Devil's child and to live from the Devil, for " No law can be sacred to me but the law of my own nature." Any careful examination of Emerson's theory of individualism, of course, reduces to zero the probability that the individual can be the Devil's child, for there is no Devil. Emerson's theodicy unfortu-nately did not provide for one. Channing, reared in the grand Miltonic tradition of a God using evil as a means for achieving good, could not afford to be so carefree as Emerson in his use of language. Doubtless, he thought, things will come right in the long run, but in the meantime, evil is very real and very terrible.

Both, however, agreed that the world has been created in an intelligible manner for a unified purpose. Emerson summed up his view in the last passages of *Nature:* " The reason why the world lacks unity, and lies broken and in heaps, is because man is disunited with himself." [50] Chan-ning, writing two years later, explained the apparent dis-order in the world in the same way. There is order, there is rule; but men lacking in the power of perception do not perceive it. ". . . One man sees all things apart and in fragments, whilst another strives to discover the harmony, connexion, unity of all." [51] This second type was, to Channing, the possessor of true wisdom.

The remainder of Channing's " Self-Culture " address is an attempt to show the advantages of culture for the ordinary man. His high view of human nature demanded that each individual cultivate whatever capacities he might have. Self-culture is made possible by the fact that the human soul has two faculties — one the power to analyze itself, and the other the ability " to discern not only what we already are, but what we may become." [52] Furthermore, through these attributes inherent in every man, we can develop ourselves both intellectually and morally, for the two realms are connected. And every man " is necessarily an end, not a means." [53] Hence no one is exempt from the responsibility his manhood entails.

But how can the working man, with all his disabilities, make the most of himself? Channing answered, characteristically enough, by telling the poor to improve their physical condition, without specifying how this laudable end was to be accomplished. Liquor in intemperate quantities was to be eschewed; perhaps even some form of prohibition was desirable. And, continuing in this hortatory vein for some pages, the Doctor urged the formation of reading groups among the laboring men, he wondered plaintively why workmen often had no pride in their labor that was so obviously beneficial to society, and he spoke soothingly of the good effect that adversity has upon the mind.

More to the point, at least to the twentieth-century mind, is Channing's desire that workingmen should become interested in politics, particularly those questions that revolve around public education. He asked for concern with " the recent exertions of our legislature and of private citizens, in behalf of our public schools." [54] He spoke with favor of Horace Mann, though not by name, and suggested that his audience support the legislature in its attempt to establish normal schools. This emphasis on political activity, general as it was, is entirely at variance with Channing's usual thought. Hence we are doubly surprised to discover him speaking emphatically in favor of the consecration of the public lands " to the education of the people " and rising in the next breath to an oratorical climax: " Mechanics, Farmers, Laborers! let the country echo with your united cry, ' The Public Lands for Education.' " [55]

The rest of the address is devoted to a defense of the dignity of labor, an exhortation to make the most of one's time, a plea for literature, " lectures, discussions, meetings of associations for benevolent and literary purposes, and in other like methods of passing the evening " as means of relaxation. Thus progress was to be furthered and the laborer was to rise to his proper worth. Contradicting his own appeal of a few minutes earlier, Channing concluded with a reminder that the workingman has many deficiencies to be remedied, but " the remedy lies, not in the ballot-box, not in the exercise of your political powers, but in . . . education." [56]

The addresses given by Channing and Emerson on the anniversaries of emancipation in the West Indies possess surprisingly little in common. Channing's Lenox Address of August 1, 1842, ought to be read in conjunction with his paper "Emancipation," since the two are devoted to the same topic. Both rejoice in the recently granted freedom of the West Indian Negro, and both reaffirm Channing's conviction of the moral worth of the individual. Emerson's speech, delivered in Concord on August 1, 1844, was chiefly devoted to a history of the emancipation movement in England. Toward the end, however, Emerson dealt with the proper response of the northerner to the slaveholding power. He advocated the use of political force, citing the imprisonment of many Negro citizens of Massachusetts as a motive for political actions:

The Congress should instruct the President to send to those ports of Charleston, Savannah and New Orleans such orders and such force as should release, forthwith, all such citizens of Massachusetts as were holden in prison without the allegation of any crime. . . . As for dangers to the Union, from such demands! – the Union already is at an end when the first citizen of Massachusetts is thus outraged.[57]

Emerson qualified his statement by adding that he knew little of politics; perhaps he need not have since his proposal was, on the face of it, absurd.

Channing was no more tender about the Union. No more a politician than Emerson, though Channing specifically abjured the use of political power to coerce the South, he called – in both the Lenox speech and in "Emancipation" – for the dissolution of any ties binding the North and South together in the maintenance of slavery. Slavery was to Channing a *moral* wrong chiefly; it had to be combated with morality, not with political means.

Both points of view must have seemed ridiculous to men

like William Lloyd Garrison. Emerson and Channing objected to slavery; very well, then, they must fight it tooth and nail, using any means at hand. Channing with his statements beginning "The Free States must," "Citizens should," and the like, would seem hopelessly naïve to the turbulent Garrison who had been jailed and whose life had been threatened in this battle against slavery. And Emerson, with his shifting of responsibility to Congress or the Commonwealth of Massachusetts, was essentially in the same bracket with Channing.

Here is the crux of the matter. Underneath the superficial differences between Channing and Emerson in their responses to specific issues lay a fundamental unity. This common foundation made them relatively immune to reform, as the word is usually interpreted. Emerson could talk complacently of the poor, and Channing think that the hardest portion of slavery was the moral degradation. Both of them, speaking from their Olympian detachment and from the coldness of their own natures, did not thoroughly sympathize with the intensely practical problems of those who were literally hungry or whose bodies were so prostrated by mistreatment that they could not think of being men.

The fatal defect of the idealistic view — that all problems are essentially those of man's relation to divinity — made both Channing and Emerson comparatively unaware of whole realms of experience. This unawareness was shocking to those of their contemporaries who did not share their view of reality. Many of the Transcendentalists and those associated with them earned the dislike of the reformers — a dislike which was reciprocated heartily. Whatever the differences (and these are not to be minimized) between Channing and the Transcendentalists, one has only to contrast them with Garrison, H. G. Wright, and May to see how great was the gap between the two modes of thinking.

Yet the Transcendentalists themselves were far from a homogeneous body. Their divisions, to be sure, were not formal. We have seen Hedge dropping off through fear of public opinion, while Orestes Brownson's stay was of the briefest, as was Isaac Hecker's. Over no question, however, was there so much disagreement as on association as an antidote to the evils of the time. The principle of association was immediately suspect to so staunch a group of individualists. Still, the difficulties of complete independence from society were impossibly great. Even Thoreau, with all his parade of isolation from the concerns of his fellows, had to borrow an axe from Alcott to get started. And what if one should ask embarrassing questions about the ultimate sources of the axe? No, complete isolation was unthinkable.

Affiliation with organizations devoted to social reform was equally unthinkable. Any popular movement was bound to contain much dross, even if its principles were acceptable. Emerson, for example, thought that the Jacksonian Democrats had the better principles but that the conservative party was made up of finer men.[58] One of Channing's chief objections to the Abolitionist movement was that its growth inevitably drew into it inferior men. Furthermore, reform per se had little attraction for most of the Transcendentalists, since they felt that evil was an individual matter to be solved by an inner rebirth. Reformers, too, were likely to be a limited lot whose horizon was bounded by their partial vision of excellence. And when they were not dogmatic like Garrison, they were apt to be sickeningly familiar. We remember Thoreau's castigation of the men who wanted to do good to him, who seemed to wrap their bowels around him.[59]

The situation seemed almost hopeless. Society as it was then organized was not propitious to the free development of the human spirit; existing reform movements were too partial and too inflexible; solitary withdrawal from the world was not possible. But one solution — or chance of a solution — remained. Suppose the men of good will should join forces: would it be possible to form little societies within the framework of the great society of the world? Could not these happy few, this band of brothers, separate themselves from a wicked world, innocently earning their own bread by the sweat of their own brows?

Time was to prove that they could not, but when the idea of Brook Farm took form in George Ripley's brain and that of Fruitlands in Bronson Alcott's, the age seemed ripe for just such an experiment. The ideas of Fourier, Saint-Simon, and Owen fermented in people's minds, and community after community was born in hope only to die in bankruptcy. With two of these communities Channing was indirectly connected: the Transcendental effort at West Roxbury, and the Fraternal Community at Mendon, Massachusetts, formed by Adin Ballou, the Universalist. Both attempts earned the Doctor's best wishes; both of them also roused his skepticism. Had he lived to see the beginning of Alcott's experiment at Harvard, his reactions would probably have been similar — though he might perhaps have been drawn to Fruitlands, since, in contradistinction to the others, it was based on the family as the fundamental unit.

Channing's reasons for doubting the ultimate success of these communal efforts were similar to Emerson's, though not so pungently phrased. Emerson asked himself in his journal, when it was suggested that he join the Brook Farm experiment, why he should raise the siege of this hencoop to march off to a pretended siege of Babylon.[60] So Channing, on being asked to subscribe to the charter of the Mendon group, wondered if many people could do together what one man would find difficult to accomplish alone. The danger, as Channing saw it, lay " in the difficulty of reconciling so many wills, of bringing so many individuals to such a unity of judgment and feeling as is necessary to the management of an extensive common concern, — in the difficulty of preventing the interference, intermeddling, harsh-judging, evil-speaking, self-will, jealousies, exactions, and love of sway, which scatter discord and woe through all our relations." [61]

He felt, too, that all associations, no matter how laudable their purpose and how select their members, were suspect merely because many were involved. Throughout Channing's " Remarks on Associations " one notices the reiteration of a single theme: " All virtue lies in individual action, in inward energy, in self-determination." [62] He admitted the obvious value of group action, but in this as in politics he feared the consequences to the individual if one relied too heavily on the assistance of others to accomplish one's aims. The very successes that associations had enjoyed strengthened Channing's suspicion of them, for as their power grew, the power of individual action must inevitably lessen. Yet, as he noted, "You can scarcely name an object for which some institution has not been formed. Would men spread one set of opinions, or crush another? They make a society. Would they improve the penal code, or relieve poor debtors? They make societies. Would they encourage agriculture, or manufactures, or science? They make societies. Would one class encourage horse-racing, and another discourage travelling on Sunday? They form societies." [63]

Nevertheless, Channing agreed with Ripley that something ought to be done, for he felt as strongly as any Brook Farmer "that it was entirely impossible to live under our civilization without being an involuntary party to great social wrong all the time." [64]   Therefore he wished the associations well, particularly since they were making the attempt to unite idealism with a productive economy. As much as Emerson, Channing insisted that the thinker must *do* something. His ideal figure at this time seems to have been Alcott, who had moved to Concord after the final failure of his Boston school and was trying to earn his own living by doing manual labor. The Doctor wrote of him to Elizabeth Peabody:

He [Alcott] little suspects how my heart goes out to him. One of my dearest ideas and hopes is the union of *labor* and *culture*. The present state of things, by which the highest and almost the only blessings of life are so often denied to those who bear its heavy burdens, is sad and must be changed. . . . Mr. Alcott hiring himself out for day labor, and at the same time living in a region of high thought, is perhaps the most interesting object in our Commonwealth.[65]

But with all the good will in the world, Channing was not sanguine about the prospects of communal action, particularly among Transcendentalists. He had seen too many of them at close range to entertain illusions about their capacity for working together. He feared that Brook Farm would attract, as in fact it did, people who were interested not so much in the goal of the movement as they were in getting something for nothing. And like Alcott, he was afraid that the family would be slighted or absorbed within the community. In spite of these objections, Channing permitted himself to hope great things of both Brook Farm and Mendon. As he wrote to Ballou, he was anxious to witness some change in the social order. Perhaps association might be the answer: " I have for a very long time dreamed of an association, in which the members, instead of preying on one another, and seeking to put one another down, after the fashion of this world, should live together as brothers, seeking one another's elevation and spiritual growth. But the materials for such a community I have not seen." [66]

The means to achieve such a Utopian order were a different matter; hence his dream remained a dream, and the hope he expressed to Miss Peabody remained only a hope. But he did not indulge himself, as did more conservative men, in fearing that the foundations of society were to be subverted by experiment in associations or by speculation on the purposes of society: " Men who think that a lecture by Mr. Emerson is to subvert Christianity, and an article of Mr. Brownson to make a wreck of property, show a want of faith in religion and society more alarming than the infidelity which they condemn." [67] In his very patience with novelty and experimentation in anything that promised to alleviate the lot of men, Channing was akin to the leading spirits of Transcendentalism. Though he could not share Ripley's faith in association as a panacea for human ills, he could welcome the evidence it brought of a spirit of improvement, which he, like Emerson and Thoreau, felt would some day surely be manifested.

George Ripley, Bronson Alcott, Waldo Emerson — these men were Channing's friends. They were all Transcendentalists, and two of them had been ministers. Frederic Henry Hedge and Convers Francis, (who was soon to be given a professorship at the Harvard Divinity School) were preachers; they were also discreet Transcendentalists. But in 1832, or shortly thereafter, a young man who was to become both a minister and an indiscreet Transcendentalist entered Channing's orbit. The name of this brash young man was Theodore Parker. It was destined to become as memorable in the history of Unitarianism as Channing's own, and the internecine war set off by the sermon " The Transient and Permanent in Christianity," in 1841, littered the theological battlefield with as many pamphlets as the Baltimore Sermon of 1819 had a generation earlier.

Parker was the *enfant terrible* of the Christian Transcendentalists. Completely without tact, he rushed in where Emerson feared to tread. Unlike Emerson, Parker had no intention of leaving the church: he tried his best to smash the sorry scheme of things entire, and tried, with somewhat less success, to remold it nearer to his heart's desire. The church moved; Theodore Parker did not. Such a firebrand,

one might think, would be profoundly uncongenial to a
man of Channing's stamp, but all the evidence points to the
opposite conclusion.

The two men had first become acquainted when Parker
was teaching at Watertown, preparatory to entering the
Divinity School. He had had the opportunity to hear
Channing in Boston the year before, but for some inexpli-
cable reason he had chosen to join the congregation of Lyman Beecher, who was fulminating against innovation in
the Park Street Church. This year at Brimstone Corner
had cured Parker of any incipient Calvinism, and it was
with a feeling of relief that he turned to the kinder teach-
ings of the Unitarians. Parker apparently made no notes
of his acquaintance with Channing until 1838, though he
was sufficiently influenced by the older man's leadership
to attend meetings of the Society of Friends of Progress, a
most informal organization which met occasionally at the
old Tremont House in the parlor of Jonathan Phillips, a
stalwart of the Federal Street Church. Miss Peabody tells
us that the group "playfully" called itself the "Club of
the Jacobins." [68] We can be sure that Phillips was not responsible for the name, since frivolity did not belong to his
temperament. He had escaped with some difficulty from
a Calvinist childhood, passed through a period of skepticism,
and found a measure of satisfaction in Unitarianism as
preached by Channing, his friend and classmate. But, as
the Doctor said, "His was an imagination which hung the
whole universe in crape." [69] His funereal view of the
universe did not unfit him for practical action, however,
for he presided over the meeting at Faneuil Hall to protest
the murder of Lovejoy.

Jacobin Club, or Friends of Progress, the group included many of the best-known Transcendentalists as well as a few who were only mildly tinged with the doctrine. Alcott was often there — what meetings did he not attend? — George Ripley too, Dr. Hedge, and occasionally Wendell Phillips, a cousin of Channing's gloomy friend. Horace Mann came frequently, as did Charles Follen, Channing's dearest companion. And Theodore Parker, not long out of Divinity School, unawed by the eminence of the Friends, contributed his own thoughts to such weighty matters as whether Emerson was a pantheist. Parker himself, no more than any of his fellow " Jacobins," was tainted with what old Dr. Ripley, Emerson's grandfather, had called " egomitism," a word he derived from *ego* and *mitto* to designate the self-sent Messiahs of the nineteenth century. Nor did Parker think Emerson belonged to that school. Channing thought that perhaps Alcott smacked of pantheism, though Parker had a different view. He was " revolted " by Alcott's conception of the progress of God: " the Almighty going forward to His own infinity — progressively unfolding Himself." [70]

By 1838, Parker's notebooks began to abound in references to Channing. The two argued about the role of conscience; Parker held it to be infallible because it acted directly, while Channing hesitated over so bold a claim. He distrusted any infallibility, whether it was ascribed to an external authority or to an intuitive one, and even questioned the human need of any infallible guide. But the two, if they discussed the matter, must have agreed in their criticism of Emerson's view of man's relation to God. In 1838, Parker, arguing with himself in his notebook, wrote:

" Mr. E. says, ' if a man is at heart just, so far he is God.'
Now, it seems that he mistakes likeness for identity. My
spirit is like God, but is it necessarily God? There are ten
peas in a pod, exactly alike in all things: are there not ten
peas, and not one alone? " [71]

In general, Channing and Parker agreed well, though we
may assume that the Doctor found it necessary to curb
some of the more strenuous utterances of his young friend.
Parker, perhaps, saw the implications of Channing's thought
rather more clearly than Channing himself did, perceiving
the similarities with his own ideas rather than the differences, and reading into the Doctor's vast silences signs of
agreement. Parker's journals are sprinkled with such words
as " he seemed to favor the hypothesis," " this he seemed
inclined to believe," " he seemed inclined to admit this,"
and the like.

The range of topics the two covered was enormous. It
extended from Strauss's *Leben Jesu*, which Channing
thought some of Kneeland's disciples might well translate,
to a discussion of the American Revolution. Parker
thought Jefferson was its outstanding figure, while Channing — surprisingly enough, considering his early opinions
— upheld the claims of Sam Adams, the most incorrigible
revolutionary of them all. The more they talked, the more
the younger man was impressed with the unconventional
quality of the Doctor's thinking. In July of 1839, Parker
confided to his journals his opinion of his friend:

If Dr. Channing could be ground over again, and come out
a young man of five-and-twenty, give all the results of his reading, experience, and life, all the insight, power, eloquence,
Christianity he now possesses, — but let him hold the same

religious, philosophical, political, and social opinions as now, and preach on them as he does, and let him, with such tracts as his "Letter on Slavery," &c., be all unknown to fame, he could not find a place for the sole of his foot in Boston, though half-a-dozen pulpits were vacant — not he.[72]

For Channing's opinion of Parker we must rely chiefly on Elizabeth Peabody, who has preserved a rather complete view of the Doctor's reaction to the South Boston Sermon of 1841. This discourse on "The Transient and Permanent in Christianity" was preached at the ordination of Mr. Shackford on the nineteenth of May. Channing was out of town at the time and did not hear of the speech until Miss Peabody wrote him at Newport, telling him it was in press and "what a breeze it had blown up." Channing dismissed the breeze by holding that "current opinions do not weigh a feather in such a case." But he had had enough experience with Parker to know that he often struck with too heavy a hand, and that in his desire for an apt image he was wont to offend tender sensibilities. "He makes truth unnecessarily repulsive; and, as I think, sometimes goes beyond truth." [73]

When Parker's sermon finally arrived in Newport (both Miss Peabody and Parker had sent copies), Channing commented in characteristic terms: "The great idea of the discourse — the immutableness of Christian truth — I respond to entirely . . . and I was moved by Parker's strong, heartfelt utterance of it." Then came the expected qualification: he was disturbed about Parker's attitude toward miracles; he feared Parker did not believe in them. And without miracles what would be the importance of Jesus? "Without them [miracles] he becomes a mere fable." And when Parker went on to say that Christ's words were valid in themselves rather than because Christ said them, Channing could not agree. "I never meet," he wrote, "a superior mind without some degree of reliance on it. From such a mind as Christ's I am sure I can hear nothing but truth. . . . This leads me to reverential study of his word as of no other." [74] If such a statement sounds strange from one who had said in another connection, "I affirm, then, that revelation rests on the authority of reason, because to this faculty it submits the evidence of its truth, and nothing but the approving sentence of reason binds us to receive and obey it," [75] we can only appeal to the Transcendental idea of inconsistency.

Still, by the time Parker had finished his discourse, he had left Christianity little but the name. As John Weiss, Parker's future biographer, sadly wrote, "What has Mr. Parker done for us? He has with justice annihilated the Transient, but where is the Permanent?" [76] Channing's reaction was similar. Parker had left him nothing — and if in Parker's sermon Channing did not recognize his own thoughts, it was no wonder, for he had never put them all together in one array. Taken separately, they had seemed innocuous enough, but when Parker performed an addition of the parts, the resulting whole somehow blotted out Channing's universe instead of illuminating it. Yet, faced with this apparent denial of his own view of Christianity, Channing was magnanimous enough to write a second letter to Miss Peabody, clarifying some points in his earlier note, and ending with a defense of Parker: "As to Mr. Parker, I wish him to preach what he thoroughly believes and feels. . . . Let the full heart pour itself forth! . . . Give my love to Mr. Parker. I shall be glad to hear from him, and in perfect freedom. . . . *I honor his virtues.* I feel that he has seized on some great truths." [77]

Channing's attitude was very different from that of most of the members of the Unitarian Association, who undertook to censure Parker in January, 1843. They accused him of deism and infidelity, and of blackening the character of the Association. Parker could easily enough refute the charge of deism by pointing out that he had never heard of any deist who maintained the possibility of an intuitive relationship with God. The charge of character assassination was the result of Parker's article on the Hollis Street Council in the *Dial*.[78] The article accused the Council of Phariseeism in its somewhat weasel-worded report on the controversy between John Pierpont and the businessmen of his congregation over the right of a minister to criticize the liquor trade by which some of his parishioners made their money.

We have seen Channing's reaction to the charge of heresy; he had heard it applied to himself too often to have much faith either in the value of the accusation or in the motives of those making it. His response to Pierpont's difficulty was equally decisive. Perhaps Channing was remembering his own problems with the Federal Street Church when he said to Pierpont: " Sir, should it be the issue of your present controversy, that some ten or twelve, of those who now oppose you, should withdraw from your society, and their places should be filled by others who sympathize with you, and will sustain you in your course, the Hollis-street pulpit would stand higher than any other in the city." [79]

Thus, differing with Parker on details, but whole-heartedly supporting him in his right to differ as well as agreeing with his broad interpretation of the function of the minister, Channing until the end of his life was hopeful of Parker. And Parker himself reciprocated that trust and affection. The entry in his journal on October 5, 1842, bears more effective testimony to his feeling for his friend than the formal eulogies he published in 1842 and in 1848:

I have to-day heard of the death of Dr. Channing. He has fallen in the midst of his usefulness. His faculties grew brighter as age came on him. No man in America has left a sphere of such wide usefulness; no man since Washington has done so much to elevate his country. His life has been spent in the greatest and best of works. A great man — and a good man — has gone home from the earth. Why, oh! my God, are so many left, when such are taken? Why could not I have died in his stead? [80]

In 1839, Parker had prophesied a " rent " in the Unitarian body. The signs had already appeared: Emerson had left the church, and Ripley was preparing to do so. And within the church itself, Parker thought, there were two parties: " one is for progress, the other says, ' Our strength is to stand still.' Dr. Channing is the real head of the first party; the other has no head." [81] In view of all the evidence it is almost impossible to contradict Parker's opinion of the Doctor. Channing knew nearly all of the Transcendentalists; he was friendly with many of them. He shared their reading habits, and many of his public utterances coincide with theirs. On the issues with which they were concerned, the Doctor invariably sided with them — with qualifications, to be sure, but what did Channing not qualify? The whole tenor of his later life shows a Tran-

scendental bias. That his disagreements with Emerson, Alcott, and Parker were many is not important, for all the
Transcendentalists disagreed among themselves: disagreement was almost an article of faith. That there were philosophical differences from a strict philosophical definition of
Transcendentalism is equally true and equally unimportant,
for American Transcendentalism was literary and romantic
rather than philosophical in character. Among Unitarians,
one may ask, does Channing belong with Norton or Parker?
And among reformers, does he belong with Garrison or
Emerson?

We have seen the answers to these questions. Thus, in
spite of Channing's reluctance to commit himself to anything, in spite of his refusal to pursue the implications of
his own thought, in spite of his never-ending qualifications,
we have no choice but to say with Emerson: " In our
wantonness we often flout Dr. Channing, and say he is
getting old; but as soon as he is ill we remember he is our
Bishop, and we have not done with him yet." [82]

CHAPTER FOUR

Channing's Views of Reform

Although Channing, like his Transcendental contemporaries, was temperamentally and intellectually aloof from the great political and social issues of his day, they irresistibly engulfed him, as they were later to engulf Emerson, Alcott, and Thoreau. The mixture of Christianity, rationalism, and self-reliance that was Channing's contribution to American thought is also the clue to his involvement in the turbulent scenes of the first half of the nineteenth century. Not content to preach an arid religion from the moral isolation of the pulpit, he sought to realize his Christian ideals in the market place of daily living, and this course drew him, half unwillingly, into political and social issues no longer so clearly defined as they had seemed to be in the realm of theory.

If the issues were confusing to Channing's mind, it was equally difficult to reduce to the single " grand idea " the prickly personalities who held the stage during this period. What was one to do with Garrison, who breathed fire and advocated non-resistance; with Jackson, the unpredictable, who was capable of staging mock apoplectic fits of anger to confound his enemies; or with the leonine Webster, his eyes like embers, who began as New England's champion and ended defending the cause of slavery? Were not these men and others like them what philosophy calls " accidental "? Was it not wise to exclude mere personality as ir-relevant to the discussion of principles? Such questions, whether implicit or overt in Channing's thought, testify to his affinity with the Enlightenment, which was preoc-cupied with general truths rather than individual instances. And yet, how could a man trusting himself and the power of his reason fail to speak out in times so obviously in need of moral leadership?

Comparatively late in his life Channing was to speak out in what for him were unequivocal terms, however measured they may have seemed to his more impetuous contempo-raries. It is a strange fact that Channing reversed the usual course by becoming more liberal and more outspoken the longer he lived. As a young man he was tentative and per-haps excessively cautious; in his middle years he spoke out boldly for religious unorthodoxy and began to take a grow-ing interest in social problems; in the last decade of his life, at an age when most men subside into disillusionment or orthodoxy, he threw himself into the reform movements of the day. In 1840 he symbolized his emancipation from con-servatism by lending the authority of his presence to the Convention of Friends of Universal Reform in the Char-don Street Chapel, Boston. This convention today lives in Emerson's description as an assembly composed of " Mad-men, madwomen, men with beards, Dunkers, Muggleto-nians, Come-outers, Groaners, Agrarians, Seventh-Day Baptists, Quakers, Abolitionists, Calvinists, Unitarians and Philosophers." [1]

As a reformer, Channing never satisfied the madmen, the madwomen, or the men with beards; indeed, he sometimes failed to please such comparative moderates as the Grimké sisters or Ellis Gray Loring. Nor did he always satisfy himself. Even in matters which he had every incentive to further and from which he could not possibly sustain any harm, he could not wholeheartedly participate. His interest in education, for example, was lifelong and his attachment to its advocates unquestioned. Yet when Josiah Holbrook, the founder of the Lyceum movement, called upon Channing and asked the use of his name " for the furtherance of his plans," Channing was unwilling to help. He wrote to his friend Orville Dewey that he was afraid of great associations, and then went on to wonder plaintively why he always mistrusted projects even when they were devoted to ends of which he completely approved. " It grieves me," he wrote, " that I am taking views of subjects perpetually, which prevent co-operation with others. I have no desire to stand alone, and on education I should joyfully do and suffer anything in my power." [2]

Later in life he partially overcame this inability to cooperate fully with others, though until the end of his days his mind was plagued with reservations about the wisdom of his course. Some of his difficulty resulted from an unwillingness to subscribe intellectually to a principle until he was ready to act upon it — and he could not act until he had some assurance of the desirability of the consequences of his action. The tendency of his age Channing diagnosed as " the habit of admitting principles which we do not act on. . . . If we were in the habit of carrying out every principle which we acknowledge, we should think more deliberately, solemnly, admit the doubtful more slowly, and at the same time have a keener, more discriminating perception of the true." [3]

The underlying assumption, of course, is the idea that principles can somehow exist independently of men and events. Hence Channing's dearest wish was for a principle isolated from the accidental corruptions of mortal interests. Such a principle he found only once, for in religion and religion alone was he to find a subject in which all the arguments were purely theoretical. He was able to isolate what he thought was the essence of religion and to announce it from his pulpit in unequivocal terms. He was not to find equal assurance in practical reforms, for in them the situation was complicated by brute facts that could not be exorcised by moral intensity. It was, therefore, greatly to Channing's credit that he could leave the comfortable Unitarian world, in which his religious reign was almost undisputed, for the noisy tumult of American life.

His moral courage was the greater since even in his own family there was objection to his career as a reformer. We have seen that he felt called upon to defend himself against the charge that through his marriage to his cousin he was living on profits made in the rum and slave trade.[4] Whatever the source of the income, there is no doubt that the Gibbses were extremely well off. It was not likely that they would wish even in theory for radical changes in the economic or political system. And on Channing's side of the family there was such pronounced objection (at least in certain quarters) to his anti-slavery activities that he asked Orville Dewey to say nothing of these activities to the Rev. Henry Channing. " My anti-slavery labours have been very painful to him as well as to some other friends — I never name the subject to him — as I wish in no way to disturb his last days." [5]

We have to bear all these facts in mind while we are examining the causes Channing interested himself in and the testimony of his writings both public and private. The most general of these interests — hence the topic on which his thought was most uninhibited — was the problem of power. Power, he thought, was of three kinds: inward power or power over ourselves, power over things, and power over other men. This last variety most interests us in a discussion of Channing's social thought, for his view of it determined his attitude toward government and the political relationships of mankind. Channing held that one part of this power was " the quickening influence of a good and great mind over other minds, by which it brings them into sympathy with itself." [6] This power is, of course, entirely commendable. In Channing's words, instead of enslaving, " it makes more and more free, those on whom it is exercised. . . . It awakens a kindred power in others, calls their faculties into new life, and particularly strengthens them to follow their own deliberate convictions of truth and duty." [7] The other part of this kind of power comprises the pernicious sway exercised by those who wish to control the lives of others. It has been wielded in the past chiefly by the priest and the civil ruler:

> The influence of almost every political and religious institution has been to make man abject in mind, fearful, servile, a mechanical repeater of opinions which he dares not try, and a contributor of his toil, sweat, and blood, to governments which never dreamed of the general weal as their only legitimate end.[8]

The fear of the arbitrary exercise of this form of power was central to Channing's view of the right relationship between government and men, for the most terrifying result of such a tyranny is that it " spoil[s] the individual of that self-direction which is his most precious right " [9] — thus he wrote in 1827. Channing's mature view of government as a necessary evil is hard to reconcile with certain passages in his earlier writings. In 1812, for example, he had written, in words reminiscent of Edmund Burke:

. . . government is a divine institution, essential to the improvement of our nature, the spring of industry and enterprise, the shield of property and life, the refuge of the weak and oppressed. . . . We are bound to respect government, as the great security for social happiness; and we should carefully cherish that habit of obedience to the laws, without which the ends of government cannot be accomplished.[10]

Though Channing seldom wrote so glowingly of government — in fact, a few pages later he went on to maintain the right of revolution [11] — he was not willing to say with Thoreau that any man more right than his neighbors " constitutes a majority of one," nor to agree with him that " As for adopting the ways which the state has provided for remedying the evil, I know not of such ways. They take too much time, and a man's life will be gone." [12] Channing did agree with Thoreau (as well as with Tom Paine) that that government was best which governed least. In his article " The Union," which first appeared in the *Christian Examiner* for May 1829, he set down his general view of the function of government of the United States in particular: " Of all governments we may say, that the good which they promote is chiefly negative, and this is especially true of the federal institutions which bind these States together. Their highest function is, to avert evil. . . . The highest political good, liberty, is negative." [13]

Furthermore, liberty, as the "highest political good," was not so much the result of legislation as its cause. It followed, in Channing's thought, that "Laws should be plain and few, intended to meet obvious wants, and such as are clearly required by the great interests of the community." They should be "intelligible, founded on plain principles, and such as common minds may comprehend." [14] If these words bear the ring of the eighteenth century's insistence on the self-evidence of all true propositions, Channing's further statement that the "only law of a free people is the will of the majority, or public sentiment; and to collect, embody, utter, and execute this, is the great end of its civil institutions" [15] is only a little less typical.

These ideas are part of the intellectual climate of the eighteenth century; it is idle to conjecture their precise source when we remember that one of Channing's favorite books on political topics was Adam Ferguson's *Essay on the History of Civil Society*. This volume, familiar and dear to Channing in his college days, provided the background of much of his thought. Channing's theory of disinterested benevolence was reinforced by Ferguson's statement that the happiness of man should be "to make his social dispositions the ruling spring of his occupations." [16] In the same way, Channing's conclusions that laws are merely the expressions of the public spirit and that they should be as simple and as few as possible were an echo of Ferguson's earlier statement:

If even the safety of the person and the tenure of property, which may be so well defined in the words of a statute, depend, for their preservation, on the vigour and jealousy of a free people, and on the degree of consideration which every order of the state maintains for itself; it is still more evident, that what we have called the political freedom . . . cannot be made to rest on any other foundation. The estate may be saved, and the person released, by the forms of a civil procedure; but the rights of the mind cannot be sustained by any other force but its own.[17]

If, as Channing thought, the standard of public conduct was to be determined by the majority will, and if the power of the state derived from the people, it follows that a formal aristocracy is a usurpation of the true end of government. No note is clearer in Channing's thinking than this detestation of an inherited aristocracy. Possibly it is laboring the point to make this detestation the result of the logical implications of a theory of human nature and government when a sufficient reason might be found in the circumstances of Channing's life. After all, he was the child of the American Revolution; he lived his mature life in what historians like to call the "national period," when it was almost fashionable to declare America's independence from the corruption of European aristocracy and to thank God that we were not as other men, but a new race destined to triumphs never dreamed of by old and decadent peoples. Channing's feelings about aristocracy as the root of political evil occasionally outran his judgment, nowhere more patiently than is his correspondence with Lucy Aikin.[18]

Their correspondence continued from 1826 until Channing's death. In it Channing revealed more of his mind than in any other extant series of letters, partly because, in the absence of a common background, he had to make explicit the bases for his conclusions. Running through the majority of the letters is the argument between Channing and

Miss Aikin concerning the social reforms that were shaking England. Try as she would, Miss Aikin could not persuade her friend that there was any real equality in English life or that there was any hope of reform in a government that was both monarchical and aristocratic. After one of her brisker defenses of English life, Channing replied:

I believe that the tendencies of aristocracy are hostile to those of Christianity and civilization; that it is a principle of *division*, whilst these bring together and harmonize mankind; that it generates a spurious self-respect and an ungrounded and un-social consciousness of superiority; that it confers on outward accidents the honour, distinction, influence due to merit alone; and that it is out of place and must be a perpetual spring of jealousy and disunion in times like the present, when we have learnt that the general weal is the only object of social institu-tions, and that every human being has a right to the means of improving his nature.[19]

Yet with all his dislike of English aristocracy and love of American democracy, Channing did not feel that democ-racy alone was the solution to the problems of man's social relations. The power of the majority was in some ways to be feared more than the power of an aristocracy; democ-racy could enforce a spirit of uniformity far greater than any minority pressure could hope to attain. As he wrote in " Spiritual Freedom " (the Election Sermon of 1830), " the power of opinion grows into a despotism, which more than all things, represses original and free thought, subverts in-dividuality of character, reduces the community to a spirit-less monotony, and chills the love of perfection." [20]

The chief end of political relationships was not the tyr-anny of the many over the few any more than it was that of the few over the many. The state existed only to foster the individuality of its inhabitants. Its success was not to be counted in material terms. In fact, material prosperity might even be a sign of moral decadence. What had been called the "public good"—the safety of the state, "its power, its prosperity, its affluence, the flourishing state of agriculture, commerce and the arts"[21]—was a good only in so far as it was based upon justice and a recognition of the rights of the individual.

Channing did not add to the doctrine of natural rights; he accepted it as it was embodied in the Declaration of Independence, buttressing the affirmation with his insistence on the claims of the individual to be regarded as an end in himself. These claims, as we have already seen, stem from three sources: the Christian view of man as a central figure in the divine drama; the rational view of man, as Tom Paine gave it classical expression in the *Rights of Man;* and the view of man as ultimately responsible only to the God in himself, as Emerson was to portray it in "Self-Reliance."

Channing attempted in 1836 to make a catalogue of the specific deductions from what he considered to be the grand right of human nature—which might be comprehended in one sentence, he thought, though volumes could not do it justice. "They [all rights] may all be comprised in the right, which belongs to every rational being, to exercise his powers for the promotion of his own and others' Happiness and Virtue."[22] If this was the "great fundamental right of human nature," particular rights inexorably followed from it. Channing listed some of these in the second chapter of his book on slavery:

Every man has a right to exercise and invigorate his intellect or the power of knowledge, for knowledge is the essential condition of successful effort for every good; and whoever obstructs or quenches the intellectual life in another, inflicts a grievous and irreparable wrong. Every man has a right to inquire into his duty, and to conform himself to what he learns of it. Every man has a right to use the means, given by God and sanctioned by virtue, for bettering his condition. He has a right to be respected according to his moral worth; a right to be regarded as a member of the community to which he belongs, and to be protected by impartial laws; and a right to be exempted from coercion, stripes, and punishment, as long as he respects the rights of others. . . . He has a right to sustain domestic relations, to discharge their duties, and to enjoy the happiness which flows from fidelity in these and other domestic relations.[23]

These theoretical bases of Channing's thought did not change appreciably in the thirty years of his life as a major public figure. What did change was his application of these principles to the practical and specific issues of the day.

By birth and early training Channing was a Federalist. As late as 1829 he could still say, " Our attachment to this party [the Federalist] we have no desire to conceal," qualifying the statement with " Our ideas of the allegiance due to a party are exceedingly liberal." And he could go on to add, " A purer party than that of the Federalists, we believe, never existed under any government." [24]   These words were written in retrospect; they sum up Channing's unconscious bias in favor of the upper classes. For all his insistence on the divine potentialities of mankind in general, he never completely freed himself from his inveterate habit of thinking of people in categories: " the poor," " the laboring classes," " the commercial classes." Never having ex-

perienced the anxieties peculiar to these groups nor the
practical problems they encountered, he inclined to treat
them a little cavalierly. One of his most unfortunate utterances is to be found in his sermon " Ministry for the Poor,"
delivered in 1835:

> That some of the indigent among us die of scanty food, is
> undoubtedly true; but vastly more in this community die
> from eating too much, than from eating too little; vastly
> more from excess, than starvation. So as to clothing, many
> shiver from want of defences against the cold; but there is
> vastly more suffering among the rich from absurd and criminal
> modes of dress . . . than among the poor from deficiency of
> raiment. Our daughters are oftener brought to the grave by
> their rich attire, than our beggars by their nakedness. So the
> poor are often over-worked, but they suffer less than many
> among the rich who have no work to do, no interesting object
> to fill up life, to satisfy the infinite cravings of man for ac-
> tion. . . . How many of our daughters are victims of *ennui*, a
> misery unknown to the poor, and more intolerable than the
> weariness of excessive toil! [25]

However generously interpreted, these words show an appalling ignorance of the real meaning of poverty, coupled
with an almost equally appalling insensitivity to the suffer-
ing of others. If Channing had had an axe to grind, such
an attitude, if not more admirable, would at least have been
understandable; but to use these words in all innocence displays an incredible naïveté. They provide the clearest evidence that he never completely transcended his class background.

Yet whatever Channing's defects of sympathy with those
whose circumstances he did not fully understand, he was
never guilty of the virulent anti-democratic pronounce-
ments of such worthies as Fisher Ames and Robert Treat

Paine.[26]   Nor did he ever agree with Hamilton's dictum that the people is a great beast.

It is true enough that in his youth Channing shared the Federalist hatred for the French Revolution and all its works; we have seen evidence of this prejudice in his activities at Harvard and in his correspondence with Shaw from Richmond.[27]   Eleven years later he was still sufficiently a Federalist to write to his grandfather William Ellery expressing the hope that Madison's election to the presidency and the end of the Embargo have " given relief to you as well as our country." [28]   But Channing's dislike for France and the French Revolution was, I think, not merely a mask for anti-democratic feeling, as it was with so many of the Federalists, though it may have been in part unconsciously assimilated from the supercharged political atmosphere in which he lived.   Perhaps we best understand his distrust of the revolution by referring it to three causes: osmosis from the anti-French feelings of the Federalists, the apparent French repudiation of Christianity and its morality, and, finally, the rise of Napoleon as a tyrant.   The first of these feelings Channing outgrew; the charge of immorality, he was finally satisfied, could be explained away as a reaction against the fearful abuses of the Bourbon regime; the last, since it involved Channing's hatred of arbitrary power, he never ceased to abhor.

Another glance at Channing's utterances on the French Revolution when he was still a lad of eighteen or nineteen shows the extent to which he shared the Federalist opinions of the day:

Should the worst happen, should my native country be prostrated . . . at the feet of France, I will curse and quit it.   I

never will breathe the same air with those who are tainted with
the foul impurities of French principles. I never will dwell
in the country where I was born free, when it is doomed to
groan under a foreign yoke.[29]

Perhaps we should not hold Channing responsible for opinions formed in extreme youth. And even allowing for
contemporary opinion of Napoleon, what are we to say
about the rhetoric of the sermon preached in 1810 on a
day of public fast?

Will it be said that he [Napoleon] wants not to conquer us,
but only wishes us to be his allies. *Allies of France!* Is there a
man who does not shudder at the thought! Is there one who
had not rather struggle nobly, and perish under her open en-
mity, than be crushed by the embrace of her friendship, — *her
alliance.* . . . Are you lovers of treachery, perfidy, rapacity
and massacre? Then aspire after the honour which Spain has
forfeited, and become the ally of France.[30]

More than thirty years later Channing no longer thought
in such abstract terms that he could condemn the French
nation wholesale. Writing the preface to the complete edition of his works, he said:

I cannot now, as I once did, talk lightly, thoughtlessly of
fighting with this or that nation. That nation is no longer an
abstraction to me. It is no longer a vague mass. It spreads out
before me into individuals. . . . It consists of husbands and
wives, parents and children, who love one another as I love my
own home.[31]

And it was with this same new understanding and wisdom
that a few months earlier he had written what was to be almost his last word on the great and vexing social problems
of his age. In Philadelphia, in his address before the Mercantile Library Company on May 11, 1841, Channing spoke

of the French Revolution in words he had never used before. The passage, long though it is, demands full quotation because it clearly establishes Channing in the great tradition of American political liberalism:

The French Revolution is perpetually sounded in our ears as a warning against the lawlessness of the people. But whence came this Revolution? Who were the regicides? Who beheaded Louis the Sixteenth? You tell me the Jacobins; but history tells a different tale. . . . They were Louis the Fourteenth, and the Regent who followed him, and Louis the Fifteenth. These brought their descendant to the guillotine. The priesthood who revoked the edict of Nantz [sic], and drove from France the skill and industry and virtue and piety which were the sinews of her strength; the statesman who intoxicated Louis the Fourteenth with the scheme of universal empire; the profligate, prodigal, shameless Orleans; and the still more brutalized Louis the Fifteenth, with his court of panders and prostitutes; these made the nation bankrupt, broke asunder the bond of loyalty, and overwhelmed the throne and altar in ruins. We hear of the horrors of the Revolution; but in this, as in other things, we recollect the effect without thinking of the guiltier cause. The Revolution was indeed a scene of horror; but when I look back on the reigns which preceded it, and which made Paris almost one great stew and gaming-house, and when I see altar and throne desecrated by a licentiousness unsurpassed in any former age, I look on scenes as shocking to the calm and searching eye of reason and virtue as the tenth of August and the massacres of September. Bloodshed is indeed a terrible spectacle; but there are other things almost as fearful as blood. There are crimes that do not make us start and turn pale like the guillotine, but are deadlier in their workings. God forbid, that I should say a word to weaken the thrill of horror with which we contemplate the outrages of the French Revolution! But when I hear that Revolution quoted to frighten us from reform, to show us the danger of lifting up the depressed and ignorant mass, I must ask whence it came; and the answer is, that it came from the intolerable weight of misgovernment

and tyranny, from the utter want of culture among the mass
of the people, and from a corruption of the great too deep
to be purged away except by destruction. I am also compelled
to remember that the people, in this their singular madness,
wrought far less woe than kings and priests have wrought, as
a familiar thing, in all ages of the world. All the murders of
the French Revolution did not amount, I think, by one fifth, to
those of the Massacre of St. Bartholomew's. The priesthood
and the throne, in one short night and day, shed more blood,
and that the best blood of France, than was spilled by Jacobinism and all other forms of violence during the whole Revolution. Even the atheism and infidelity of France were due
chiefly to a licentious priesthood and a licentious court. It was
religion, so called, that dug her own grave.[32]

This passage is a far cry from the Francophobia of Channing's early years; it is almost as far from the easy moralizing of the two essays on Napoleon in which he had declared
that France's revolution had not given her freedom because
her " character forbade her to be free." [33] Reading such
empty, facile phrases, we can understand Matthew Arnold's
estimate of Channing's works: that they were " the flower
of moral and intelligent mediocrity." [34] But in spite of occasional lapses into clerical cant, Channing's view of Napoleon was sufficiently just to warrant the high praise which
the nineteenth century in general awarded it.

The chief ground of Channing's objection to Napoleon
was the military despotism with which the usurper had
saddled France. Military dominance, the Doctor thought,
was the worst abuse of the power to control others, in itself
so dangerous. His thinking on this topic had not changed
for forty years; in 1799 he had written to his friend Shaw
that a standing army was a " hot-bed of vice," and had
added that he agreed with the man who said, " for five dol-

lars worth of whisky, they [soldiers] would every man of them sacrifice their country, and sell its liberties." [35]   And in 1841, thinking of military courage, he wrote: " Almost any man, under the usual stimulants of the camp, can stand fire. The poor wretch, enlisted from a dramshop and turned into the ranks, soon fights like a hero." [36]   With men of this type at his disposal a military genius would find it easy to subdue a whole nation to his will.   But such a despotism is diabolical, and Channing reserved for the tyrant his strongest words:

> He who lifts a parricidal hand against his country's rights and freedom; who plants his foot on the necks of thirty millions of his fellow-creatures; who concentrates in his single hand the powers of a mighty empire; and who wields its powers, squanders its treasures, and pours forth its blood like water, to make other nations slaves and the world his prey, — this man, as he unites all crimes in his sanguinary career, so he should be set apart by the human race for their unmingled and unmeasured abhorrence, and should bear on his guilty head a mark as opprobrious as that which the first murderer wore.[37]

These are not Federalist reasons for opposing Bonaparte; they are an enduring and powerful indictment of tyranny. This hatred of the domination of men over others was the mainspring of Channing's thinking on political subjects.   It is apparent in his earliest letters to Shaw, even though partially concealed under Federalist prejudice; it shines brighter in the two essays on Napoleon, even though obscured by the superficial moralizing of the preacher.   And it glows most strongly and almost without hindrance in the great speeches written at the end of his life.

Channing's final rejection of the Federalist viewpoint did not come until 1829, and even then it was tempered by many a backward glance. This rejection was not a negative one stemming from Channing's fear of the domination of the few over the many. Rather it was the result of his perception that the Federalists as a group lacked faith in the possibilities of man, that they lacked faith in democracy: "By not confiding in the community, they lost its confidence. By the depressed tone with which they spoke of liberty, their attachment to it became suspected. The taint of anti-republican tendencies was fastened upon them by their opponents, and this reproach no party could survive." [38]

Temperamentally a cautious man himself, Channing failed to see any active danger to the democratic community in Federalism: he thought its leaders were impelled by the same caution that impelled him. Consequently, he never believed of the Federalists what their enemies said about them. It never, I think, occurred to him that the party was at heart anti-democratic, nor that the Hartford Convention was anything more than a somewhat rash protest against the policies of the national government. Whether Channing's ignorance is to be condoned is another question. He was a fairly close friend of John Quincy Adams, who was in full possession of the facts. He was friendly with many of the leaders of the party — in fact, some of them were his own parishioners. Yet he walked among them in his almost incredible innocence, apparently without being greatly affected by the society in which he moved.

He was redeemed from the practical excesses of Federalism by his own faith in the capacities of mankind and by

his own integrity of mind which refused assent to propositions he was not willing to act upon. The first real crisis
came in 1812, when the New England community, restive
under the Jeffersonian Embargo and Mr. Madison's war,
was muttering threats of rebellion. Much as Channing
hated war and much as he disapproved of a *de facto* alliance
with Napoleon, he nevertheless braved the wrath of Boston
in his sermons which concern the declaration of war against
Great Britain. In the extracts collected under the title
" Duties of the Citizen in Times of Trial or Danger,"
Channing gave his views on the responsibility of citizens to
their government.

The nature of the situation prevented him from an absolutely clear-cut definition of principles, for many contradictory issues were involved. In the first place stood his
uncompromising hatred of war. We have only to recall the
impoverishment of Newport during the last two decades
of the eighteenth century to recognize one of the sources
of this hatred. Growing up, as he did, in a town and on an
island devastated by the British during their long occupation must have impressed upon the young boy a strong sense
of the desolation that combat wrought, even for the victors.
Then there was the hereditary suspicion of England as a
monarchy and hence forever the enemy of a republican
nation. But perhaps more strongly than anything else, the
thought of Napoleon, the symbol of everything Channing
hated, must have urged him to condemn America's policy.
One might dislike England, but one despised France. Furthermore, as a New Englander, Channing could not have
been sympathetic with the " War Hawks "; as an anti-
imperialist he could not have looked with favor on the

grandiose plans to annex Canada.   How, then, could he resolve these contrary tensions?

His answer on the war with Great Britain was clear: he
did not think it justifiable.   The next question was, " What
conduct belongs to a good citizen in our present trying
condition? " [39]   Apparently the answer was submission to
the lawful government because:

Resistance of established power is so great an evil, civil commo-
tion excites such destructive patterns, the result is so tremen-
dously uncertain, that every milder method of relief should first
be tried, and fairly tried.   The last dreadful resort is never
justifiable, until the injured members of the community are
brought to despair of other relief, and are so far united in views
and purposes as to be authorized in the hope of success.[40]

One does not have to imagine an extremist's reaction to such
a statement, for Thoreau has provided a stinging rebuke in
his " Civil Disobedience ": " All men recognize the right
of revolution; that is, the right to refuse allegiance to, and
to resist, the government, when its tyranny or its ineffi-
ciency are great and unendurable.   But almost all say that
such is not the case now.   But such was the case, they
think, in the Revolution of '75." [41]   Thoreau went on to
attack the kind of thinking exemplified in Channing's
second sentence by contradicting the source from which
it was drawn, *The Principles of Moral and Political Philosophy*, by William Paley.[42]   Thoreau did not ask himself
whether it was expedient to do right, as Paley's utilitarian-
ism demanded he should.   He insisted on right action, no
matter what the consequences.

Channing, however, felt that the mere existence of a
republican government precluded a rebellion because the

government itself provided for change. At the same time, he held that freedom of speech must be preserved if the government was not to turn into a tyranny. The right of suffrage itself was meaningless without freedom of opinion, freedom of speech, and freedom of the press. Consequently, any attempt on the part of the government to inhibit these rights, even in time of war, was inimical to the true interests of the nation. The hushing of opposition because the country was at war seemed to Channing the ultimate in folly:

A sentiment more unworthy of a free country can hardly be propagated. If this doctrine be admitted, rulers have only to declare war, and they are screened at once from scrutiny. At the very time when they have armies at command, when their patronage is most extended, and their power most formidable, not a word of warning, of censure, of alarm must be heard. . . . Admit this doctrine, let rulers once know, that, by placing the country in a state of war, they place themselves beyond the only power they dread, the power of free discussion, and we may expect war without end.[43]

Two years later, when the invasion of Boston by the British seemed imminent, Channing spoke in a different vein. Still paying his respects to Madison, he declared:

However unjustifiable may have been the measures by which we have been reduced to this mournful extremity, our right to our soil and our possessions remains unimpaired; the right of defence can never be wrested from us. . . . We should resolve that we will be true to ourselves, to our fathers, and to posterity . . . that whilst God gives us power we will not receive law as a conquered people.[44]

There is no word here of resistance to the government. And we seem to detect an almost jesuitical note, for if the war against Great Britain was unjust in its beginnings, it is difficult to understand why, when the tide of battle has turned against us, the right of self-defense becomes a moral absolute.

Channing never fully faced up to the problem of war. He was, like most normal people, against aggressive war, yet he was not a pacifist. Wars of defense seemed just to him — but he never realized the practical impossibility of establishing whether any given war is aggressive or defensive. Perhaps the ambiguity of his attitude toward war may be due in some part to the circumstances of his life. His Grandfather Ellery had been one of the signers of the Declaration of Independence, and the young Channing had of course grown up believing in the absolute justice of the American cause. Wars, then, sometimes were justifiable. But then there was the desolation of Newport — the picture of Dr. Hopkins' church must often have appeared in his mind. And, believing as he did in the evils of military power, Channing must have regarded all military exploits with a deep-seated suspicion. There was no lack of contemporary testimony concerning the evils of war. The years of Channing's youth and early manhood had rung with the echoes of the French Revolution and the Napoleonic battles.

The constant rumors of war against the French (would such war be justifiable since it involved the extermination of an incarnate devil?) and the final outbreak of open conflict against the English in 1812 contributed to Channing's bafflement concerning the meaning of war. Nor did the cessation of hostilities in 1815 end the almost constant bickering between the United States and Great Britain. The Oregon question, supposedly settled by the Treaty of Ghent in 1814, simmered uneasily for a generation; the argument over the Maine boundary dragged on for nearly forty years, culminating in the Aroostook "disturbance" of 1838. Equally irritating to Great Britain was the poorly timed and tactless support that unofficial groups in this country gave to the ill-starred Canadian revolt.

Indian wars, of course, were constant throughout the years of Channing's life; and on our southern border, the settling of the Mexican province of Texas by Stephen F. Austin and his fellow colonists was to provide a fertile source of conflict between the United States and Mexico —a conflict which Channing foresaw as the prelude to a long career of imperialistic war.

Thus the Doctor had ample experience of war and threats of war. Born in the midst of one conflict, in maturity he had to face the prospect of an imminent invasion, and in old age the menace of a third major conflict. Yet his contemporaries looked to him in vain for any adequate solution to the problem of war. He never seemed to realize completely the true nature of its causes, nor did he ever provide convincing leadership in the agitation for peace. It is true that he made a number of speeches decrying the evils of armed conflict, that he dwelt at some length on the physical and moral ravages of war, that he feared the consequences of military despotism, that the Peace Society of Massachusetts was founded in his parsonage. But in summing up his position in the introductory remarks to the collected edition of his works, Channing wrote: "If, indeed, my country were invaded by hostile armies, threatening without disguise its rights, liberties, and dearest interests,

I should strive to repel them, just as I should repel a criminal, who should enter my house to slay what I hold most dear, and what is intrusted to my care." [45]   In short, his position in 1812 was substantially his position in 1841.

In the intervening years he had written much on the subject. The "Lecture on War," delivered in the early months of 1838, is the most remarkable of his statements; in addition to his usual comments on the physical and moral destructiveness of war, Channing here made his closest approximation to an analysis of the causes of war. In doing so, he contrived to marry to this new analysis his old theory of the evil tendencies of power. Speaking of the mistaken conclusion of some apologists that wars would become fewer as commercial relations were developed between nations, he commented:

Wealth breeds power, and power always tempts to wrong. Communities which at once grow rich and licentious, breed desperate men, unprincipled adventurers, restless spirits, who unsettle social order at home, who make freedom a cloak and instrument of ambition, and find an interest in embroiling their country with foreign foes. Another consequence of growing prosperity is the rapid growth of population . . . and communities are tempted to throw off this dangerous load, this excess of numbers, in foreign war. . . . Let us not speak of industry, commerce, and wealth, as insuring peace. . . . Does trade cherish nothing analogous to the spirit of war in ordinary pursuits? Is there no fighting on the exchange? Is bargaining nothing but friendship and peace? [46]

The rest of the lecture is devoted, like the sermon of 1812, to a discussion of the duties of a citizen when his country wages an unjust war. It is necessary to resist such a war, apparently, even at the price of martyrdom.

When Channing sent a copy of this address to Lucy Aikin, she lost no time in going to the heart of his argument. After complimenting him on his perspicuity in understanding that the increase of commerce did not necessarily imply a lessening of wars (a somewhat more pessimistic view than Channing usually took of commerce), Miss Aikin criticized his contention that war is sometimes necessary and just:

I do not see how any Christian can stop short of Quakerism on this point without allowing himself to regard these non-resisting principles as local or temporary in their intention. You, I suppose, take this view, as you permit self-defence. But in many cases this is permitting all. Practically, the line dividing offence from defence is often very evanescent. Once allow war not to be utterly unlawful, and we may listen to considerations of state, expediency, utility. . . . Thus each case of hostilities comes to be discussed on its own merits or demerits, and the application of the religious scruple comes to be matter of opinion.[47]

Channing, of course, did not admit to religious scruples against war; he based his case on a moral imperative depending on the nature of things. But the difference in terms does not make any practical difference in the validity of Miss Aikin's argument, and if Channing answered her, his letter is not preserved.

Further ambiguity in Channing's views of war and violence is found in his treatment of the Lovejoy case. This episode is especially significant for an understanding of his attitude toward the problems of his times: it displays him at his best and at his worst, bold in his cause but timid in his fear that his actions might be misunderstood, entirely devoted to the theoretical principle but fearful that practical action might commit him further than his conviction warranted.

On the surface, the situation seemed simple enough. Elijah Lovejoy, a young man from Maine, at the age of thirty-two had become editor of the *Observer*, an Abolition paper in St. Louis. The opposition of the people of St. Louis became so severe that, as the result of threats from the citizenry, Lovejoy decided to move himself and his paper to Alton, Illinois. He was no more successful there; his press was twice destroyed by a mob. Assisted by his friends and determined to take a stand on his constitutional rights, Lovejoy went ahead and ordered a new press in spite of the efforts of a committee of local citizens to discourage him. The press was installed, the mob rose again — but this time Lovejoy, attempting to defend himself and his property, was killed.

The riot and murder took place on the night of November 7, 1837. The news did not reach Boston for twelve days, but when it came it produced an explosion of feeling among those sympathetic to the anti-slavery movement as well as those whose devotion to the ideal of free speech transcended their antipathy to abolition. The matter, at least in so far as Channing was concerned, came to a head on November 24, when he suggested to his friend Samuel E. Sewall that a petition should be drawn up asking the use of Faneuil Hall for a protest meeting. When Sewall had drawn the petition, he sent a copy to the Doctor and asked for his signature, adding, " I think your name will have greater weight than that of any other person in the city." [48] Channing replied immediately by signing the petition " very cheerfully," and then proceeded to take the bloom off the idea by trusting that " it will not be presented unless you have reason to hope an effective meeting." He went on to regret that his voice was not fitted to public speaking in Faneuil Hall, and concluded by hoping that " the names next offered may be such as to save the petition from being regarded as the act of any party." [49]

When the petition was presented to the mayor, it was denied by him and the board of aldermen on the grounds that whatever took place in Faneuil Hall was " often considered, in other places, as the expression of public opinion in this city." The mayor and the board further felt that the expression of opinion they anticipated from the meeting "ought not to be regarded as the public voice of this city." [50] The threat to free speech was so apparent that a meeting of citizens was held in response to a second call written by Channing. This plea took the form of an open letter to the citizens of Boston; in it Channing disclaimed any intention of supporting Lovejoy because of his Abolition activities. He was interested, Channing said, only in deprecating lawlessness: " I cannot, I will not, tamely and silently, see these rights of freedom trampled down in the person of a fellow-citizen, be he rich or poor, be he friend or foe, be he the advocate or the opposer of what I deem the truth." [51] This call was so successful that the protest meeting was finally acceded to by the city authorities and scheduled for the eighth of December.

Behind the scenes Channing was still dubious. On Saturday, the second of December — the same day the open letter appeared in the *Boston Daily Advertiser* — he wrote to a friend active in the affair that he hoped " we may have a meeting which will *unite* the people of our city . . . and for this end exasperating views of one or another party should be conscientiously kept out of sight." The Abolitionists, he suggested, would do well to show themselves as " the settled foes of violence and mobs " — and stop there. He hoped, too, that he might " be excused from all participation in it." [52]

When the day came, however, Channing was equal to the occasion. Repudiating the suggestion that the meeting had been arranged to give aid and comfort to the Abolitionists, Channing explained that its purpose transcended party, and took upon himself responsibility for its having been called:

> I claim to know something of its origin; for I believe its existence is due to me as much as to any other person. . . . I said that I wished that the citizens of Boston would in some public manner express their abhorrence of the lawless spirit which had prompted to this and to kindred deeds. . . . I felt that the citizens could preach a more awakening sermon than all our ministers. . . . I received a petition from my friend embodying the suggestion I had made. . . . To this petition I affixed my name. . . . I signed the petition with the full understanding that the meeting should bear no relation to party but should comprehend all citizens of whatever sect or party whose spirits had been stirred, as mine was, by the fearful progress of lawless force.[53]

The meeting, as we have seen, was a complete success for Channing and his friends. And yet within a few days he had written to one of the prime movers, his friend Ellis Gray Loring, that the actions of Lovejoy in resorting to violence were troubling him. He also suggested that the Abolitionists themselves had condoned violence — an accusation he had made earlier in his career and was to make again in the future. Loring took exception to Channing's criticism, pointing out his ambiguous attitude: " You say, we *owe* the adoption of the Peace Principle to the Country. As much I think, and no more than (I say it, with entire respect) yourself. — You are also formidable to the South. More so, I think and they say, than a hundred societies." [54]

If we apply Loring's criticism to Channing's whole attitude toward violent resistance, we can begin to understand why there were so many facets of the Doctor's thought — why he seemed consistent to himself, evasive to his friends, and pusillanimous to his enemies. What these circumstances were appeared perfectly clear to him; they were not so lucid to others. Conversely, circumstances which to others seemed to justify (or at least extenuate) the use of violence did not seem sufficient to Channing. Lacking almost entirely the power of self-criticism, he literally could not understand that his conclusions might seem untenable to others, or that the actions he chose to take might seem capricious or even cowardly to those who did not share his ideas.

In the Lovejoy case Channing could not entirely exculpate the Abolitionists, for he felt they had somehow drawn the citizens' wrath upon themselves through their intemperateness. Not that he defended the actions of the mob — but he would have preferred a more clear-cut issue. He could not understand that he himself, moderate and well-balanced as he thought himself to be, had incurred the same hatred that Lovejoy had, that Lovejoy's final resort to armed resistance was precisely the response that, on Channing's own reasoning, he should have made.

Channing's true dimensions appear in these circumstances. With all his faults of temperament and with all his inability to put himself in another's shoes, he did not do the easy thing and relapse into silence. Instead, he downed his doubts, forbore the facile rationalizations that would have excused him, and took part in an action which not only put him in some physical danger but also compromised his position in the pulpit. Never the unthinking radical and never carried beyond himself by the heady wine of cant that has done so much to justify reformers to themselves, Channing, in the crisis, nevertheless took his place in the van.

As we have seen, Channing had similarly qualified his role in the anti-slavery controversy.[55] We can see, from the perspective of more than a century, how immense his influence was as well as how dilatory and fainthearted his efforts seemed to the reformers. As early as 1834, Garrison had personally tried to interest Channing in giving formal support to the Abolition movement:

> In a cause like this, there are two things to be remembered — 1st, that a tremendous responsibility rests upon him who perverts his influence; and 2nd, that an equally fearful responsibility *rests upon him who withholds his influence.* . . .
> I thought of beseeching you in this letter, to exert your victorious influence for the deliverance of this country from impending ruin. But if the slaughter of two millions of victims who have gone down to their grave with their chains around them . . . have failed to move you, it is scarcely possible that any appeal can succeed from me. . . .[56]

Channing, completely in the liberal tradition, went his own way, and consequently earned for himself the liberal's reward: the hatred and suspicion of the extremists on either side of the controversy.

In the last analysis, Channing's rejection of slavery was based on his view of the sacredness of the individual, the fact that all men had natural rights, and on his deep hatred for the abuse of power. And this rejection was, of course, amply fortified by the simple humanitarian instincts of a man who had seen slavery in action and knew firsthand of its degrading effects both on the slave and on the slave-holder. His pamphlet " Slavery," which appeared in 1835, is Channing's fullest expression on the subject. None of the other works — such as the " Letter to Henry Clay," " Remarks on the Slavery Question," " The Abolitionists," the two essays " The Duty of the Free States " and " Emancipation," or even the Lenox Address — add anything essential to his position. In many ways, " Slavery " and these other pamphlets are Channing's best work, for he showed un-wonted zeal in gathering relevant facts. He besieged John Quincy Adams, Nathan Appleton, Congressman Robert C. Winthrop, Charles Sumner, Justice Story, and others for the latest government information on slavery and related matters. Written thus from his own personal knowledge as well as from the most authoritative and complete in-formation available, Channing's work had relevancy and force which his more abstract discourses often lacked.

The argument of " Slavery " is arranged under eight headings. In the first Channing claimed that a human being could not be considered as property, using the *argumentum ad hominem* that if any man could be so held, then all men, even white, could be enslaved. His second argument, from natural rights, has been sufficiently developed. His third section, dealing with the view that the slaveholder was not necessarily guilty, drew down upon him the Abolitionists' wrath. Sarah M. Grimké demolished his arguments point by point, taking issue with him on his assumption that a man might be a good man though he held slaves. Miss Grimké thought that the slaveholder might be good in other directions, but in slaveholding he was violating a law of God and hence was deserving of blame. And to Channing's statement that some slaveholders held their slaves from a disinterested benevolence for the slaves' own good, she pointedly replied it was a strange benevolence indeed that required a man to enslave another and to profit from that slavery. To Channing's fear that anti-slavery propaganda might be the cause of violence, she answered that there was no other way to awaken the slaveholder except by propaganda.[57]

Channing was on firmer ground in the fourth and fifth points of his argument; he spoke of the evils of slavery and attacked the arguments from Scripture with which the southerners were beginning to buttress their " peculiar institution." The last three sections of the pamphlet — dealing with the inadvisability of emancipation at the present time, the author's fears about the rashness of the Abolitionists, and his warning to the men of the North that they would need " calm energy " to remain free, that they must be " firm, but also patient, forbearing, and calm " [58] — represent Channing's inevitable qualification of his position.

Samuel J. May has left us a straightforward account of the Abolitionists' reception of " Slavery ":

To his [Channing's] chapters in "Property in Man," "Rights," and "Evils of Slavery," we could take no exceptions. But his chapter entitled "Explanations" seems to us, as Mr. Garrison called it a chapter in *recantation*, a disastrous attempt to make it appear as if there could be sin without a sinner.[59]

And to Channing's contention that the Abolitionists were too precipitate, too violent, that they should rely on the good will of other philanthropists, May replied:

Are they the men to bear the brunt of a moral conflict? "Not many wise," as this world counts wisdom, — "not many rich, not many mighty," were ever found among the leaders of reform. God has always chosen the foolish to confound the wise. . . . Else why was not the abolition of slavery attempted and accomplished long before by that "better class"? [60]

Yet, as May was willing to admit, Channing's "Slavery" was of extraordinary importance in the development of the anti-slavery controversy. In spite of its concessions to the South (the same concessions that so irritated Miss Grimké, May, and Loring, to say nothing of Garrison and Maria Weston Chapman), the reaction was as violent as if the Doctor had offered to lead a servile insurrection. "Friends of the South" wrote pamphlets refuting Channing's statements; Senator Leigh of Virginia arose to address the Senate on the misrepresentation of the southern character, and proclaimed that southern gentlemen would never dream of illicit relations with their female slaves; and the same James T. Austin who was to rise to such bad eminence in the Lovejoy affair sprang to the defense of slavery in a pamphlet bearing the title "Remarks on Doctor Channing's Slavery; by a Citizen of Massachusetts."

Judged by its results rather than by its timidities, Channing's pamphlet served its purpose well. If it did not approach the single-mindedness of a Garrison, it perhaps made up for lack of intensity by creating in the popular mind a greater faith in the disinterestedness of its author's motives. In a characteristic way the volume was testimony to the sincerity of Channing's statement to Joseph Tuckerman, written during the Doctor's stay in St. Croix:

Hardly a day passes without spreading and strengthening my sympathies with the mass of men, the poor, the forsaken. The sights which are most familiar here turn my thoughts continually on the need of great revolutions in our present social order. The selfish, all-grasping spirit, which everywhere sacrifices the mass to the few or leaves the many to suffer without pity or the means of improving their lot, must be resisted as it has not been.[61]

The fact of slavery was also a stimulus to Channing's thinking in other areas. He first awakened fully to the horrors of slavery on St. Croix; those horrors brought others to his mind. As he wrote to his friend Andrews Norton:

I have never been brought so much in contact with it [slavery] before — and though I see it in one of its mildest forms, I look on it with increasing aversion. I do not however waste all my indignation on the evil which is immediately under my eye. When the planter tells me that his slave has more comforts than the labouring classes in most other countries, I feel that he says the truth, and I am led to think of the sad aspects which society presents even among ourselves. No where does Christianity seem to have writ below the surface.[62]

Once the condition of workingmen had been brought home to Channing, he never lost his interest in projects for ameliorating their lot. Here, as in other reforms in which he was active, his approach was at first conservative and moralistic, growing more liberal and more practical as time went on.

Yet, liberal and practical as his views finally became, Channing had only glimpses into the nature of the society in which he lived. One might view with mingled complacence and alarm the advance of the nineteenth century — but as a professional moralist and acknowledged leader, one had also to devise some program for the solution of the century's most pressing problems. Since, however, the truly vital work of the century was the abolition of slavery and the preservation of the Union, reformers — at least in the first part of the century — may possibly be excused for giving only partial attention to those difficulties, present then, which now harass the twentieth century.

Even with this qualification, Channing's attitude toward the problems resulting from the increasing industrialization of the country seems a little innocent to the modern mind. Two underlying assumptions contributed to the unreality of Channing's approach: his inveterate tendency to regard people as members of different social groups rather than as individuals, and his determination to look at human life in the large, with little or no attention to detail. Such an attitude could suggest no practicable remedy for the conditions which so tormented the age. We know, however, that the Doctor was optimistic, for while still at St. Croix he had written: " I trust . . . that causes are at work which are to give a new aspect to this and other oppressed parts of the world. I think that great changes are at hand, and I anticipate happy ones, though I may not live to see them.

It seems to me that the claims and rights of human beings . . . are better understood." [63]

This sublime faith in unspecified " causes " and " great changes " often proved disturbing to the less idealistic-minded who were impatient to get at some specific task and were armed with facts, figures, and social theories. All his life Channing remained aloof from such impedimenta. The great controversy of the Jackson administration over the second Bank of the United States touched him hardly at all, and yet the social consequences of this struggle far transcended the implications of all his speeches on the dangers of wealth or the perils of commercialism. Volu-minous though it is, Channing's extant correspondence shows almost no trace of any real understanding of the issues or even of any great interest in them. For example, in 1834, writing to Nathan Appleton — who combined the character of a wealthy cotton manufacturer with that of a congressman — Channing interrupted his request for a reference in behalf of a friend to ask:

Have you not a pamphlet giving your views of the bank-system? If so, I should be pleased to see it. My ignorance of the subject, or my want of general principles, has prevented my giving any attention to the question which is now agitating the country. I can see injustice and usurpation in the course of the Executive — but of its bearings on the general interest I cannot judge. I fear more and more the exaggerations of politicians on all such matters. If I can get light without more labour than I can afford, I shall be glad to have it.[64]

This admission of ignorance concerning the real merits of the argument — perhaps he had received the pamphlet — did not keep Channing, a few months later, from writing to Miss Aikin:

The warfare of our headstrong, arbitrary President with our National Bank has turned our prosperity into commercial distress. . . . It is hoped that the usurpation of the President will be put down, and that he will be the means or occasion of introducing improvements into our Banking system, which, without a check, might have produced wide mischief.[65]

Three years later Channing was still sufficiently concerned with the difficulties of money and banking to send John Quincy Adams an enclosure from a correspondent in Edinburgh and to ask Adams' opinion of the correspondent's economic theory. Adams replied, succinctly enough, that he was not acquainted with the author's reputation, but feared that he understood " the subject upon which he writes less than you." Adams added that he was sorry that the Doctor had not found time to write on the " moral and religious " view of banking and paper currency.[66] Fortunately for us, it is not difficult to deduce Channing's " moral and religious " view of these topics.

As a moralist, he was not greatly perturbed by the depression that followed the curbing of the power of the Bank; after pointing out that the " spirit of commercial gambling, or what is called by courtesy speculation " had ended in disaster for the nation, he was sure that " people will find out, at length, that money is not the supreme end of the social compact." [67] Four months later, in a letter written in August, 1837, Channing still felt that the man of commerce was endangering his virtue. The cure was to be found in religion:

Much might be done by a strong, clear exposition of the rights and duties, the true principles, and the perils of trade. . . . The unmastered, immeasurable passion for gain lies at the root of the evil, and this is to be met by a higher, wiser application of Christian truth.   The moral sense on this subject is to be *created*.[68]

Whatever the reason, there could be no doubt in Channing's mind that something was somehow wrong in the social system.   He saw about him squalor and wretchedness; indeed, he had been aware of it for many years.   Was it not to redeem this wretchedness that he and his friend Joseph Tuckerman had inaugurated the Ministry at Large [69] as long ago as 1826?   But earnest and high-minded though the attempt had been, could Channing, looking back over a decade of experience with the project, honestly say that poverty had been lessened or that its degrading effects on bodies and minds had been significantly reduced?   Channing felt, of course, that the Ministry had been a good thing, and that even if it had accomplished little except temporary amelioration, in the future it would prove of incalculable value.   Yet, with all the moral energy expended on the Ministry at Large, one may doubt if it really was anything more than a sort of liaison between the formal ministry and the " visitation of the poor " — an institution (dear to the heart of the nineteenth century) whose deficiencies have been so thoroughly exposed by Kingsley:

And there's another mistake in your charitable great people, sir.   When they see poor folk sick or hungry before their eyes, they pull out their purses fast enough, God bless them; for they wouldn't like to be so themselves.   But the oppression that goes on all the year round, and the want that goes on all the year round, and the filth, and the lying, and the swearing, and the profligacy, that go on all the year round, and the sickening weight of debt, and the miserable grinding anxiety from rent-day to rent-day, and Saturday night to Saturday night, that crushes a man's soul down, and drives every thought out of his head but how he is to fill his stomach, and warm his back, and keep a house over his head . . . they never felt this.[70]

We may, in Channing's defense, point out that America in the first forty years of the nineteenth century was an almost complete stranger to the wretched English poverty that appalled Melville in 1839, as he recorded so tellingly in *Redburn* ten years later. And for all that Nathan Appleton had said that America's ability to export cotton goods successfully was due to " cheapness of the otherwise unemployed female labor," [71] the factories at Lowell and Waltham were models of their kind. What if the employees did work long hours and their pay was only three dollars a seventy-four-hour week? The girls were strong; they apparently had sufficient energy left over to play the pianos in their company boarding houses, to read in the company libraries, and to produce their own stories and poems which they went on to publish themselves in their own papers, of which the *Lowell Offering*, though a few years later than Channing's time, was the most famous. More to the point is the fact that neither Dickens nor Harriet Martineau, both of whom knew poverty and bad working conditions when they saw them, had anything but admiration for the New England cotton factories. If the conditions were far from idyllic by present-day standards, they were also far above the average of their own day.

Channing himself was inclined to think that the panic of 1837 and its aftermath was largely confined to the mercantile classes. Writing in 1842 to his English correspondent, William Rathbone, he said:

The truth is, that *as a people*, we know nothing yet of distress. I have spent three or four months in the interior, partly in Pennsylvania, partly in Massachusetts, and I see nothing but comfort and abundance. I have met but one beggar, a stout French Canadian, wandering about with his family to get work, and looking as if he and they were living on the fat of the land. . . . The trading community suffer much, and this must be, not only from past rashness, but because we have twice as many people in trade as the exchange of the products of the country requires.[72]

And yet other men, perhaps quicker to see than Channing, found poverty and wretchedness enough. Horace Greeley, after recording instances of extreme poverty, wrote:

But worst to bear of all was the pitiful plea of stout, resolute, single young men and young women; " We do not want alms; we are not beggars; we hate to sit here day by day idle and useless; help us to work, — we want no other help: why is it that we can have nothing to do? "[73]

One may suspect that in Channing's reaction to the depression, the moralist overcame the man; for it is certain that when he recognized the existence of poverty, he was the first to deprecate it, and he was not unaware that if " any member of the social body suffer, all must suffer with it."[74] He felt, further (and it is a measure of his distance from the dominant thinking of Boston), that " much can be accomplished by a generous, affectionate mode of speech and action among those classes of society which it has been thought can only be reached by menace, sternness, and terror."[75] But with all his humanity, all his perception of the evils of a commercial society, all his desire to understand the causes of poverty, Channing never transcended the barriers of class, education, and temperament. He could not believe that poverty was often the direct result of the social system. In no way did he anticipate Marx, or even Henry George. Perhaps the conditions of American life exonerated him from making a thoroughgoing social diagnosis. That the failure of the price structure (which more than doubled the price of flour in less than two years) could be responsible for poverty rather than the individual moral deficiencies of the laborer was a concept Channing never understood — though others, like Orestes Brownson, were quick enough to see.

Consequently, Channing's approach to the alleviation of poverty was not through a revision of the social system itself but through an individual appeal, first to the wealthy classes to be more Christian in their dealings with the poor, and second to the poor themselves to rise above their lamentable addiction to alcohol, their sinful lies, and their want of education. It was, however, everlastingly to Channing's credit that he did not succumb to one of the major temptations of his age — to write off the poor as lesser breeds without the law. His view of the temperance movement, for example, was comparatively free from the facile moralizing and the revivalistic excesses of the American Society for the Promotion of Temperance. Channing did not think that man, as a sinful being, naturally took pleasure in sottishness; he believed that many people took refuge in liquor to escape the intolerable burdens of their lives: "Multitudes, to earn subsistence for themselves and their families, are often compelled to undergo a degree of labor exhausting to the spirits and injurious to health. Of consequence, relief is sought in stimulants." [76] He saw, too, that there was a deep psychological reaction to the American insistence on competitive excellence, that in a society in which by definition only a few could ever really succeed, the vast majority were doomed to comparative failure and the feeling of insecurity that followed: " Just as far as wealth is the object of worship, the measure of men's importance, the badge of distinction, so far there will be a tendency to self-contempt and self-abandonment among those whose lot gives them no chance of its acquisition." [77]

Channing, of course, would not have been a man of his times if he had not included among the causes of intemperance the bad example set by the rich and the prevailing materialism of the age, but these aspects of his thought are not labored. The weight of his attempt to deal with the problem lies in his recognition of intemperance as a social evil rather than as individual wickedness. Nevertheless, his proposals for reducing the evil were hopelessly naïve. True to his doctrine of individual reform, Channing thought that " moral strength, force of principle " would have to be inculcated in " the less prosperous classes of society." [78] This was to be accomplished by providing the laboring class with other forms of amusement than drinking. He thought that music should be introduced among the poor, that they should be encouraged to take up dancing, and that recitations should be furnished for them. This last diversion was to take the place of theatrical performances, which, he felt, were perhaps too depraved to be entirely recommended. Nor was literature to be overlooked in the enumeration of the sources of innocent merriment. And lastly, the physical health of the poor was of the utmost importance.

With the laboring classes thus rescued from the perils of boredom and ill health, two other steps would have to be taken before the danger of intemperance could be effectively diminished. The upper classes would have to give up their bad example and set a good one by abstention from liquor. With the triumph of principle among the well-to-do, it would be easy for those of less material fortune to make the sacrifice. And, anticipating his conclusions in the Hollis Street Church controversy, Channing also suggested that the sale of liquor should be discouraged and that " the vending of them [spirits] by respectable men should be regarded as a great public evil." [79]

One can hardly expect 1837 to regard alcoholism as a disease; thus, according to the light of his time, Channing was surprisingly modern in his analysis of the reasons for intemperance and in his suggestions for its cure. But if his diagnosis was accurate and some of his suggestions for alleviation were psychologically sound, he failed notoriously to mention any immediately practical steps. Some of what he said was indubitably true; what he failed to recognize was that none of his suggestions stood any chance of being translated into fact in the foreseeable future. The Ministry at Large and the activities of well-meaning reformers like Eliphalet Nott, the president of Union College, in proving that drinking was unscriptural, were almost completely inadequate as means through which the Doctor's reforms were to be effected. As might have been expected, the temperance movement fell into the hands of moral fanatics like Lyman Beecher and Gerrit Smith (unlike in so many ways), and Channing's sensible though impracticable suggestions dropped out of sight in the intense moral crusade of the late 1830's, which bred such an intense reaction that the movement lost much of its momentum.

Since the laborers were to conquer intemperance by their own efforts, though aided by the helping hands of their more fortunate brothers, so they were to conquer their deficiencies of education. In disagreement with the insistence of Alcott and Parker on the infallibility of the private conscience, Channing's views of education were comparatively orthodox. His friendship with Horace Mann, that eminently practical reformer, helped to save him from theoretical excess. Alcott, as we may well imagine, had his own opinion of the Doctor's reluctance to accept the new truths that were being demonstrated in Alcott's own school. He wrote in his journal:

Dr. C., from the deficiency of his own knowledge on this subject and a still lingering tinge of that scholastic discipline by which his mind was formed, sets a much higher value on mere historical knowledge than belongs of right to it in a scale of human acquirement. He says that he is daily reminded of his own deficiencies and is compelled to recur to authorities, when, as I feel, he should have the facts in his own mind. History, he thinks, is one of the most effectual revelations of human nature — the facts of the past are the manifestations of the capacities of the human race. . . .

Now, while I would not take from his view of the importance of this knowledge, yet I think much knowledge of our nature can be derived from the study of individual life. History is rather the exhibition of the power of the individual than of the people.[80]

In spite of this difference between the attitude of the radical Alcott and the temperamentally conservative Channing, there was entire agreement between them on the importance of education. The Doctor's "Remarks on Education," published in the *Christian Examiner* for March 1833, explains to the modern reader one of the reasons Alcott was, for a time at least, so great an admirer of the older man. Channing had written: "There is no office higher than that of a teacher of youth, for there is nothing on earth so precious as the mind, soul, character of the child. No office should be regarded with greater respect. The first minds in the community should be encouraged to assume it." [81] Alcott must have read these words with entire approval. And he must also have approved of the Doctor's dynamic view of the kind of ability a teacher ought to have:

The highest ability is that, which penetrates farthest into human nature, comprehends the mind in all its capacities, traces out the laws of thought and moral action, understands the perfection of human nature and how it may be approached, understands the springs, motives, applications, by which the child is to be roused to the most vigorous and harmonious action of all its faculties, understands its perils, and knows how to blend and modify the influences which outward circumstances exert on the youthful mind.[82]

These words, curiously modern in their insistence on the importance of understanding child psychology and their evident concern with the problem of motivation, go far to establish Channing's place in the progressive tradition, though his position fell somewhat short of what the extremists demanded. The fact that he sent his daughter Mary to study with Elizabeth Peabody, an ardent Pestalozzian, also indicates where his sympathies lay.

With this approval of progressive education and its encouraging view of human nature, Channing rejected the idea that education is a process of cramming the mind with facts. He thought with Miss Peabody and Alcott that the " true end of education . . . is to unfold and direct aright our whole nature." The multitude, on the other hand, felt " that to educate a child is to crowd into its mind a given amount of knowledge, to teach the mechanism of reading and writing, to load the memory with words, to prepare a boy for the routine of a trade." [83]   To Channing, this mechanical transference of skills did not seem sufficient to prepare the young child for his duties as a man and a citizen. But if more was needed and if sufficiently high-minded teachers were to be secured, money and adequate training were necessary; the source for both of these would have to be, as the Doctor admitted, " the opulent." [84]

Education, then, was a heaven-sent opportunity for the rich to indulge their disinterested benevolence toward the poor by giving the depressed classes a chance to rise above their station as individuals and through individual education awaken to new horizons. Here was no attempt to legislate poverty or low morals and manners out of existence — here was the way the door to better things could be opened for the poor. Yet on no account were the rich to be taxed into support of universal education. Such taxation, at least so Channing thought in 1837, would be morally wrong, for it would deprive the wealthy of their property without their consent. How, then, were the money and the adequate training of teachers to be provided for? Channing's answer was typical:

If, however, the enlightened among the laboring classes and their enlightened friends will set in motion a system of improvement which promises good and great results, the rich will not be found wanting in sympathy and benevolent aid. They cannot and ought not to be driven; but many among them would contribute liberally and joyfully to any wise practicable effort for elevating the laboring classes.[85]

But Channing's position was not always so doctrinaire.[86] He found himself able to give public support to Horace Mann's effort to improve the educational standards of Massachusetts — an effort which resulted in the establishment of three normal schools, a substantial increase in teachers' salaries, the expenditure of many millions in the construction of new school buildings, and the lengthening of the school year.

Most of Mann's work was to be accomplished after Channing's death; the Doctor's views remained theoretical, though he did live long enough to witness the foundation of the normal school system. Unfortunately, little survives to tell us whether Channing approved (or even noticed) the fact that support for these institutions as well as for the other reforms came from taxation as well as from disinterested benevolence.

Channing's suggestion that the wealthy give free rein to their benevolent inclinations in response to " the enlightened among the laboring classes " obviously depended upon the spread of enlightenment among these classes. Unlike some of his State Street parishioners, the Doctor did not fear the spread of knowledge, though in one isolated passage he suggested that any education for the lower classes " should include the means of inuring the people to manual labor. By this labor the multitude must subsist. An education unfitting them for work would make their future lives useless and dishonorably dependent. Accordingly, there is no need of costly institutions for universal education." [87]

Such acceptance of the *status quo* was contrary to the

main direction of Channing's thought. Seldom did he display so callous an attitude toward the situation of the laboring class, though there is evidence that he regarded the commercial distress of the years following 1837 as the result of too much education. The depression, he wrote, "is a natural consequence of the spread of education and will correct itself in time. An educated man would rather live by his wits than his hands, and consequently there has been a great rush into trade, where, it was supposed, that by the union of shrewdness with enterprise, men might grow rich with little toil." [88] This position, though characteristic enough of a particular aspect of Channing's thinking, was certainly at variance with the tenor of his " grand ideas ": these, whatever the minor reversals of the current, were steadfastly oriented toward the basic equality and worth of all men. Yet, as I have pointed out, this fundamental drift was often obscured by the inherited Federalism of Channing's thought, as well as by his temperament, which was cautious in the extreme.

More typical of his public utterances and more consonant with his religious and philosophic backgrounds was Channing's statement in " Self-Culture " which dealt unequivocally with the charge that education for all meant the unfitting of the minds of the lower classes for their natural work:

I reply, that a social order, demanding the sacrifice of the mind, is very suspicious, that it cannot indeed be sanctioned by the Creator. Were I, on visiting a strange country, to see the vast majority of the people maimed, crippled, and bereft of sight, and were I told that social order required this mutilation, I should say, Perish this order.[89]

Yet even this statement is to be qualified, for in his two
lectures " On the Elevation of the Laboring Classes," given
in 1840, Channing disclaimed any intention of relieving
mankind of the necessity of work. Indeed, dwelling with
great satisfaction on the moral benefits derived from con-
quering obstacles, he spoke of physical labor with the enthusiasm of one who had never indulged in it. He came to
the satisfying conclusion that manual labor " is a school, in
which men are placed to get energy of purpose and character, a vastly more important endowment than all the
learning of all other schools." [90]

Perhaps illogically, he felt that physical effort was no
impediment to the activity of the mind. He had thought
Alcott at the plow was the most inspiring sight in Massachusetts; it is as well that he was not to know of Hawthorne's conclusions about the effect of labor on the mind —
conclusions backed by sad experience of playing nursemaid
to Transcendental heifers [91] and long hours of toil in the
" gold-mine." [92] Whether Channing's acceptance of labor
was the result of a subconscious Calvinist identification of
worldly prosperity with a state of grace, whether it
stemmed from his Federalist inheritance, or whether it
sprang out of an agrarian conviction that work in the land
was the only socially profitable source of income, we cannot
know; we can, however, be sure that it was a cardinal point
of Channing's social thought.

The elevation, then, of the laboring classes — an elevation to be realized through education — was not to mean
freedom from toil, nor was it to mean absorption into the
socially acceptable group. It was to mean " elevation of
soul." Channing was aware that the phrase was vague and

he proceeded to qualify it by adding that this elevation implied the release of thought in its relation both to material objects and spiritual understanding. The mind was to comprehend certain " great ideas " (a term dear to Channing), among which were the idea of God, the idea of man, of virtue, of human life. These ideas do not necessarily depend on outside aids like libraries and teachers; they come from within.

Having thus disposed of the misconceptions about education for the laboring classes, Channing went on in his second lecture to attack some of the preconceptions about society that stood in the way of full realization of his view of life. He categorically rejected the notion that hereditary rank was necessary for a stable society. But more than that, he rejected the findings of the classical economists, especially Malthus, that population tended to outstrip the means of subsistence and that wages in a free market were necessarily at the subsistence level. In view of Channing's own hesitations about reform and the obvious fact that they were in part due to his upbringing and unconscious desire to preserve a state of affairs most congenial to his private fortune, however hard it may have been on the laborer, his objections to the doctrines of Smith, Ricardo, and Malthus had a double force. He replied to their theories by questioning their motives; when men say nothing can be done about the state of affairs, Channing said, it was well to consider the source of the statement:

It comes generally from men who abound, and are at ease; who think more of property than any other human interest; who have little concern for the mass of their fellow-creatures; who are willing that others should bear all the burdens

of life, and that any social order should continue which secures
to themselves personal comfort or gratification.[93]

Nor was this the sum of Channing's objection, for he
added that:

. . . no community has seriously set itself to the work of improving all its members, so that what is possible remains to be
ascertained. No experiment has been made, to determine how
far liberal provision can be made at once for the body and
mind of the laborer. The highest social art is yet in its infancy. Great minds have nowhere solemnly, earnestly under-
taken to resolve the problem, how the multitude of men may be
elevated. The trial is to come.[94]

Now that the pretensions of the more ardent nineteenth-
century reformers — that all would be well if suffrage were
extended, or the wealth shared, or education made available
to all — have been seriously questioned by the march of
events in the twentieth century, Channing's words have a
prophetic quality. Much can be forgiven in a man who
could see so clearly into the future, who was not taken in
by the catchwords of reform, and who yet preserved a
faith in the possibilities of all men.

If we can examine Channing's mind so pitilessly through
the lens of a century's passage and say, " Here the Federalist speaks," or " Here he is blinded by his own self-
interest," or " Here he is being inanely idealistic," it is because he was so honest in exposing the whole of his mind to
us. His contemporaries did not mistake his position: the
men of State Street rejected his preaching and the workingmen rejoiced in him as an ally. They speak in the words
of the Slaithwaite Mechanics Institute:

Rev'd Sir/ Through the medium of Mr. Smith Gray, we beg to hand you two resolutions passed in our Society.

Res^d That the warmest thanks of the members of this Institute are due and hereby given to Dr. Channing of Boston America for his valuable books written to elevate the working Classes.

That the members are truly grateful for the two Books ' Self Culture ' and ' Lectures on Labor ' and hope that the Author of all things will long preserve a life so valuable to the human race and particularly to the working Classes of Britain.

> Signed on behalf of the Institute by
> Jabez Meal Flax Spinner Pres^t
> Thomas Sykes Miller Vice-
> John Farley Weaver Sec^y [95]

CHAPTER FIVE

The Man of Letters

Recognition of Channing's influence was not confined to the operatives of Great Britain, for his work as a religious writer also was known and respected in England in the 1820's. Even those who disagreed with his theology saw much in his work to admire. Felicia Hemans, for example, found it possible to rise above the barriers of sect and write to her friend Joanna Baillie (who had been much impressed with Channing's Dudleian lectures of 1821 on "The Evidences of Christianity"):

> He [Channing] is an Unitarian, and, as you will observe from his Essay on Milton, a zealous advocate of that cause; but surely there is enough in that path which we all tread together, to make us feel that we are "the children of one Father," and to prevent our allowing difference of opinion to divide our hearts.[1]

But Channing's fame was destined to extend far beyond the partisan respect usually accorded to religious writers, and the clue to his English reputation is discovered in Mrs. Hemans' reference to his "Remarks on the Character and Writings of John Milton," which first appeared in the *Christian Examiner* in 1826. This essay and the three that followed — "Remarks on the Life and Character of Napoleon Bonaparte," "Remarks on the Character and Writings of Fénelon," and "Remarks on National Literature," which appeared at the rate of one a year in the *Christian Examiner* between 1827 and 1830 — partially account for Channing's literary reputation, although, as the anonymous author of a series of sketches of American writers printed in the *Athenaeum Journal* during the first two months of 1835 remarked:

The *lay* productions, on which the literary reputation of this great divine is founded, are very few: a small volume of Essays comprises them all. Yet, in these small limits, the hand of the master are [*sic*] so visible — the thoughts are of such broad sculpture — the language is so severely beautiful — and the truth and loftiness of the author's mind are so stamped upon every line, that, if he were not the leader of a powerful sect, and should he never write more, his fame would have pedestal enough: the Essay on Napoleon alone would make a reputation.[2]

Even if we add the "Remarks on National Literature" to the "small volume" called *Discourses, Reviews, and Miscellanies,* the twentieth-century reader is inclined to think that Channing's four "lay productions" must have provided far too narrow a pedestal to support the weight of his reputation. The truth of the matter, one suspects, is that though these essays did much to strengthen Channing's literary fame and to acquaint a wider audience with his works, they could not have been the sole cause of the esteem in which he was held. If he had not already achieved an international reputation as a preacher, if his utterances had not been regarded as the voice of American Unitarianism, one wonders whether his reflections on secular topics would have excited the attention they did.

Even from the beginning of his preaching career, Channing had aroused more than ordinary interest. His sermons attracted an audience less interested, perhaps, in doctrinal subtlety and logical demonstration than in aesthetic and emotional response. Contemporary testimony to his extraordinary effectiveness as a pulpit orator is overwhelming in its unanimity, for his listeners were all agreed that Channing's power lay in his complete absorption in his message. When his colleague Ezra Stiles Gannett attempted, twenty-five years after the Doctor's death, to analyze the secret of his power, he came to the same conclusion:

> There was little of close reasoning in his discourses: — why attempt to prove that which, distinctly seen, must commend itself by its own character? . . . The recognition of truth by his hearers was the aim of Dr. Channing's preaching. Hence his annunciation of truth was positive, authoritative, conclusive; yet neither dogmatic nor dictatorial: at once profoundly personal and sacredly impersonal, because his own experience was the channel through which it passed from the Source of truth. His audience left the house, smitten, stirred, determined, through the sympathy with his own deep conviction into which he had drawn them.[3]

This personal sincerity, coupled with a totally unaffected manner, did much to redeem Boston preaching from the cold, affected mathematical deductions from Scripture that Moses Stuart had complained of.[4] The author of the articles in the *Athenaeum Journal*, who apparently had heard Channing preach and seems to have been familiar with the sermons of the Unitarian ministers in Boston, spoke in his sketch of Channing of the " brilliant, poetical sermon," the absence of cant, " the perfect adoption of tone, style, and delivery " of the Unitarians and he attributed their skill to the fact that they bore " the impress of their great master," [5] who, of course, was Channing himself.

Channing's pre-eminence in Boston inevitably made him the spokesman for American Unitarianism, and his opinions as they were recorded in the *Christian Examiner* — a quasi-official organ of the Unitarians — achieved wide circulation. The controversy between the Unitarians and the orthodox also attracted attention, even from those not directly involved in the theological niceties of the arguments, because Channing soon became a symbol of the liberal progressive, and his attitude on questions of the day was eagerly awaited by both sympathizers and opponents.

Against this background, then, the reasons for Channing's success as a literary figure become clear. His obvious sincerity, his refusal to be bound by the conventions of party or sect, his intellectual honesty recommended him to the attention of those who ordinarily were not interested in religious controversy, while his importance to those whose main intellectual interest was religious, those who supported the large trade in religious tracts and volumes of sermons, needs no further explanation.

Furthermore, with the exception of his article on Fénelon, Channing was extremely fortunate in his choice of subjects. His first major attempt to reach a wider audience was his essay on Milton. This took the form of a review of Milton's *A Treatise on Christian Doctrine*, a book which had been lost for more than two hundred years. Its publication was, naturally, of the greatest significance, and Channing took advantage of the general interest to give his views of the poet. He devoted only about a third of his review to Milton's treatise, mostly by way of summary, with occasional interpolations of criticism, of Milton's method or conclusions. Channing was not particularly impressed with the book, for he had expected a more unconventional treatment of the great philosophical questions which had so long exercised his mind. But where Milton was too bold, as in his treatment of polygamy and divorce, Channing was too shocked to follow. After citing Milton's position on divorce, he could write only one sentence: " On this topic we cannot enlarge." [6]

The first two-thirds of the essay, in which Channing discusses the poetry and prose of Milton, is the most interesting to the modern reader, and seems to have provided, as well, the stimulus to Brougham's bitter attack on Channing in the *Edinburgh Review*. The Doctor began his essay with a consideration of Milton's relation to poetry, and was delighted to find himself in agreement:

We agree with Milton in his estimate of poetry. It seems to us the divinest of all arts; for it is the breathing or expression of that principle or sentiment, which is deepest and sublimest in human nature; we mean, of that thirst or aspiration, to which no mind is wholly a stranger, for something purer and lovelier, something more powerful, lofty, and thrilling, than ordinary and real life affords.[7]

Lest it be supposed that Channing's view of poetry was hopelessly, wildly idealistic, his qualification of this extreme position (a qualification curiously reminiscent of Coleridge's view of the creative imagination) must be added:

It [imagination] indeed finds its elements in what it actually sees and experiences in the world of matter and mind; but it combines and blends these into new forms and according to new affinities; breaks down, if we may so say, the distinctions and bounds of nature; imparts to material objects life, and sentiment, and emotion, and invests the mind with the powers and splendors of the outward creation.[8]

Since Channing had always enjoyed reading poetry as well as listening to it, he was anxious to defend it against those severer moralists who, in the Platonic tradition, objected that poetry was a begetter of lies and false illusions. To this objection Channing's reply was twofold. In the first place, even admitting that poetry did deal in shadow and illusion, it was perhaps weaning mankind away from the narrow realities of physical well-being and self-gratification. Perhaps it was not " the least service which poetry renders to mankind, that it redeems them from the thraldom of this earth-born prudence." [9] But the chief purpose of poetry was to give men glimpses of a higher truth than earth could otherwise provide.

Milton, Channing thought, possessed this power of raising man above himself; he suggested further that Milton's freedom and boldness of conception had " no need of the minute, graphic skill, which we prize in Cowper or Crabbe." [10] Milton's grand sublimity was best exemplified in the two first books of *Paradise Lost*, dominated as they are by the figure of Satan, who seemed to Channing to excite " an awe not unmixed with mysterious pleasure . . . as a miraculous manifestation of the power of mind." [11]

The phrase " power of mind," the clue to Channing's admiration for Milton, betrayed him into a position his detractors eagerly seized upon. He had written in defense of Milton's Latinisms and involved style, pointing out that simple clarity is not necessarily the chief goal of a writer:

The best style is not that which puts the reader most easily and in the shortest time in possession of a writer's naked thoughts; but that which is the truest image of a great intellect, which conveys fully and carries farthest into other souls the conceptions and feelings of a profound and lofty spirit. To be universally intelligible is not the highest merit. A great mind cannot, without injurious constraint, shrink itself to the grasp of common passive readers.[12]

The Addisonian style was, in Channing's opinion, desirable, but when its principles were codified and turned into strait jackets to restrict the efforts of genius, then it was time to speak out boldly.

Nine years after the publication of *Discourses, Reviews, and Miscellanies,* which contained Channing's essay on Milton, and thirteen years after the original publication of the article in the *Christian Examiner,* Henry Brougham used the Doctor's apology for Milton as a stick to beat American literature. The reason behind Brougham's attack seems to have been the *Edinburgh Review's* old bias against all things American — a bias that went back at least to Sidney Smith's famous question of 1820, "Who reads an American book? " Perhaps a more proximate cause of the attack lay in a favorable notice in *Fraser's Magazine,* which we shall consider presently, or in Harriet Martineau's laudatory account of Channing in her *Retrospect of Western Travel,* published in 1838. At any rate, whatever Brougham's motive, the running title of the article, ostensibly a review of a reprint of Channing's Milton essay, left no doubt of Brougham's intentions: it reads " False Taste — Dr. Channing." [13]

Brougham began by saying that Channing's name stood

high in American literature — and immediately added that from the article on Milton no one would ever guess why. Getting down to specific instances, he criticized the Doctor's style: " The taste which it displays is far from being correct; his diction is exceedingly affected; and his affectation is that of extreme vigour and refinement of thought, often when he is only unmeaning, contradictory, or obscure." [14] Brougham took exception to Channing's observations on style by distorting his meaning into an apology for willful obscurity: " Anything more pernicious, more hurtful to all good writing, and indeed more prejudicial to accurate thinking, cannot be imagined, than the propagation of such wild absurdities, under the authority of considerable names." [15]

Channing professed himself unable to understand the reasons for Brougham's attack, particularly since he considered him to be " a fellow-labourer in the cause of freedom." [16] Lucy Aikin had apparently relayed to her friend the opinion of old Samuel Rogers, once an arbiter of literary taste and still retaining some of his influence, that Brougham was motivated by jealousy of Channing's attainments. The Doctor did not agree: " Lord B. and myself have too little in common for envy. Our paths are too distinct to let us jostle one another. Then he must be conscious that his gifts, by their *kind*, to say nothing of their extent, have given him a conspicuousness before which my reputation makes little show." [17]

Brougham's criticism was, without serious question, absurd.[18] Channing had no illusions that he was another Milton; he realized the scope of his talents, and freely admitted his own deficiencies. As he wrote to an English friend after seeing his Lenox speech on emancipation through the press:

> I feel, that such efforts bring me before the publick as a *pamphleteer*, not a very exalted name in literature — But this is the readiest way to the publick mind, and as my pamphlets do not withdraw me much from the investigations and pursuits to which my life has been given, I could not decline the task without self-reproach.[19]

Channing's own style was limpid enough; as befits a pamphleteer, his chief interest was in clarity, and whatever obscureness his writing shows comes from an uncritical use of abstractions rather than excessive compression of thought or a desire to be obscurely profound.

Channing's second major secular writing was his review of Sir Walter Scott's *The Life of Napoleon Bonaparte.* In this task all occasions conspired to produce a work that was sure to be eagerly read. The intense and pervasive interest in Napoleon, popular curiosity to see what Scott's treatment would be like, and Channing's own position as arbiter of Boston's culture assured attention to his review. The Doctor sat down to the work with due solemnity — partly induced, no doubt, by the consideration of nine fat volumes of Scott. Andrews Norton had asked him to do the job for the *Christian Examiner,* and Channing agreed, " on the reasonable condition, that on reading the work, I shall find myself possessed of sufficient materials to form a fair judgment. I deem it of great importance to the interests of freedom and humanity that a just estimate should be formed of the modern conqueror, and I confess, I fear that Scott will not do his work faithfully." [20]   Then, after his usual forebodings of bad health and questionings of his fitness for the task, Channing went on to suggest another difficulty: " I am [not] sure that my views will be thought reasonable.   I find that lively abstract thinking on human nature has given me an abhorrence of despotism and a love of liberty which no active career could have inspired, and to some, I may seem rash and fanatical." [21]   A few days later, Channing again wrote to Norton.   He had procured a copy and found it longer than he had expected it to be; he asked for an extension, maintaining that he could not possibly do justice to Scott in time for the next number of the *Christian Examiner*.   And, after reading a few pages, he found he did not care for it: " I am sorry to find the work no better than I expected.   It is written with great negligence, often with a graceful ease, but I fear it still oftener clogged with verbiage.[22]

After a decent interval the review was finally finished, but it took up more space than Channing had at first expected, and occupied two numbers of the *Examiner*.   The criticism of Scott's work took only two pages in which Channing noted the stylistic deficiencies (mentioned in his letter to Norton) and commented on Scott's impartiality. The rest of the essay was devoted to a consideration of the life and deeds of Napoleon, a consideration which flowered, as was Channing's wont, into reflections on the nature of power, the ends of government, and man's relation to the Deity.

The article, as might be expected, drew both favorable and   unfavorable   notices — favorable   from   those   who agreed in advance with Channing's point of view, and unfavorable from those who differed with him. Lucy Aikin's reaction was typical of the former. She was especially pleased with the essay because she found that its analysis of Napoleon's character agreed perfectly with her father's opinion: " he, like you," she wrote to Channing, " regarded him [Napoleon] as in most respects a man of vulgar mind, a mere soldier of fortune, and he expressed the same indignation against those who, calling themselves friends of freedom, yet ranked among his partizans." Miss Aikin went on to express her admiration for the style of the article, and added (without revealing the name of her friend) that she had heard a literary acquaintance " a few days since, decidedly pronouncing Dr. Channing the most eloquent writer of the English language." [23]

Miss Aikin was not alone in her acclaim. A writer in *Fraser's Magazine* praised the article on Bonaparte as highly as that journal a few months earlier had praised the one on Milton: he wrote that in the essay " we discern the traces of a master-mind," and added that " few writers so charm and rivet by the magic influence there is breathed from every period." [24] Eight years earlier, the *Westminster Review* had paid its respects to the Doctor, dwelling in almost mystical language on the beauties of his style and the profundity of his thought.[25] The same magazine had already broken precedent by condescending to review one of Channing's sermons. They did not usually do this, they said, but these sermons were " so full of novel and of elevating views, conveyed in a language emphatic and majestic, like the finest passages of Milton's glorious prose " that they could not help opening their columns to a notice.[26]

But all the comments were not so favorable, and one of them has achieved a dubious immortality because it came from the pen of William Hazlitt. Hazlitt, of course, was a great admirer of Napoleon, and when an edition of Channing's writings appeared in 1829, he saw a great opportunity to accomplish two ends with one effort. He could further the *Edinburgh Review's* policy of attacking American writers and at the same time aim a blow at his hero's detractor. After a brief warming up in which Hazlitt dismissed Charles Brockden Brown as a Godwin without material, and labeled Cooper a drudge who " labours under an epilepsy of the fancy," [27] he bent to his task of destroying Channing. He gave him, to be sure, a condescending pat on the head for the sermon " On the Duties of Children " and a word of encouragement for the essay on Fénelon, but after questioning Channing's intellectual honesty,[28] he added that the Doctor's writings

. . . cannot be called mere common-place, but they may be fairly termed ambitious common-place: That is, he takes up the newest and most plausible opinion at the turn of the tide, or just as it is getting into vogue, and would fain arrogate both the singularity and the popularity of it to himself. He hits the public between what they are tired of hearing, and what they never heard before.[29]

Hazlitt's criticism, except for its implication of opportunism and intellectual dishonesty, is difficult to refute. There is little in Channing's writings to rivet the attention; his work is not remarkable for profundity of thought or striking originality of expression. It had oft been thought before, and, regrettably, had also been oft as well expressed. Yet if Channing was not a prime mover, he was, in the best sense of the word, a publicist who was able to sense the direction of the thought of his times and to formulate it before it became the possession of most thinking people. Indeed, perhaps a formulation was necessary before it could be received into the minds of men and be accepted by them.

Hazlitt, of course, was speaking for England rather than America. So good an authority as Emerson, many years later, was able to write:

> I attribute much importance to two papers of Dr. Channing, one on Milton and one on Napoleon, which were the first specimens in this country of that large criticism which in England had given power and fame to the Edinburgh Review. They were widely read, and of course, immediately fruitful in provoking emulation which lifted the style of Journalism.[30]

The essay on Fénelon was of the same character, but since its subject met less response in the public mind than either Milton or Napoleon, it did not receive the acclaim given the two earlier articles. Nevertheless, the Fénelon paper is of interest because it gives Channing's views on religious writing and helps us to understand why his own works have partially escaped the dustbin that swallowed up the great mass of theological controversy and religious tracts once so popular.

As Emerson told his wife, " in composition the *What* is of no importance compared with the *How*. The most tedious of all discourses are on the subject of the Supreme Being." [31] Channing's view was not less severe: " It is too true, and a sad truth, that religious books are preeminently dull. If we wish to impoverish a man's intellect, we could devise few means more effectual, than to confine him to what is called a course of theological reading." [32]

This was remarkable, thought Channing, because the religious impulse, rightly understood, ought to produce the
very flower of literary culture, for its themes are the highest
of which the mind is capable. And yet:

It is wonderful how men can think and write upon religion
to so little effect . . . that such a subject should be treated
so monotonously as to be proverbially dull, that its professed
explorers should be able to plant their footsteps so exactly in
the track of their predecessors, that the boundlessness of the
field should so seldom tempt an adventurous spirit from the
beaten way, is wonderful, and might seem a miracle to a man
unacquainted with the vassalage which has broken down the
mind in the department of religion.[33]

The remainder of Channing's essay on Fénelon dealt
with familiar themes: the necessity for self-respect (here
Channing attacked Fénelon's concept of the annihilation
of self as the first requirement for holiness), a call for union
with God, and a reasoned plea for a literature which should
recognize man's dependence on his Creator. Channing
felt that a purely secular culture was bound to produce a
wholly superficial literature — superficial because it ignored
the most fundamental need of man. And, as might be expected from one who had seen so clearly the banality of
religious writing when it was divorced from other areas of
human experience, he suggested that a reintegration would
not necessarily result in the production of pious tracts.
There was no reason why such a union should not prove
fructifying both to theology and literature. Religion was
not necessarily heavy and solemn, nor was it necessarily a
barrier to the expression of lighter emotions — in fact, it
should prove helpful to any honest and deep-seated expression of human potentiality. Religion would increase man's

understanding of even the most terrifying passions and experiences. More than this, it would enable us to assimilate these tragic experiences into our own lives, as Channing suggested it had enabled Shakespeare to become a wiser man: " though he painted so faithfully and fearfully the storms of passion, [Shakespeare] was a calm and cheerful man." [34]

The " Remarks on National Literature," first published in 1830, presents the fullest account of Channing's view of literature and its function. Since we have already looked at this essay in some detail,[35] we need only recall how startlingly similar it is in thought to Walt Whitman's call for a national literature in *Democratic Vistas*. Both Channing and Whitman demanded a new literature for a new people; neither thought of culture as the polite accomplishment of a few. They agreed that spiritual fulfillment rather than material prosperity was the criterion of a nation's development. And both thought of the poet's function (using the phrase in its broadest sense) as prophetic.

These four essays — on Milton, Napoleon, Fénelon and National Literature — comprise Channing's title to fame as a literary figure. They are his only formal excursions into criticism. Yet they do not cover the whole of his views, and before we try to make up our minds on his significance, we should think about his informal criticism — his opinions of the books he read and his recommendations to others. The most remarkable aspect of this informal criticism is the narrowness of Channing's range of intellectual sympathy, for with all his generosity in public toward the personality of others and with all his attempts to give every

devil his due, he was entirely capable of letting a precon-
ception about a man's moral character interfere with a just
appreciation of the man's works. Joseph Blanco White
noticed this defect in Channing before they had started to
correspond, and mentioned it in a letter to a friend: " I
have lately read Channing's Sermons. . . . They are admirable; and yet Channing himself does not seem totally
free from theological intolerance. Witness what he says
against the English Unitarians." [36]

As early as 1815, Channing had repudiated identification
with English Unitarian materialists like Priestley; [37] sixteen
years later he was arguing with Lucy Aikin about Priestley,
still, apparently, without having given much attention to
the study of his works: " I know little of his works, and
probably shall not read them, for I have little sympathy
with his ethical and metaphysical doctrines, and seldom
turn my thoughts to the religious controversies on which
he spent so much of his zeal." [38] Channing's real reason
for not reading Priestley seems to have been his intense distrust of the Englishman's morality. He admitted, by way
of faint praise, that Priestley was probably a good man personally, but continued, " I have had many doubts of his
moral greatness. It is not a good sign when a man carries
out his speculations without the least fear or hesitation,
when they seem to shock the highest moral principles." [39]
Strange words from one who had spent the last fifteen years
of his life writing to " shock the highest moral principles "
of the Calvinists!

Channing's dislike of men and books whose heretical
tendencies were different from his own extended to historians as well as philosophers. He was anxious to protect

his young friend Eloise Payne from the ravages of infidelity, and wrote to her in 1809 apropos of historians:

> I can tell you whom I do not like. Hume and Gibbon are names which, I hope, excite in me no unchristian asperity, but I cannot pronounce them without feelings of strong displeasure. I view them as enemies of the virtue, hopes, consolations and best interests of mankind. They have labored to extinguish in us every fear of death, to blot out from creation every trace of divine wisdom and love, and to wrap futurity in hopeless darkness.[40]

As if this indictment were not sufficient, he added, " I think his [Gibbon's] forced, affected stile [sic] a serious objection to his work." And then, with typical caution, Channing appended a postscript: " I have spoken with too little limitation on infidel writers. When they write on subjects which have no connection with religion and morality, my remarks will not apply." [41]

If the Doctor was insistent on a canon of correct moral feeling in historical and philosophical writing, he was even stricter in his demands on fiction. Elizabeth Peabody reported that he " expressed the fear that to lose oneself in imaginative sympathy with beautiful heroes and heroines, sympathizing as we always do with the noble, and gratified by the poetic justice which was dealt all the characters, satisfied us with ourselves, though our own life was of a lower tone." [42] And in a letter to Miss Peabody, written some time after she had started her bookshop and lending library in Boston, he remonstrated with her about the type of books she was buying: " You sent me some volumes of Balzac — I have feared, the French novels could not be circulated without putting some readers in peril — and ought not to be in your library." [43]

All of Channing's literary perceptions were not so starkly moral in nature. Novelty in itself had no fears for him; he had been among the first in Boston to welcome Wordsworth as a great poet, and remained an ardent admirer for the rest of his life. Fifty years after the event, Bronson Alcott remembered that Channing had been the first to mention the name of Wordsworth to him, and added that he questioned " whether a single townsman of mine had ever heard of Wordsworth at that time." [44] And near the end of his own life Channing still remembered his short interview with the poet and some of the comments that had been made about Wordsworth's growing conservatism. He wrote of these matters to Felicia Hemans, revealing a loyalty that was perhaps only the obverse of his prejudice against infidels:

I grieve at the privation of sight which you think him [Wordsworth] doomed to suffer. . . . I was told, when in England, after I had seen him, that he had been injured by the notice of the great, that he had forgotten the nobility of genius and lofty sentiment in the presence of the *artificial* aristocracy of this world, that he had sunk into a position, that even that low passion, the love of money, had settled upon him. I could not and would not believe that a man, to whom my heart and mind owed so large a debt, was so fallen — and yet I could not escape an uneasy suspicion, that prosperity had found some weak part in him. Your letter did much to give me back the sentiment with which I used to contemplate him.[45]

Coleridge was another whom the Doctor admired, and the admiration was apparently reciprocated. Coleridge, in a letter to Washington Allston, wrote that though he had known Channing in part before his visit, it was a " gratification to converse with him and to find that he was

" amiable " and " discriminating," and possessed the " love
of wisdom and the wisdom of love." [46] Some years later,
when the letter was recalled to Channing's mind, he rem-
inisced: " I was amused . . . on my return to America,
to read in a letter he [Coleridge] had written to Mr. Allston, that he had seldom met a person so interested in conversation as Mr. Channing; for my part was simply inter-
rogative: I made not a single original remark! " [47] Later
in the same conversation he defended Coleridge's turn
toward conservatism, holding that though he repudiated
Unitarianism, he spared the personality of the Unitarians,
and that he remained more liberal than either Wordsworth
or Southey.[48]

Paradoxically enough, considering his distaste for novels
because they tended to make the reader satisfied with his
low lot, Channing was fond — with reservations — of Scott:

> He was anything but a philosopher. But in *extent* of obser-
> vation, in the quick perception of the endless varieties of human
> character, in the discovery of their signs and manifestations . . .
> where will you find his equal? . . . I do not say he ever touches
> the highest springs within me, but he had bound me by new
> sympathies to my race.[49]

Goethe, too, Channing liked in the same way, and in the
same way found him lacking in high moral purpose. Miss
Peabody reports that it took the Doctor a whole winter to
get through *Wilhelm Meister*. He appreciated " its artistic
merit and meaning," she tells us, but he would often turn
from it to one of his old favorites, Miss Mitford.[50]

He thought Mrs. Hemans a great poet, if somewhat too
inclined to gloom. His view of Byron is what might be
expected:

That a mind so gifted should have been left to devote its energies to the cause of impiety and vice, and should be so soon and suddenly taken, without making reparation to insulted truth and virtue, — that such a mind is to live for ages in its writings only to degrade and corrupt, — in all this we see the mysterious character of God's providence.[51]

The one unexpected note in Channing's approach to literature was his acceptance, patronizing as it was, of Shelley. He had read some of Shelley's work and had heard something of his life from Southey, who, the Doctor thought, "did not interpret him profoundly." Channing suggested, anticipating Arnold, that "Shelley was a seraph gone astray, who needed friends that he never found in this world."[52] In view of Shelley's opinion of Christianity, Channing's tolerance seems strange, for he had condemned Godwin out of hand: "There are some errors which show such a strange obliquity of intellect as to destroy my confidence in the judgment of those who adopt them. Godwin does not believe in a god, and such a mind must be as unsound as one which should not believe in the existence of the sun."[53]

Taken all in all, Channing's literary judgments show the same eclecticism (stiffened by a high sense of the individual's moral importance) that we have seen in his philosophical, religious, and social views. The difficulties of applying such a congeries of feelings, concepts, and prejudices are sufficiently obvious to the twentieth-century reader; one may almost say that Channing succeeded in being an impressive figure in spite of his theories. And in literary criticism these difficulties are fatal.

In short, Channing was a moralist rather than a critic,

and only men infused with the same religious intensity — in an age like the nineteenth century — could have confused the two. Besides Hazlitt, only two major critical figures of the nineteenth century had anything to say about Channing: Coleridge was agreeably impressed by the Doctor in his capacity as listener and moralist; Matthew Arnold, as we have seen, dismissed Channing as " the flower of moral and intelligent mediocrity." And with this judgment, as applied to Channing's criticism, we shall have to concur.

A word or two remains to be said concerning Channing as a writer. Organization was not his strong point, though he was at times capable of arranging his writing into more or less logical divisions — as in his slavery pamphlets. He wrote easily, and seldom (as his manuscripts testify) felt the need for extensive revision. In light of his writing habits and method of composition, this is to be wondered at. Harriet Martineau, an indefatigable writer herself, was amazed to find that he thought only two hours in twenty-four could be profitably expended in composition for publication. She wrote in her autobiography that Channing's practice, when he was in Rhode Island, was " to saunter round the garden once every hour, and then come back to the desk; and when in Boston, he went to the drawing-room instead, or walked about in his library. . . . I wondered how he could ever get or keep his ideas in train, under such frequent interruption." [54]
The virtues of Channing's style are those of oratory. First and most important, he was almost invariably clear. At times, as we have seen, his clarity was achieved perhaps as the result of a somewhat dubious oversimplification; but

in the main his writing is entirely lucid. It boasts, as well, an occasional epigrammatic touch, though he was never so successful at epigram as Emerson. Yet Channing could, on occasion, produce a striking phrase, as in his description of Jonathan Phillips as one who hung the universe in crape; or a striking image, as in his famous likening of Calvinism's insistence on the redemptive power of the blood of Christ to a religion which placed a gallows in the center of the world and bade men worship it. He was able also to build a fine oratorical climax, as in his addresses on Napoleon.

Renan's contention that Channing became a writer without premeditation is only partly true, and his statement that Channing's " works do not bear witness to any literary ambition. There is not in them a single passage where the least pretension to art or style is to be remarked " [55] is simply not true at all. Even though Channing did eschew florid ornamentation and did not search out literature for apposite references, he was deeply concerned with delivering his message as effectively as possible. Plainness, however, he thought a virtue; consequently he seldom made use of literary tropes to adorn his thought.

On the other side of the ledger, we must account as unfortunate his habit of using abstractions. Far better, if, like Emerson, he could have made use of the meal in the firkin and the milk in the pan to give his ideas point and relevancy. And his constant repetition, however desirable a device it may have been in making sure that a listening audience understood his sermon, is thoroughly vexatious to the modern reader.

With these objections in mind, we may well wonder at the opinion of the *North American Review* writer that

Channing was the stylistic equal of Irving. Channing's style, he wrote, " is equally elegant, and a little more pure, correct and pointed than that of Mr. Irving." [56] But worse was to come: the writer went on to announce that Channing was superior to everyone in this country, and to Coleridge and " Carlile " in England.[57]

We are likely to regard such an opinion as pure extravagance, and to agree with Emerson when he wrote:

> I cannot help seeing that Doctor Channing would have been a much greater writer had he found a strict tribunal of writers, a graduated intellectual empire established in the land, and knew that bad logic would not pass, and that the most severe exaction was to be made on all who enter these lists. . . . It is very easy to reach the degree of culture that prevails around us; very hard to pass it, and Doctor Channing, had he found Wordsworth, Southey, Coleridge, and Lamb around him, would as easily have been severe with himself and risen a degree higher as he has stood where he is.[58]

These words, hard though they are, sum up Channing's position in American literary culture. He lived at a time when good writers were few. Both his stylistic virtues and his sincerity stood him in good stead, and he achieved a literary reputation greater, perhaps, than would have been his in any other period of our country's history.

CHAPTER SIX

The Significance of Channing

More than a hundred years ago, when W. H. Channing had gathered his materials for a biography of his uncle and sat down at his desk with the purpose of presenting a full-scale portrait of Dr. Channing, he had to confess failure. He found the task impossible: to write a book that would avoid, on the one hand, the extreme of a coherent picture achieved by sacrificing the truth of the portrait to the prejudice of the biographer, as well as on the other, the extreme of a colorless picture presenting, without selection, all facets of the man as equally important. He chose what seemed the simplest expedient — that of gathering together his uncle's utterances on as many subjects as possible, of arranging them into more or less plausible categories, and then letting the Doctor speak for himself. But when the modern reader finishes the *Memoir*, he remains baffled by the character he has been studying. The nephew has included too much. The thought of a lifetime has been gathered into three volumes, often without distinction of date or of importance to the writer; connecting links are omitted, and the reader is left to flounder in a mass of contradictory and apparently unrelated facts.

The problem, then, in dealing with Channing is one of selection. There are enough materials in the three volumes of the *Memoir* to construct the lives of half a dozen men.

And in the four large collections of Channing manuscripts in the possession of the American Unitarian Association, the Boston Public Library, the Houghton Library at Harvard, and Henry M. Channing — to say nothing of the collection of sermon manuscripts at the Meadville Theological School and the minor accumulations at the Rhode Island and the Massachusetts Historical Societies, as well as the various odd repositories of a letter or two — there are sources enough to discourage the most avid student. Nor is this all: a glance at the catalogue of any large library proves, if the investigator had not already guessed, that most of Channing's contemporaries had a word to say about him during their lifetimes, and that they or their literary executors piously recorded innumerable letters and reminiscences of the relationship.

As reflected in this mass of material, Channing's figure assumes a Protean shape. A rationalist reading these accounts would easily perceive that Channing was a rationalist, a socialist would as easily prove the Doctor a socialist at heart, the Transcendentalist would recognize the lineaments of Transcendentalism, the Federalist would welcome his spiritual brother, the humanist would cite chapter and verse to prove Channing was of his persuasion, and the theist would establish his theism.

As we have seen, Channing proved equally puzzling to his more single-minded contemporaries, particularly the militant souls engaged in the anti-slavery controversy. But even Alcott, usually so mild and even-tempered, had a sharp word to say about the Doctor's refusal to stand still in one place long enough to be counted. In 1837 he wrote in his journal:

Dr. Channing's efforts have been put forth to good purpose on many occasions — always, however, by way of quieting and allaying. He never makes an Idea; but, after these have begun to work and have put the public mind into action, then does he give his assent to them — usually, however, with so much compromise and timid modification, lest he should stir up the fears and passions of conservatives, that much of their good effect is lost. Dr. Channing always has the last word to say, never the first. Hence he gets the credit of wisdom which belongs of right to those who have set this wisdom afloat in a community, and opened the eyes of men.[1]

We might write off Alcott's criticism as petulance resulting from Channing's failure to support the Temple Street School as warmly as Alcott thought it deserved, except for the fact that Alcott's judgment tallies almost exactly with the criticism Hazlitt had written of Channing seven years earlier: " He keeps an eye on both worlds; kisses hands to the reading public all round; and does his best to stand well with different sects and parties. He is always in advance of the line, in an amiable and imposing attitude, but never far from succour." [2]

Coming as they do from sources entirely independent of each other and reinforcing Arnold's judgment that Channing's work was the flower of intelligent mediocrity, the two criticisms cannot be easily dismissed. The best that can be said for Channing is that both Hazlitt and Alcott misconstrued his motives. There is not a line in Channing's voluminous private correspondence to indicate that he ever took a public position at variance with his truest thought in an attempt to avoid public displeasure. Indeed, he was constantly on guard, both in his letters to his friends and in his own self-examination, against any inference not justified by the facts as he saw them. He constantly attached postscripts to his letters to qualify some position — or, having mailed a letter, hastened to send another behind it to clarify what he had written. And to an old friend who had been trying for some time to establish a school he wrote a long series of advisory letters, warning her in one of them against too quick acceptance of new doctrines: " I wished to suggest that there is a process of mind, which in the schools is called patient research, which should precede conviction — I wished to say that we may be *pleased* and may be *moved* by what is not *altogether* true, that there is danger taking anything by the lump." [3]

Such preternatural caution meant that Channing would never make a decision to act unless he had first tested the grounds for it so long and so thoroughly that less timid minds grew impatient with his delay. If by his caution he had achieved a high level of consistency, his hesitation in reaching conclusions might have been more easily forgiven by his contemporaries and extenuated by posterity. But, as we have noticed, his delay in making up his mind was not balanced by any corresponding gain in consistency of thought. In one sense, his faith in the potentialities and goodness of all men was perfectly consistent. Yet in theory it rested upon more or less contradictory assumptions, and in practice it was weakened by the fact that it did not so much supplant the Federalism of the Doctor's youth as it merely added onto the Federalist foundation. That the two formed a rather rickety and drafty intellectual structure Channing never seemed to notice.

Thus, in spite of Hazlitt's unfounded aspersions on the Doctor's intellectual honesty, we must admit a large mea-

sure of truth in his suggestion that Channing "hits the
public between what they are tired of hearing, and what
they never heard before." And Alcott's conclusion, independently arrived at, that Channing "gets the credit of
wisdom which belongs of right to those who have set this
wisdom afloat in a community, and opened the eyes of
men," complements Hazlitt's analysis. But, although these
conclusions are true, are they so damning as their authors
imply?

The real question is not whether Channing was a primary
figure. Admittedly, he was not. He instigated no movements, but the nature of his thought gathered no disciples,
brought about no reforms. His function was to codify, to
translate, and to make available to a dominantly middle-class
culture a synthesis of ideas which — however confused
they were in statement and however halting in practice —
helped to solidify and give contemporary expression to
American liberalism, social as well as religious.

Channing's enormous contemporary reputation was mer-
ited; and he deserves an important place in the history of
our culture, for he was far more than the comfortable
purveyor of truisms, the sedative of the bourgeois conscience, that some modern critics have taken him for. In
spite of his timidities and hesitations, the great mass of people both in this country and in Europe thought of him as
a great liberal leader. The precise, practical results of
Channing's influence cannot be measured. We can only
speculate, for instance, when we encounter his name in an
unexpected circumstance — as when Beethoven professed
interest in his works, or, as in the brief statement recorded
by Carl Sandburg:

When Fell [Jesse W. Fell of Bloomington] talked with enthusiasm about Channing's sermons, Lincoln showed such a keen interest that Fell asked Lincoln if he would like to have a complete collection of the sermons. So Fell bought a special edition for Lincoln, who put it in his little library.[4]

Clearer indications of Channing's influence on the minds of his contemporaries are to be found in the long and affectionate correspondence that passed between him and the English literary figures he was proud to name among his friends: Felicia Hemans, Jane Roscoe, William Roscoe, Lucy Aikin, Harriet Martineau, Joseph Blanco White, and Joanna Baillie. We have seen Channing in correspondence with some of the great French social thinkers of his day; in 1826, the Rev. Mr. Nichols of Portland, Maine, to whom Channing had earlier proposed a ministerial association, thought enough of his friend's European acquaintance to ask him for letters of introduction for " Henry Longfellow " who was going to France " with a view of acquiring some of the principal modern languages and of perusing the general literature." [5] In 1830 Channing was writing letters of introduction to Wordsworth and Southey. And in 1840 James G. Birney, of anti-slavery fame, asked Channing to introduce him abroad. These, of course, did not exhaust the stream of introductory notes from his pen. His personal friends were not slow to use his name to help them in England and Europe, and a steady procession of Cambridge and Boston notables — Nortons, Tuckermans, Channings, Farrars, and others — streamed through Lucy Aikin's house, bearing notes from the Doctor.

Nor was the traffic in letters of introduction entirely

from West to East. Even before Hazlitt's blast in the *Edinburgh Review*, England had been aware of Channing's reputation. A Mr. Adam, for instance, had written rather breathlessly to Andrews Norton in 1831, and for all his exaggeration of phrasing, his note can be taken as representative of the response to Channing in certain circles:

> I long to see his [Channing's] Review of Scott's Life of Napoleon of the existence of which I only know by an extract from it which I met with in the Morning Chronicle. It is spoken of with enthusiastic admiration. Dr. Channing is one of those few men who can command the attention of the civilized world and he should be entreated to embody the noble and generous conceptions of his enlightened mind in some permanent memorial worthy of the genius with which he is endowed and of the age which is opening upon us.[6]

With such recommendations to attention, it can hardly be doubted that the cultivated visitor to America would wish to make the Doctor's acquaintance. The most famous visitors were Harriet Martineau, who had provided herself with an introduction from N. P. Willis (which she was cautioned not to use if she could obtain one from anybody who knew Channing better), Lord Morpeth, and Charles Dickens, who was introduced by Edward Everett, then the American ambassador to England.

Miss Martineau has left an account of Channing both in her memoirs and her *Retrospect of Western Travel*, where she devoted an entire chapter to her recollections of him. Lord Morpeth, whose visit preceded Dickens' by a little over a month, was as enthusiastic, though briefer, than Miss Martineau. He recorded in his diary: " You found a fragile frame and a dry manner, but you soon felt that you were in a presence in which nothing that was impure, base, or selfish could breathe at ease." [7]   And Dickens did Channing the credit of mentioning him favorably in his *American Notes for General Circulation:*

I mention the name of this distinguished and accomplished man (with whom I soon afterward had the pleasure of becoming personally acquainted), that I may have the gratification of recording my humble tribute of admiration and respect for his high abilities and character, and for the bold philanthropy with which he has ever opposed himself to that most hideous blot and foul disgrace — Slavery.[8]

If these acknowledgments of Channing's superiority seem to contradict the opinions of Alcott and Hazlitt, we shall have to admit the fact — and appeal once again to the suggestion that his was an extraordinarily complex character in which observers had a tendency to find reflected whatever they were looking for.   Another instance of the contradictions of the Doctor's character is found in his attitude toward personalities in controversy.   As we have seen, he was especially tender of the slaveholder and did not want to alienate him; in the same way, he did not wish to indulge in name-calling in his theological battles.   In this area he had a certain success, outstanding in the case of Moses Stuart.   His real opinion of Stuart he made clear to Andrews Norton in 1832 (although not a word of it was breathed into his published exchange of letters with Stuart):

The wrongheadedness of this vain and rash man is a reason for not setting down . . . [his] gross misstatements as intentional departures from truth — so great is my desire to purify controversy from personalities, that I incline to let him off as easily as consists with self respect.[9]

This avoidance of personality in controversy was both a virtue and a defect of Channing's method. On the one hand, it lifted the argument out of the realm of private loyalties; on the other, the sharpness of the attack was weakened by its apparent lack of focus. And, in part, the accusation that he was timid is based on Channing's firm conviction that no dispute should ever be argued in personal terms.

His own age, as we have seen, regarded Channing with mixed emotions; how are we, looking at his work a hundred years and more after his death, to estimate his place as a figure in our intellectual history? If his reputation as a literary figure can be dismissed so cavalierly, if his activities as a reformer have proved so equivocal, if his relationship with the Transcendentalists seems now approving and now merely tolerant, if his religious synthesis has been called in question by humanists and theists alike, what remains of a figure who was admitted by his critics as well as his friends to play a decisive part in wrestling with the intellectual and social problems of his times? Channing's peculiar gift, it seems to me, was the capacity (deplored by Hazlitt and Alcott) to stand in a dual relationship with his contemporaries: to perceive more deeply than the mass of people — more deeply than the majority of intellectual leaders, even — without losing their confidence. This, perhaps, is the clue to the complexities of the Doctor's personality which so baffled his nephew; Channing becomes comprehensible when we recall that, rather than originating ideas, he reflected the intellectual cross currents that swirled about him. No stormer of intellectual or moral outposts, he nevertheless had the power of consolidating the gains of others and of pacifying the newly occupied territory so well that his successors have hardly realized that the ground on which they stand was once a battlefield.

It is the destiny of such a man, once the conflict has ended, to be forgotten; yet his life may be as deeply woven into our national tradition as that of more spectacular figures whose names are still remembered. This has been Channing's fate; it does not detract from his significance. Because he was a minister, a generation impatient of theology has ignored him, without realizing that its freedom from religious dogma was in great part his work. Because he flourished at a time commonly described as intellectually arid, his philosophy has been dismissed along with that of his contemporaries. Because his was one of the first voices raised in the slavery crisis, and because he died twenty years before the Civil War, his work as a reformer has been drowned in the thunder of that conflict. And because he was the precursor of the most brilliant period of American literature, his light has been dimmed by the greater brilliance which succeeded him.

Bibliography

To keep the Bibliography within manageable compass, I have included only books discussed in the text, mentioned in the Notes, or bearing more or less directly on the figure of Channing. Otherwise one would have to mention whole battalions of pamphlets and armies of memoirs of contemporary figures — most of which would be of a merely corroborative nature. For the same reason I have omitted standard works of reference unless I have quoted from them in the text.

[Alexander, James Waddel; Dod, Albert Baldwin; Hodge, Charles]. *Two Articles from the Princeton Review, Concerning the Transcendental Philosophy of the Germans and of Cousin, and its Influence on Opinion in This Country*, [ed. Andrews Norton]. Cambridge, 1840.

The American Notebooks by Nathaniel Hawthorne. Based upon the Original Manuscripts in the Pierpont Morgan Library, ed. Randall Stewart. New Haven, 1932.

Arnold, Matthew. *Essays in Criticism*. London and Cambridge, 1865.

Brooks, Charles T. *William Ellery Channing: A Centennial Memory*. Boston, 1880.

[Brougham, Henry]. Review of Channing's "Milton," in *The Edinburgh Review, or Critical Journal*, LXIX, 139 (April, 1839), 214–230.

Calvin, John. *Institutes of the Christian Religion*. Philadelphia, [n.d.], 2 vols.

Chadwick, John W. *William Ellery Channing, Minister of Religion*. Boston and New York, 1903.

Channing, George G. *Early Recollections of Newport, R. I., from the Year 1793 to 1811*. Newport, 1868.

Channing, William Ellery. *Channing's Note-Book: Passages from the Unpublished Manuscripts of William Ellery Channing*, ed. Grace Ellery Channing. Boston, 1887.

Channing, William Ellery. *Discourses, Reviews, and Miscellanies*. Boston, 1830.

Channing, William Ellery. *A Letter to the Rev. Samuel C. Thacher, on the Aspersions Contained in a Late Number of the Panoplist, on the Ministers of Boston and the Vicinity*. Boston, 1815.

Channing, William Ellery. *Remarks on the Rev. Dr. Worcester's Letter to Mr. Channing, on the "Review of American Unitarianism" in a late Panoplist*. Boston, 1815.

Channing, William Ellery. *A Sermon Delivered at the Ordination of the Rev. John Codman, to the Pastoral Care of the Second Church of Christ in Dorchester, Dec. 7, 1808.* Boston, 1809.

Channing, William Ellery. *A Sermon Preached in Boston, April 5, 1810, The Day of the Public Fast.* Boston, 1810.

Channing, William Ellery. *Works.* See *The Works of William E. Channing.*

"Channing's Literary and Political Essays. Remarks on Milton," in *Fraser's Magazine for Town and Country,* XVII, 101 (May, 1838), 627–635.

"Channing's Literary and Political Essays. Remarks on Napoleon Bonaparte," in *Fraser's Magazine for Town and Country,* XVIII, 105 (September, 1838), 286–297.

[Channing, William Henry]. *Memoir of William Ellery Channing, with Extracts from His Correspondence and Manuscripts,* second edition. Boston, 1848, 3 vols.

Chorley, Henry F. *Memorials of Mrs. Hemans, with Illustrations of Her Literary Character from Her Private Correspondence.* New York and London, 1836, 2 vols.

Commager, Henry S. *Theodore Parker,* second edition. Boston, 1947.

Cooke, George Willis. *Ralph Waldo Emerson: His Life, Writings, and Philosophy.* Boston and New York, [1881].

The Correspondence of Thomas Carlyle and Ralph Waldo Emerson, 1834–1872, ed. Charles Eliot Norton. Boston, 1883, 2 vols.

Curtis, George W., et al. *Homes of American Authors; Comprising Anecdotal, Personal, and Descriptive Sketches.* New York, 1853.

Dewey, John. *Reconstruction in Philosophy,* enlarged edition. Boston, 1948.

Dickens, Charles. *American Notes for General Circulation.* New York, 1842.

Dorfman, Joseph. *The Economic Mind in American Civilization 1606–1865.* New York, 1946, 2 vols.

"Dr. Channing and the Edinburgh Review," in *Southern Literary Messenger,* VI, 1 (January, 1840), 2–12.

Edgell, David P. "A Note on Channing's Transcendentalism," in *New England Quarterly,* XXII (September, 1949), 394–397.

[Evarts, Jeremiah]. Review of "American Unitarianism," in *The Panoplist, and Missionary Magazine,* XI, 6 (June, 1815), 240–272.

Ferguson, Adam. *Essay on the History of Civil Society.* London, 1768.

Greeley, Horace. *Recollections of a Busy Life: Including Reminiscences of American Politics and Politicians, from the Opening of the Missouri Contest to the Downfall of Slavery; to Which Are Added Miscellanies: "Literature as a Vocation," "Poets and Poetry," "Reforms and Reformers," A Defence of Protection, etc., etc. Also a Discussion with Robert Dale Owen of the Law of Divorce.* New York, 1868.

Harriet Martineau's Autobiography, ed. Maria Weston Chapman. Boston, 1877, 2 vols.

[Hazlitt, William]. Review of Channing, in *The Edinburgh Review, or Critical Journal*, L, 99 (October, 1829), 125–144.

The Heart of Hawthorne's Journals, ed. Newton Arvin. Boston and New York, 1929.

Hicks, Granville. "When Dickens Met Channing," in *Christian Register*, July 18, 1929, p. 604.

Holmes, Oliver Wendell. *The Professor at the Breakfast Table*. Boston and New York, 1894.

Holmes, Oliver Wendell. *Ralph Waldo Emerson*. Boston, 1885.

Hopkins, Samuel. *The System of Doctrines, Contained in Divine Revelation. Explained and Defended. Shewing Their Consistence and Connexion with Each Other. To Which Is Added, a Treatise on the Millennium.* Boston, 1811, 2 vols.

Hutcheson, Francis. *A System of Moral Philosophy, in Three Books.* London, 1755, 2 vols.

The Journals of Bronson Alcott, ed. Odell Shepard. Boston, 1938.

Journals of Ralph Waldo Emerson with Annotations, ed. Edward Waldo Emerson and Waldo Emerson Forbes. Boston and New York, [1909], 10 vols.

Kingsley, Charles. *Yeast a Problem*. London, 1881.

Ladu, Arthur I. "Channing and Transcendentalism," in *American Literature*, XI (May, 1939), 129–137.

Le Breton, Anna L., ed. *Correspondence of William Ellery Channing, D.D., and Lucy Aikin, from 1826 to 1842*. Boston, 1874.

Lee, Eliza Buckminster. *Memoirs of Rev. Joseph Buckminster, D.D., and of His Son, Rev. Joseph Stevens Buckminster*. Boston, 1849.

The Letters of Ralph Waldo Emerson, ed. Ralph L. Rusk. New York, 1939, 6 vols.

The Literary Diary of Ezra Stiles, ed. Franklin B. Dexter. New York, 1901, 3 vols.

"Literature of the Nineteenth Century. America," in *The Athenaeum Journal of English and Foreign Literature, Science, and the Fine Arts*, No. 375, pp. 10–12.

Long, Orie W. *Frederic Hedge: A Cosmopolitan Scholar*. Portland, 1939.

Martineau, Harriet. *Retrospect of Western Travel*. New York, 1838, 2 vols.

May, Samuel J. *Some Recollections of Our Antislavery Conflict*. Boston, 1869.

Morison, Samuel E. *Three Centuries of Harvard 1636–1936*. Cambridge, 1936.

Morse, Jedidiah, ed. "*American Unitarianism, or a Brief History of 'The Progress and Present State of the Unitarian Churches in America.'* Compiled from Documents and Information Communicated by the Rev. James Freeman, D.D., and William Wells, Jun. Esq., of Boston, and from other Unitarian Gentlemen in this Country, By Rev. Thomas Belsham, Essex Street, London. Extracted from his 'Memoirs of the Life of the Reverend Theophilus Lindsey,' published in London, 1812, and now published for the benefit of the Christian Churches in this country, without note or alteration," third edition. Boston, 1815.

[Paiker, Theodore]. "Hollis Street Council," in *The Dial*, II (October, 1842), 201–221.

Patterson, R. L. "The Theology of Channing and the Via Affirmativa," in *Anglican Theological Review*, XXVI (October 1944), 229–235.

Peabody, Elizabeth. *Reminiscences of Rev. Wm. Ellery Channing, D.D.* Boston, 1880.

Pickard, Samuel T. *Life and Letters of John Greenleaf Whittier.* Boston and New York, 1894, 2 vols.

Pierpont, John. *A Discourse Occasioned by the Death of William Ellery Channing.* Boston, 1842.

Price, Richard. *A Review of the Principal Questions in Morals, Particularly Those respecting the Origin of our Ideas of Virtue, its Nature, Relation to the* DEITY, *Obligation, Subject-matter, and Sanctions. The Third Edition Corrected, and Enlarged by an Appendix, Containing Additional Notes, and a Dissertation On the Being and Attributes of the Deity.* London, 1787.

Renan, Ernest. *Studies of Religious History.* London, 1893.

Review of Channing's "Ministry for the Poor," in *North American Review*, LXXXIX (October, 1835), 366–406.

Review of Dr. Channing's Discourse at the ordination of Frederick A. Farley, in *Westminster Review*, X, 19 (January, 1829), 98–101.

Review of Dr. Channing's works, in *Westminster Review*, XII, 24 (April, 1830), 472–491.

Rusk, Ralph L. *The Life of Ralph Waldo Emerson.* New York, 1949.

Sandburg, Carl. *Abraham Lincoln: The Prairie Years.* New York, 1927.

Schlesinger, Arthur M., Jr. *The Age of Jackson.* Boston, 1946.

Schneider, Herbert W. *The History of American Philosophy.* New York, 1946.

Services in Memory of William E. Channing, D.D. Boston, 1867.

Shaftesbury, Anthony, Earl of. *Characteristics of Men, Manners, Opinions, Times. With a Collection of Letters.* [n.p.], 1757, 3 vols.

Shepard, Odell. *Pedlar's Progress: The Life of Bronson Alcott.* Boston, 1937.

Skeel, Emily Ellsworth Ford, ed., and Ford, Emily Ellsworth Fowler, comp. *Notes on the Life of Noah Webster.* New York, 1912, 2 vols.

Sketches of the Life of the Late Rev. Samuel Hopkins, D.D. Pastor of the first Congregational Church in Newport, Written by Himself; Interspersed with Marginal Notes Extracted from His Private Diary: To Which Is added; A Dialogue, By the Same Hand, On the Nature and Extent of True Christian Submission; Also, a Serious Address to Professing Christians: Closed by Dr. Hart's Sermon at His Funeral: With an Introduction to the Whole, by the Editor. Hartford, 1805.

Stewart, Randall. *Nathaniel Hawthorne, A Biography.* New Haven, 1948.

Stuart, Moses. *A Letter to William E. Channing D.D. on the subject of Religious Liberty.* Boston, 1830.

Stuart, Moses. *Letters to the Rev. Wm. E. Channing, Containing Remarks on His Sermon, Recently Preached and Published at Baltimore,* second edition. Andover, 1819.

Thayer, A. W. *The Life of Ludwig von Beethoven.* New York, 1921, 3 vols.

Thom, Joseph H. *The Life of the Rev. Joseph Blanco White.* London, 1845, 2 vols.

Weiss, John. *Life and Correspondence of Theodore Parker, Minister of the Twenty-eighth Congregational Society, Boston.* New York, 1864, 2 vols.

Wells, Ronald V. *Three Christian Transcendentalists: James Marsh, Caleb Sprague Henry, Frederic Henry Hedge.* New York, 1943.

Whitehead, Alfred N. *Science and the Modern World.* The New American Library, 1948.

Woods, Leonard. *Letters to Unitarians Occasioned by the Sermon of the Reverend William E. Channing at the Ordination of the Rev. J. Sparks.* Andover, 1820.

The Works of Ralph Waldo Emerson, Standard Library Edition. Boston and New York, [1883], 14 vols.

The Works of William E. Channing, D.D. Third Complete Edition, with an Introduction. Boston, 1842, 6 vols.

The Works of William E. Channing, D.D. With an Introduction. New and Complete Edition, Rearranged. To Which Is Added The Perfect Life. Boston, 1888.

The Writings of Henry David Thoreau. Boston and New York, 1906, 20 vols.

Notes

In the case of material drawn from manuscripts, I have used the following abbreviations to indicate the location of manuscript collections:

AUA	American Unitarian Association, Boston
HMC	Collection of Henry M. Channing, Sherborn, Mass.
Norton Papers	Andrews Norton papers, Houghton Library, Harvard University
RIHS	Rhode Island Historical Society, Providence

William Ellery Channing is generally referred to here as "WEC." Except where the 1888 edition (one volume) is specifically indicated, "WEC, *Works*" refers to the 1842 edition (six volumes) of *The Works of William E. Channing*.

Initials are used also in the following cases:

ABA, *Journals*	The Journals of [*Amos*] Bronson Alcott (1938)
WHC, *Memoir*	William Henry Channing's *Memoir of William Ellery Channing* (1848)
RWE, *Journals*	Journals of Ralph Waldo Emerson (1909)
RWE, *Letters*	The Letters of Ralph Waldo Emerson (1939)
RWE, *Works*	The Works of Ralph Waldo Emerson (1883)
HDT, *Writings*	The Writings of Henry David Thoreau (1906)

Details of publication for these and other books (many of them referred to by short titles) appear in the Bibliography (pp. 235–239).

1. Channing's Life

[1] *Literary Diary of Ezra Stiles*, II, 426–427.

[2] *Sketches of the Life of Samuel Hopkins*, p. 78.

[3] WHC, *Memoir*, I, 33. This passage is quoted by W. H. Channing as part of the sermon "Christian Worship," but it does not exist in printed versions of the text.

[4] WEC, *Works*, IV, 348.

[5] *Idem*.

[6] WHC, *Memoir*, I, 34–35.

[7] George G. Channing, *Early Recollections of Newport*. George Channing gives a colorful account of the personalities and the school life of the period. Among his recollections is the memory of a threadbare

calico smock, passed down to him, the youngest, through eight earlier brothers and sisters.

[8] WHC, *Memoir*, I, 43.

[9] WHC, *Memoir*, I, 44.

[10] WHC, *Memoir*, I, 45. Quoted from a letter written by Joseph Story to W. F. Channing. For further details of Harvard of the Channing period see Morison, *Three Centuries of Harvard*, Chap. 8. Morison's account does not add substantially to that compiled in WHC, *Memoir*.

[11] WHC, *Memoir*, I, 60.

[12] And yet in his junior year he wrote to Allston: "I have no inclination for either divinity, law, or physic." WHC, *Memoir*, I, 73.

[13] WHC, *Memoir*, I, 65–66.

[14] WHC, *Memoir*, I, 64–65.

[15] WHC, *Memoir*, I, 69–70.

[16] WHC, *Memoir*, I, 72.

[17] WHC, *Memoir*, I, 99–100.

[18] Letter from William Ellery to WEC, April 13, 1799. (HMC.)

[19] WHC, *Memoir*, I, 116.

[20] WHC, *Memoir*, I, 110.

[21] WHC, *Memoir*, I, 108.

[22] WHC, *Memoir*, I, 92.

[23] WHC, *Memoir*, I, 88–89.

[24] WHC, *Memoir*, I, 93.

[25] WHC, *Memoir*, I, 126–127.

[26] WHC, *Memoir*, I, 126.

[27] WEC, *Works*, IV, 337.

[28] WHC, *Memoir*, I, 157.

[29] WHC, *Memoir*, I, 161.

[30] Lee, *Memoirs of Rev. Joseph Buckminster and of Rev. Joseph Stevens Buckminster*, pp. 324–325.

[31] Skeel and Ford, *Notes on the Life of Noah Webster*, II, 77.

[32] Brooks, *William Ellery Channing*, p. 105.

[33] WEC, *A Sermon Delivered at the Ordination of the Rev. John Codman*, p. 16.

[34] Letter from WEC to William Ellery, July 2, 1813. (AUA.)

[35] Jedidiah Morse (1761–1826) was the "Father of American Geography" and a stern "Old Light" Calvinist. J. W. Chadwick, a hostile critic, succinctly described his activities: "No man ever lorded it over God's heritage as Dr. Morse. He was the head and front of orthodox opposition to the liberal offending. At every stage of that opposition he was, if not easily first, always well in the lead. The institution of the General Association, the attempted Consociation, the arming of the *Panoplist*, the criticism of Ware's Harvard appointment, the Andover counterblast to this, the building and manning of the Park Street Church, — in all these pithy and momentous enterprises his was an active and aggressive part." Chadwick, *William Ellery Channing*, pp. 127–128.

[36] WEC, *A Letter to the Rev. Samuel C. Thacher*, pp. 13–14.

[37] Letter from John Ware to Andrews Norton, Jan. 12, 1817. (Norton Papers.)

[38] Letter from Samuel A. Eliot to Andrews Norton, May 6, 1819. (Norton Papers.)

[39] Stuart, *Letters to the Rev. Wm. E. Channing*, p. 178.

[40] Hence the irreverent name given to the interchange by the detached portion of the laity, "The Wood 'n' Ware Controversy."

[41] Later torn down to make room for the Vanderbilt mansion which now occupies the site.

[42] The *Boston Directory* for 1818 lists Channing as living on Beacon Street. The record thenceforward is confusing, for we next find him listed in 1821 as in Tremont Place. Then there is a gap of four years, partly accounted for, no doubt, by his European trip in 1822 and 1823. In 1826 we find him at Summer Street for six years; then in 1833 at 49 Mt. Vernon until 1837, when he moved to 61 Mt. Vernon, where he apparently lived until his death. (The entry for 1838 reads 81 Mt. Vernon, but I suspect it to be a misprint.)

[43] Proprietors' records of the Arlington Street Church (formerly the Federal Street Church), p. 259 *et seq.*

[44] Peabody, *Reminiscences of Rev. Wm. Ellery Channing*, p. 368.

[45] Letter from Andrews Norton to George Bancroft, April 29, 1820. (Norton Papers.)

[46] WHC, *Memoir*, II, 217-218.

[47] Letter from Catherine Norton to Samuel Eliot, Jan. 8, 1823. (Norton Papers.)

[48] WHC, *Memoir*, II, 219-220.

[49] Letter from Catherine Norton to Samuel Eliot, Oct. 5, 1823. (Norton Papers.)

[50] RWE, *Letters*, I, 137.

[51] Rusk, *The Life of Ralph Waldo Emerson*, p. 103. See also Holmes, *Ralph Waldo Emerson*, p. 51; and Cooke, *Ralph Waldo Emerson*, pp. 23-24.

[52] WHC, *Memoir*, I, 218.

[53] WEC, *Works*, III, 238.

[54] WEC, *Works*, IV, 98-100.

[55] Typewritten excerpt from a sermon "If I Were a Layman" by P. R. Frothingham. (AUA.)

[56] RWE, *Letters*, I, 307-308. For corroboration of the report, see Le Breton, *Correspondence of William Ellery Channing, D.D., and Lucy Aikin*, p. 60.

[57] Letter from WEC to Andrews Norton, Jan. 24, 1831. (Norton Papers.)

[58] *Idem.*

[59] Letter from WEC to Andrews Norton, April 1, 1831. (Norton Papers.) The manuscript is torn, and the letters between brackets in the quotation are missing.

[60] Frothingham, "If I Were a Layman," *loc. cit.*

61 Needless to say, the records of the Arlington Street Church are all sweetness and light on this transaction.

62 *Harriet Martineau's Autobiography*, II, 273.

63 Peabody, *Reminiscences*, p. 363. Miss Peabody said (to posterity) that she saw it in the *Liberator*. But posterity has never been able to find it.

64 May, *Some Recollections*, pp. 173–174.

65 Pickard, *Life and Letters of John Greenleaf Whittier*, II, 642.

66 *Harriet Martineau's Autobiography*, I, 368. Where Miss Martineau got the figure of two years is not clear, since Texas was not annexed until 1845. There is not much question, however, about the importance of Channing's pamphlet in publicizing a most iniquitous situation.

67 WHC, *Memoir*, III, 215.

68 May, *Some Recollections, passim.*

69 WHC, *Memoir*, III, 229.

70 Schlesinger, *The Age of Jackson*, p. 146.

71 WEC, *Works*, VI, 178.

72 WEC, *Works*, VI, 176–177.

73 WEC, *Works*, VI, 417–418.

74 WEC, *Works*, VI, 419.

75 *Idem.*

76 Thayer, *The Life of Ludwig van Beethoven*, III, 283.

2. The Rational Christian

1 Dewey, *Reconstruction in Philosophy*, pp. 100–101.

2 Schneider has suggested a part of this classification in *The History of American Philosophy*, p. 61.

3 WEC, *Works*, IV, 110.

4 Calvin, *Institutes*, II, 201.

5 Shaftesbury, *Characteristics of Men*, II, 34–35. Shaftesbury, of course, was not a clerical writer.

6 Hopkins, *The System of Doctrines*, I, 52–53.

7 Price, *Questions in Morals*, pp. 74–75.

8 The essay was first printed in 1699. It seems to have had no appreciable influence until its republication in 1711 in the second volume of *Characteristics*. The title is usually given as *An Inquiry Concerning Virtue and Merit;* but I have used the form of the 1757 edition of *Characteristics*.

9 Hutcheson, *A System of Moral Philosophy*, I, 174–175.

10 Price, *Questions in Morals*, pp. 56–57.

11 *Ibid.*, p. 92.

12 *Ibid.*, p. 171 *et. seq.*

13 *Ibid.*, p. 387.

14 Weiss, *Life and Correspondence of Theodore Parker*, I, 108–109. In this excerpt, the "understanding" means the lower faculty; it is equivalent to Price's "reason." Channing consistently used such words as

"mind," "reason," and "conscience" interchangeably. They all mean
the faculty by which truth is apprehended.

15 RWE, *Works*, I, 122.
16 WEC, *Works*, III, 209.
17 Le Breton, *Correspondence of Channing and Lucy Aikin*, p. 403.
18 See above, pp. 42, 43.
19 WEC, *Works*, VI, 199, 200.
20 WEC, *Works*, VI, 204, 205.
21 WEC, *Works*, VI, 216.
22 WEC, *Works*, VI, 200.
23 WEC, *Works*, VI, 219.
24 WEC, *Works*, VI, 223, 224.
25 WEC, *Works*, III, 232, 233.
26 WEC, *Works*, III, 233.
27 See above, pp. 62–63.
28 Alexander, *et al., Two Articles from the Princeton Review*, p. 65.
29 For a very interesting paper on this topic, see Patterson, "The
Theology of Channing and the Via Affirmativa." Patterson contends
that Channing's position was that God's attributes are maximized human
qualities, and that Channing departed from traditional theology by holding that we can know *what* God is. Patterson says that Channing rejected the *analogia entis* — i.e., that our qualities may perhaps resemble
God's — in favor of the assumption that our qualities are actually the
qualities of the Deity. It seems to me that though Channing's thought
tends in that direction, and that at least once (in the sermon "Likeness
to God") he says as much, he withdrew from the implication when it
came to him from someone else's mouth. See below, pp. 145–147, for his
reaction to Parker's South Boston Sermon.
30 Hopkins, *The System of Doctrines*, I, 111.
31 *Ibid.*, I, 86.
32 Hutcheson, *A System of Moral Philosophy*, I, 69.
33 *Ibid.*, I, 60. The same analogy occurred to Samuel Hopkins. See
The System of Doctrines, I, 68.
34 Hopkins, *The System of Doctrines*, I, 479.
35 Holmes, *The Professor at the Breakfast Table*, p. 16. "T'other
fellow," one may guess, was probably Theodore Parker.
36 See above, pp. 23–24.
37 WEC, *Works*, III, 205–206.
38 Letter from WEC to the Rev. Mr. Nichols, Sept. 15, 1817.
(AUA.)
39 Calvin, *Institutes*, I, 335.
40 Hopkins, *The System of Doctrines*, I, 196.
41 *Ibid.*, I, 55–56.
42 WEC, *Works*, III, 21.
43 Price, *Questions in Morals*, p. 96.
44 WEC, *Works*, IV, 342–344.
45 The influence of Hopkinsian thinking has been underestimated. If
Hopkins can be trusted, the movement spread rapidly between the death

of Jonathan Edwards and the beginning of the nineteenth century. Hopkins wrote in his autobiography, shortly before his death in 1803: "About forty years ago there were but few, perhaps not more than four or five who espoused the sentiments, which have since been called *Edwardean*, and *new divinity*, and since, after some improvement was made upon them, Hopkintonian, or Hopkinsian sentiments. But these sentiments have so spread since that time among ministers, especially those who have since come on the stage, that there are now more than one hundred in the ministry who espouse the same sentiments, in the United States of America, and the sentiments appear to be coming more and more into credit, and are better understood, and the odium which was cast on them and those who preached them, is greatly subsided." *Sketches of the Life of Samuel Hopkins*, pp. 102–103.

[46] WEC, *Works*, III, 60.
[47] WEC, *Works*, III, 60.
[48] WEC, *Works*, III, 60.
[49] WEC, *Works*, III, 63.
[50] WEC, *Works*, III, 64.
[51] Stuart, *Letters to the Rev. Wm. E. Channing* (1819), pp. 10–11.
[52] *Ibid.*, p. 24.
[53] WEC, *Works*, III, 75.
[54] Stuart, *Letters to the Rev. Wm. E. Channing* (1819), p. 45.
[55] WEC, *Works*, III, 85.
[56] WEC, *Works*, III, 87.
[57] WEC, *Works*, III, 100.
[58] Woods, *Letters to Unitarians*, p. 21.
[59] *Ibid.*, pp. 21–22.
[60] *Ibid.*, p. 23.
[61] *Ibid.*, p. 27.
[62] WEC, *Works*, III, 86.
[63] Woods, *Letters to Unitarians*, p. 62.
[64] *Ibid.*, p. 82.
[65] WEC, *Works*, III, 93.
[66] Woods, *Letters to Unitarians*, p. 115.
[67] *Ibid.*, p. 131.
[68] *Ibid.*, p. 149.
[69] Le Breton, *Correspondence of Channing and Lucy Aikin*, p. 6.
[70] WEC, *Works*, III, 197.
[71] WEC, *Discourses, Reviews, and Miscellanies*, page vii.
[72] Stuart, *A Letter to William E. Channing* (1830), p. 36.
[73] *Ibid.*, p. 37.
[74] Le Breton, *Correspondence of Channing and Lucy Aikin*, p. 17.
[75] WEC, *Remarks on the Rev. Dr. Worcester's Letter*, p. 20.
[76] Whitehead, *Science and the Modern World*, p. 75.
[77] WEC, *Works*, III, 212–213.
[78] WEC, *Works*, III, 210.
[79] WEC, *Works*, III, 213.
[80] WEC, *Works*, III, 222.

[81] WEC, *Works*, III, 230.
[82] WEC, *Works*, III, 238–239.
[83] WEC, *Works* (1888), p. 942.
[84] RWE, *Works*, I, 68.
[85] WEC, *Works* (1888), p. 928. The quotation is from W. H. Channing's introduction to *The Perfect Life*.
[86] WEC, *Works*, III, 233–234.
[87] See above, pp. 62–63.
[88] Price, *Questions in Morals*, p. 142.
[89] WEC, *Works* (1888), p. 939.
[90] *Services in Memory of William E. Channing, D.D.*, p. 27.
[91] *Idem.*
[92] WEC, *Works*, III, 241.
[93] WEC, *Works*, III, 238.
[94] Le Breton, *Correspondence of Channing and Lucy Aikin*, p. 81.
[95] WEC, *Works*, V, 304.
[96] WEC, *Works* (1888), p. 1003.
[97] WEC, *Works*, III, 303.
[98] RWE, *Works*, II, 9.
[99] WEC, *Works*, I, xviii.
[100] WEC, *Works*, IV, 34.
[101] WEC, *Works*, IV, 35.
[102] WEC, *Works*, IV, 36.
[103] Price, *Questions in Morals*, p. 16. See above, p. 102, for a further statement of Price's view.
[104] WEC, *Works*, IV, 109.
[105] WEC, *Works*, I, v–vi.

3. Channing and the Transcendentalists

[1] See Ladu, "Channing and Transcendentalism," for an able exposition of the difficulties in placing Channing among the Transcendentalists.
[2] Letter from Andrews Norton to WEC, April 11, 1840. (Norton Papers.) The pamphlet in question is a reprint of two articles from the *Biblical Repertory and Princeton Review*, which are devoted to the destruction of infidelity as the editors thought it manifested itself in the Transcendental movement. The *Review* also reprimanded Norton, but in his reprint he saw fit to omit that section. This letter has been printed in Edgell, "A Note on Channing's Transcendentalism." See also above, p. 70.
[3] RWE, *Letters*, I, 45.
[4] RWE, *Letters*, II, 451.
[5] *Services in Memory of William E. Channing, D.D.*, pp. 28–29.
[6] Curtis, *et al.*, *Homes of American Authors*, p. 231.
[7] ABA, *Journals*, p. 15.
[8] RWE, *Letters*, I, 194.
[9] ABA, *Journals*, p. 32.
[10] ABA, *Journals*, Aug. 2, 1836, pp. 77–78.

[11] Peabody, *Reminiscences*, pp. 356-357.

[12] ABA, *Journals*, p. 105. Channing's criticism of the school was still bothering Alcott in 1856, for in that year he finally vindicated himself in his own mind by dreaming that Channing had suggested that the teachers in the Concord School should be invited to lecture at the Divinity School in Cambridge. See ABA, *Journals*, pp. 420-422.

[13] RWE, *Letters*, I, 439 (note 31).

[14] Peabody, *Reminiscences*, pp. 403-404.

[15] Letter from John Brazer to Andrews Norton, Nov. 7, 1836. (Norton Papers.)

[16] Quoted in Stewart, *Nathaniel Hawthorne*, p. 89.

[17] Letter from Charles W. Upham to Andrews Norton, Nov. 5, 1836. (Norton Papers.) He went on to say that *Sartor Resartus* is "infidelity without dispute," and to wonder why "our Theological School" published it. He might well wonder, if it had — but there is no evidence that the Divinity School had anything to do with its publication.

[18] Letter from Charles W. Upham to Andrews Norton, Dec. 21, 1839. (Norton Papers.)

[19] Peabody, *Reminiscences*, p. 370.

[20] RWE, *Letters*, II, 135.

[21] RWE, *Letters*, II, 293-294.

[22] See, for example, *The Correspondence of Thomas Carlyle and Ralph Waldo Emerson*, II, 14-15.

[23] *Ibid.*, I, 304-305.

[24] Peabody, *Reminiscences*, p. 414.

[25] *The American Notebooks by Nathaniel Hawthorne*, p. 168.

[26] Peabody, *Reminiscences*, p. 365. One suspects that the italics represent Miss Peabody's emphasis rather than Channing's own, though there is no way of telling.

[27] Rusk, *The Life of Ralph Waldo Emerson*, pp. 275-276.

[28] See Long, *Frederic Hedge: A Cosmopolitan Scholar*, and Wells, *Three Christian Transcendentalists*.

[29] RWE, *Works*, I, 129.

[30] Peabody, *Reminiscences*, p. 372 *et seq.*

[31] *Ibid.*, pp. 379-380.

[32] *Ibid.*, p. 381.

[33] RWE, *Works*, I, 132-133.

[34] WEC, *Works*, III, 261.

[35] WEC, *Works*, III, 267.

[36] WEC, *Works*, III, 267.

[37] RWE, *Works*, I, 143.

[38] WEC, *Works*, III, 274.

[39] Holmes, *Ralph Waldo Emerson*, p. 115.

[40] WEC, *Works*, I, 243 *et seq.*

[41] WEC, *Works*, I, 254-255.

[42] WEC, *Works*, I, 257.

[43] WEC, *Works*, I, 259.

[44] WEC, *Works*, I, 271.

[45] WEC, *Works*, I, 267.
[46] WEC, *Works*, I, 270.
[47] WEC, *Works*, II, 372.
[48] WEC, *Works*, II, 381.
[49] WEC, *Works*, II, 381.
[50] RWE, *Works*, I, 77.
[51] WEC, *Works*, II, 363.
[52] WEC, *Works*, II, 355.
[53] WEC, *Works*, II, 369.
[54] WEC, *Works*, II, 396.
[55] WEC, *Works*, II, 398.
[56] WEC, *Works*, II, 411.
[57] RWE, *Works*, XI, 161–162.
[58] RWE, *Works*, III, 200–201.
[59] HDT, *Writings*, XI, 264–265.
[60] RWE, *Journals*, V, 474.
[61] WHC, *Memoir*, III, 120.
[62] WEC, *Works*, I, 291.
[63] WEC, *Works*, I, 282.
[64] Peabody, *Reminiscences*, p. 406.
[65] *Ibid.*, p. 414.
[66] WHC, *Memoir*, III, 119.
[67] Peabody, *Reminiscences*, p. 416.
[68] *Ibid.*, p. 407.
[69] *Ibid.*, p. 255.
[70] Weiss, *Life and Correspondence of Theodore Parker*, I, 106.
[71] *Ibid.*, I, 114.
[72] *Ibid.*, I, 109.
[73] Peabody, *Reminiscences*, p. 420.
[74] *Ibid.*, p. 423 *et seq.*
[75] WEC, *Works*, IV, 40.
[76] Quoted in Commager, *Theodore Parker*, p. 76.
[77] Peabody, *Reminiscences*, p. 429.
[78] [Theodore Parker], "Hollis Street Council," in *The Dial*, II (October 1842), pp. 201–221.
[79] Pierpont, *A Discourse Occasioned by the Death of William Ellery Channing*, p. 6.
[80] Weiss, *Life and Correspondence of Theodore Parker*, I, 183.
[81] *Ibid.*, I, 119.
[82] Peabody, *Reminiscences*, p. 371.

4. CHANNING'S VIEWS OF REFORM

[1] RWE, *Works*, X, 352.
[2] Letter from WEC to Orville Dewey [n.d.]. (HMC.) This letter was probably written around 1827 or 1828, for Holbrook had founded the Lyceum movement in 1826 and was trying (with great success) to expand its operations in the years immediately following. The letter is included, with slightly different wording, in WHC, *Memoir*, III, 98.

[3] WHC, *Memoir*, III, 172. This passage was written on Nov. 10, 1835.

[4] See above, p. 44.

[5] Letter from WEC to Orville Dewey, April 18, 1839. (HMC.)

[6] WEC, *Works*, I, 140. For Channing's thought on this kind of power, see the "Discourse at the Dedication of Divinity Hall, Cambridge, 1826" in WEC, *Works*, III, 257-286.

[7] WEC, *Works*, I, 143.

[8] WEC, *Works*, I, 144.

[9] WEC, *Works*, I, 143.

[10] WEC, *Works*, V, 412-413. True, these words were written to curb Federalist opposition to the War of 1812; yet they represent one facet of Channing's thought. See also his article "The Union," in WEC, *Works*, I, 333-367.

[11] "So far is an existing government from being clothed with an inviolable sanctity, that the citizen, in particular circumstances, acquires the right, not only of remonstrating, but of employing force for its destruction." WEC, *Works*, V, 415.

[12] HDT, *Writings*, IV, 368.

[13] WEC, *Works*, I, 336.

[14] WEC, *Works*, I, 344.

[15] WEC, *Works*, I, 356.

[16] Ferguson, *Civil Society*, p. 88.

[17] *Ibid.*, p. 277.

[18] Lucy Aikin (1781-1864) was the daughter of John Aikin the biographer, the niece of Mrs. Barbauld, and the author of several historical works which earned her considerable popularity in her own day.

[19] Le Breton, *Correspondence of Channing and Lucy Aikin*, p. 223.

[20] WEC, *Works*, IV, 83.

[21] WEC, *Works*, II, 40.

[22] WEC, *Works*, II, 34.

[23] WEC, *Works*, II, 35.

[24] WEC, *Works*, I, 361.

[25] WEC, *Works*, IV, 267.

[26] Paine was christened Thomas, but dropped the name in 1801— apparently fearing the anathema which Boston hurled upon the author of *The Age of Reason*.

[27] See above, pp. 13, 17.

[28] Letter from WEC to William Ellery, May 15, 1809. (HMC.)

[29] WHC, *Memoir*, I, 95.

[30] WEC, *A Sermon Preached in Boston, April 5, 1810*, p. 14.

[31] WEC, *Works*, I, xxvii.

[32] WEC, *Works*, VI, 175-176.

[33] WEC, *Works*, I, 130.

[34] Arnold, *Essays in Criticism*, p. 188.

[35] WHC, *Memoir*, I, 89.

[36] WEC, *Works*, VI, xxvi.

[37] WEC, *Works*, I, 81.

[38] WEC, *Works*, I, 363.

[39] WEC, *Works*, V, 412.

[40] WEC, *Works*, V, 415.

[41] HDT, *Writings*, IV, 380.

[42] Channing is undoubtedly in agreement with Paley here, though it is out of character for the Doctor to plead expediency as a motive for acting or refraining from action.

[43] WEC, *Works*, V, 418–419.

[44] WEC, *Works*, V, 428.

[45] WEC, *Works*, I, xxviii.

[46] WEC, *Works*, V, 128.

[47] Le Breton, *Correspondence of Channing and Lucy Aikin*, pp. 347–348.

[48] Letter from Samuel E. Sewall to WEC, Nov. 25, 1837. (HMC.)

[49] Letter from WEC to Samuel E. Sewall, Nov. 25, 1837. (Typescript copy in the Boston Public Library.)

[50] May, *Some Recollections*, p. 226.

[51] WHC, *Memoir*, III, 205.

[52] Letter from WEC to ——, Dec. 2, 1837. (Typescript in the Boston Public Library.) The original of this letter does not seem to be available. The library dates the letter Dec. 23, and states that the addressee was William Lloyd Garrison. Both of these conjectures are almost certainly wrong. The date must be Dec. 2, because the meeting Channing refers to was held on Sunday, Dec. 3, 1837, in the Supreme Court rooms. Furthermore, Channing also refers to "conversations with you," and he never met Garrison to speak to. I think, from internal evidence, that the letter was probably written to Samuel E. Sewall.

[53] Quoted from the manuscript in possession of Henry M. Channing. The text differs somewhat in wording from that printed in WHC, *Memoir*, III, 209.

[54] Letter from Ellis Gray Loring to WEC, Dec. 17, 1837. (HMC.)

[55] See above, pp. 42–47.

[56] Letter from William Lloyd Garrison to WEC, Jan. 20, 1834. (Manuscript copy in the Boston Public Library.)

[57] Letter from Sarah M. Grimké to WEC, June 1837. (HMC.)

[58] WEC, *Works*, II, 143–144.

[59] May, *Some Recollections*, p. 178.

[60] *Ibid.*, p. 184.

[61] Letter from WEC to Joseph Tuckerman, Feb. 12, 1831. (HMC.)

[62] Letter from WEC to Andrews Norton, Jan. 24, 1831. (Norton Papers.)

[63] WHC, *Memoir*, III, 141.

[64] Letter from WEC to Nathan Appleton, Feb. 9, 1834, in possession of David P. Edgell.

[65] Le Breton, *Correspondence of Channing and Lucy Aikin*, pp. 203–204.

[66] Letter from John Quincy Adams to WEC, Aug. 11, 1837. (RIHS.)

[67] WHC, *Memoir*, III, 264.

[68] WHC, *Memoir*, III, 264-265.

[69] The Ministry at Large was an attempt on the part of the Unitarian clergy to extend their usefulness beyond the pulpit and their own parishioners. Its goal was to carry the advantages of religion into the homes and lives of those who through poverty, ignorance, or both, did not enjoy the benefits of church membership.

[70] Kingsley, *Yeast a Problem*, p. 52. Kingsley, whose theory of reform was fundamentally the same as that of Channing, saw far more deeply and acutely, it seems to me, into the real nature of the problem.

[71] Dorfman, *The Economic Mind in American Civilization*, II, 635.

[72] Letter from WEC to William Rathbone, Aug. 10, 1842. (HMC.)

[73] Greeley, *Recollection of a Busy Life*, p. 145.

[74] WEC, *Works*, VI, 103.

[75] WEC, *Works*, VI, 119.

[76] WEC, *Works*, II, 312.

[77] WEC, *Works*, II, 315.

[78] WEC, *Works*, II, 318.

[79] WEC, *Works*, II, 339.

[80] ABA, *Journals*, p. 50.

[81] WEC, *Works*, I, 374.

[82] WEC, *Works*, I, 377.

[83] WEC, *Works*, I, 381.

[84] WEC, *Works*, I, 387.

[85] WHC, *Memoir*, III, 69.

[86] See above, p. 133.

[87] WHC, *Memoir*, III, 68.

[88] Letter from WEC to William Rathbone, Aug. 10, 1842. (HMC.)

[89] WEC, *Works*, II, 400.

[90] WEC, *Works*, V, 159.

[91] *The Heart of Hawthorne's Journals*, p. 69.

[92] *Ibid.*, p. 73.

[93] WEC, *Works*, V, 203-204.

[94] WEC, *Works*, V, 205-206.

[95] Manuscript in the collection of Henry M. Channing.

5. The Man of Letters

[1] Chorley, *Memorials of Mrs. Hemans*, I, 114-115.

[2] "Literature of the Nineteenth Century. America," in *Athenaeum Journal*, Nos. 375, 377, 380, 382 (Jan. and Feb., 1835). Channing is described in the first article, pp. 10-11.

[3] *Services in Memory of William E. Channing, D.D.*, pp. 11-12.

[4] See above, pp. 23-24.

[5] *Athenaeum Journal, loc. cit.*

[6] WEC, *Works*, I, 55.

[7] WEC, *Works*, I, 7.

[8] WEC, *Works*, I, 8.

[9] WEC, *Works*, I, 10.

[10] WEC, *Works*, I, 12.

[11] WEC, *Works*, I, 16.

[12] WEC, *Works*, I, 21.

[13] Brougham's review of Channing's "Milton," p. 214.

[14] *Ibid.*, p. 214.

[15] *Ibid.*, p. 217.

[16] Le Breton, *Correspondence of Channing and Lucy Aikin*, p. 352.

[17] *Idem.*

[18] See, for example, "Dr. Channing and the Edinburgh Review," in the January 1840 issue of the *Southern Literary Messenger*. This article is a page-by-page refutation of Brougham's criticism; its conclusion is that "Dr. Channing . . . is acknowledged by competent judges, to be one of the best writers of the day." And two years earlier *Fraser's Magazine* had exaggerated Channing's position, albeit in the other direction from Brougham, by calling him "unquestionably the finest writer of his age," and speaking of his "force of style, his beauty and freshness of thought and diction." See "Channing's Literary and Political Essays. Remarks on Milton," in *Fraser's Magazine*.

[19] Letter from WEC to William Rathbone, Aug. 10, 1842. (HMC.)

[20] Letter from WEC to Andrews Norton, Aug., 1827. (Norton Papers.)

[21] *Idem.* There is a tear in the manuscript, but the word "not" is clearly indicated by the context.

[22] Letter from WEC to Andrews Norton, Aug. 5, 1827. (Norton Papers.)

[23] Le Breton, *Correspondence of Channing and Lucy Aikin*, p. 16. For an equally uncritical appreciation, see below, p. 231, the letter from Mr. Adam to Andrews Norton.

[24] "Channing's Literary and Political Essays. Remarks on Napoleon Bonaparte," in *Fraser's Magazine*, p. 290.

[25] Review of Dr. Channing's works, in *Westminster Review*.

[26] Review of Dr. Channing's Discourse at the ordination of Frederick A. Farley, in *Westminster Review*, p. 99.

[27] William Hazlitt's review of Channing, in *Edinburgh Review*, p. 127.

[28] See above, p. 227.

[29] Hazlitt's review of Channing, p. 141.

[30] RWE, *Works*, X, 320.

[31] RWE, *Journals*, IV, 211.

[32] WEC, *Works*, I, 167.

[33] WEC, *Works*, I, 168.

[34] WEC, *Works*, I, 213–214.

[35] See above, pp. 128–130.

[36] Thom, *Joseph Blanco White*, II, 69. See also Harriet Martineau's *Retrospect of Western Travel*, in which she takes issue with Channing's treatment of Priestley.

[37] See above, p. 27.

[38] Le Breton, *Correspondence of Channing and Lucy Aikin*, pp. 110–111.

[39] *Ibid.*, p. 81.

[40] Letter from WEC to Eloise Payne, Nov., 1809. (AUA.)

[41] *Idem.*

[42] Peabody, *Reminiscences*, p. 267.

[43] Letter from WEC to Elizabeth Peabody, undated. (HMC.)

[44] ABA, *Journals*, p. 464.

[45] Draft of a letter from WEC to Felicia Hemans, undated. (HMC.)

[46] WHC, *Memoir*, II, 218–219.

[47] Peabody, *Reminiscences*, p. 76.

[48] *Idem.*

[49] Le Breton, *Correspondence of Channing and Lucy Aikin*, p. 158.

[50] Peabody, *Reminiscences*, pp. 336–337.

[51] WHC, *Memoir*, II, 343.

[52] Peabody, *Reminiscences*, p. 339.

[53] Le Breton, *Correspondence of Channing and Lucy Aikin*, p. 85.

[54] *Harriet Martineau's Autobiography*, I, 327.

[55] Renan, *Studies of Religious History*, p. 262.

[56] Review of Channing's "Ministry for the Poor," *North American Review*, p. 366.

[57] *Ibid.*, p. 372.

[58] RWE, *Journals*, VI, 105–106.

6. The Significance of Channing

[1] ABA, *Journals*, p. 85.

[2] Hazlitt's review of Channing, p. 132.

[3] Letter from WEC to Eloise Payne, Nov. 4, 1811. (HMC.)

[4] Sandburg, *Abraham Lincoln: The Prairie Years*, p. 415.

[5] Letter from John Nichols to WEC, April 28, 1826. (HMC.)

[6] Letter from W. Adam to Andrews Norton, Sept. 2, 1828. (Norton Papers.)

[7] Quoted in Hicks, "When Dickens Met Channing," p. 604.

[8] Dickens, *American Notes*, p. 13.

[9] Letter from WEC to Andrews Norton, Sept. 3, 1832. (Norton Papers.)

Index